Radio Drama

Radio Drama brings together the practical skills needed for radio drama, such as directing, writing and sound design, with media history and communication theory. From the early audio broadcasts of 1914 and the development of General Electric's New York *WGY* station in 1922, through Orson Welles's startling Hallowe'en broadcast of *War of the Worlds* in 1938, to more recent radio spoofs and the subversive challenge from 'media guerrillas', Tim Crook explores the history and contemporary practice of radio drama. Challenging the belief that sound drama is a 'blind medium', *Radio Drama* shows how experimentation in radio narrative has blurred the dividing line between fiction and reality in modern media. Using extracts from scripts and analysing radio broadcasts from America, Britain, Canada and Australia, the book explores the practicalities of producing drama for radio. Tim Crook illustrates how far radio drama has developed since the first 'audiophonic production' and evaluates the future of radio drama in the age of live phone-ins and immediate access to programmes on the Internet.

Tim Crook has written, directed and produced award-winning radio plays, series and documentaries. He is the Head of Radio at Goldsmiths College, University of London, and is the author of *International Radio Journalism*.

Radio Drama

Theory and practice

Tim Crook

London and New York

First published 1999
by Routledge
11 New Fetter Lane, London EC4P 4EE

Simultaneously published in the USA and
Canada by Routledge
29 West 35th Street, New York, NY 10001

Routledge is an imprint of the
Taylor & Francis Group

© 1999 Tim Crook

Typeset in Perpetua and Bell Gothic by
RefineCatch Limited, Bungay, Suffolk
Printed and bound in Great Britain by
Biddles Ltd., Guildford and King's Lynn

British Library Cataloguing in Publication Data
A catalogue record for this book is available
from the British Library

Library of Congress Cataloging in Publication Data
Crook, Tim, 1959–
Radio drama / Tim Crook.
p.   cm.
Includes bibliographical references and index.
1. Radio plays — History and criticism.   I.
Title.
PN1991.65.C66   1999
809.2′22—dc21   99–26899
                                                              CIP

ISBN 0–415–21602–8 (hbk)
ISBN 0–415–21603–6 (pbk)

Contents

Contents

Plates

Acknowledgements

This book is the result of a personal odyssey lasting twenty years. Radio drama and radio drama-documentary expression are undoubtedly the most understated creative, dramatic and literary art forms and seem to have suffered an element of cultural neglect in terms of the volume of critical publication rather than the quality. I think that this area has been under-explored from the point of view of academic study compared with other dramatic media. This medium of drama offers the dramatist considerable control and a fast route to the centre of human consciousness and psychological engagement. It is probably the most efficient and cost-effective way of reaching a huge audience, but it is also one of the more interesting and enjoyable storytelling forms to access the world of media and communications theory. Through audio drama you can explore the rich and intellectually fulfilling world of cultural history, semiotics, psychology of communication, sociology, study of audiences and other theoretical concerns centred in the field of human communication and society.

I have tried to write an enabling book to open doors and windows in the world of practice and theory and to give students in media and communications an exciting and enjoyable journey that truly articulates an interplay or integration of the thinking and the doing, the education as well as the training.

I have sought to explore key subjects such as media history, sound, writing, directing and the distinction between fiction and reality for audiences with as much international perspective as I have been able to research. I realise that I have neglected much. I could not pretend to offer a comprehensive text on the entire subject. I have also had to leave out considerable amounts of research and writing that I had undertaken for the project. Detailed questions of representation and political economy have not been engaged: they deserve a separate volume. I have explored radio acting through the perspective of directing since a book focusing on radio performance has recently been published. I also think that much could be gained by performers appreciating the director's perspective and recognising the common aesthetic and professional concerns.

I would like to thank the following people and organisations who have been a source of inspiration, help and challenge to me in the writing of this book.

Marja Giejgo, the guru of Independent Radio Drama Productions (IRDP), who has brought judgement and maturity to a rather emotionally wrought community and whose technological and design skills created the UK's first Internet Play of the Month.

Richard Shannon, my co-director in IRDP. We have taken risks, pioneered together and brought opportunities to writers and actors, and pleasure to listeners.

Keith Waghorn, studio manager at Goldsmiths College, University of London, and all my colleagues in an enlightened and internationally renowned Department of Media and Communications. I single out **John Beacham**, Head of Practice and brilliant teacher and lecturer in television drama, for supporting me in my development in further education, and **Christine Geraghty**, Head of Department at Media and Communications (at the time of writing), for further support and providing valuable research time to complete the writing of this text.

I am grateful to **Rebecca Barden**, senior editor at Routledge, **Christopher Cudmore**, assistant editor, for constructive guidance and patience over the development of the text, and **Kate Chenevix Trench** for desk editing.

David Blake, **Gail Johnson**, **Paul Rogers** and the Woolwich Building Society (now **Woolwich PLC**) for being committed and consistent sponsors of new writing in radio.

Janet Lee, Deputy Head of Programming at the UK Radio Authority, a consistent supporter and progenitor of cultural programming in commercial radio.

Sue Timothy, **Lawrence Baylis**, **Robert Gordon-Clarke**, **Jonathan Brill** and the **London Arts Board** (formerly Greater London Arts) for recognising and funding radio drama as an art form independent of the BBC.

Peter Thornton, **Philip Bacon**, **Charles Cox**, **Robin Malcolm**, **Nigel Charters**, **Charles Golding**, **Nikki Townley**, **Catherine Lee** and **Trevor Aston**, current and former programming executives at LBC, Britain's first independent commercial station, which has consistently supported and developed innovation in radio drama broadcasts.

The **BBC** and a myriad of radio producers, directors and editors who have inspired, provoked and provided the impetus to challenge and be experimental.

Kate Rowland, in charge of BBC Radio Drama Production (at the time of writing).

Tom Morris and the **BAC**, for being an innovative and supportive theatre which has successfully explored the symbiosis between theatre and radio.

James Roy, Damiano Pietropaolo, Gregory Sinclair, Dave Carley and **Keith Hart** at CBC, Canada, and **Charles Potter**, colleague, friend and distinguished independent radio drama producer in New York.

Andy Trudeau, enlightened cultural programming editor at NPR, Washington, DC.

Glen Barnham at Equity.

I thank all the contributors of views and opinions through interviews conducted for this book. They include the directors and dramaturgists photographed. The exigencies of space mean that many interviews and dimensions of research could not be included. Thanks too are due to the writers, the actors, the directors and the listeners who have all participated in and continue to enjoy the world of audio drama.

Dr Fred Hunter, a trusted and important mentor, has hunted down useful references and loaned me journals and books which are difficult to find.

Peter Everett, the self-effacing former BBC Radio 4 Network editor, for giving permission to use his practical advice on feature making.

My students both in professional and educational contexts. I single out the following because some of their essays have helped crystallise conclusions and research dimensions on my part: **Rikke Houd, Mette Højrup, Emer Shaw, Simon Bolger, Colin Burgess** and **Lance Dann**.

I apologise profusely for failing to acknowledge anyone who recognises any influence on this text. Every effort has been taken to secure permission for the quotation of extracts. Where this has not been achieved I offer an advance apology and explain that the trail of research has not been able to reach you. I beg your indulgence to include the information for the purposes of scholarship, review and educational learning.

Part I

Practice meets theory

Chapter 1

A new media history perspective through audio drama

There's no romance in television: it's just the Wal-Mart of the mind. Radio is infinitely sexier.

(Garrison Keillor, *Radio Romance*, 1991)

And more particularly:

I live right inside radio when I listen. 'The Medium Is The Message'.

(Marshall McLuhan, *Understanding Media*, 1964)

Radio drama has been one of the most unappreciated and understated literary forms of the twentieth century and the purpose of this book is to demonstrate that this neglect should not continue into the twenty-first century. Academics, media theorists and writers in most cultures have not fully appreciated that the medium of sound has provided an environment in which a new storytelling genre has been born. It has developed with sophistication and explosive energy; it now occupies a significant position in the cultural lives of societies throughout the globe. Even where the dominance of long-form popular dramas has transferred to television, the audio drama narrative is central to the short narrative communication of radio commercials. Huge traditions, styles and movements have been established and remain largely undocumented. Even now, radio drama is regarded as an adjunct of radio production practice. The shelves of the library at Goldsmiths College, University of London disclose the following ratio of critical publication space between novels and poetry, theatre texts, film/television and radio drama: 64, 21, 14 and 1.[1]

There are strong signs that this neglect is being challenged. The international radio academy, which includes practitioners as well as philosophers, is gathering to debate, discuss and present papers.[2] In Britain, drama lecturer Alan Beck at the University of Kent has undertaken the first and most significant comprehensive research into the history of British radio drama, which will have an impressive output in CD-ROM publication. Many aspects of previous academic evaluation of the subject are unreliable. This is not due to intrinsic failings in individual approach. It is more a case of underdeveloped radio theory and a continuing struggle to legitimise sound art or radio drama in terms of its equality as an art form.[3]

I began with hubris from Garrison Keillor and the phrase for which Marshall McLuhan is most remembered: 'The medium is the message'. If this is the case, radio or audio drama has to begin with the medium of recorded sound and the dynamics of its transmission. These phases clearly predate radio. There is no evidence that I can find of researchers or writers who have even considered the significance of 'electrophones' during the period from 1900 until the advent of licensed broadcasting. So much store is placed on the first 'drama broadcast' or transmission of the 'first radio play written for the wireless'. This is perfectly valid. History requires datelines to frame development. Fortunately texts exist to point to defining moments. The BBC's first Chief Engineer, Captain P. Eckersley, in his *The Power behind the Microphone* (1942), describes a radio drama experiment transmitted on 17 October 1922 from the research station at Writtle, near Chelmsford, Essex:

> We did a wireless play. We chose the balcony scene from Cyrano: it is played, on the stage, in semi-darkness with virtually stationary players and so it seemed very suitable for broadcasting. 'Uggy' Travers, a young actress and her brother came to help. We sat round a kitchen table in the middle of the wooden hut, with its shelves and benches packed with prosaic apparatus, and said our passionate lines into the lip of our separate microphones . . .
>
> It was all rather fun. Doubtless at times I was horribly facetious, but I did try to be friendly and talk with, rather than at, my listeners . . . We failed to take ourselves seriously, and broadcasting, as we saw it, was nothing more nor less than an entertainment, for us as much as the listeners.[4]

Evidence of an early experiment in the broadcast of audio drama emerges from a study of the history of radio in California by John Schneider, which is available on the World Wide Web. In his narrative about the history of KQW and radio programming pioneer Charles 'Doc' Herrold, Schneider states:

> About this time [1914], Herrold's station attempted its first remote broadcast. The event was a play being performed in the auditorium at Normal College

(now California State University at San José). The carbon button microphones Herrold used had very limited pick-up range, and his students improvised a reflector to collect the sound out of an old wooden chopping bowl. The signal was transmitted to the bank building through an ordinary telephone connection. Newby related: 'We would use a phone, and they would take the receiver off of the hook and we would hold the receiver on the other end at the microphone of the transmitter. And it would go through; voices would go through pretty good.' He told of another incident when they tried to broadcast a harp recital. They had to keep the microphone very close to the strings to pick up the harp with enough volume, and the mike upset the harpist so much that she couldn't play a thing.[5]

American radio history is complex and chaotically documented. It would be a brave scholar who confidently asserted that the first US radio drama had been identified with a particular date and on a certain radio station. There are some references, for example 1922 has been marked as the year when General Electric's New York station WGY in Schenectady broadcast 'the first dramatic series . . . and the first sound effects were used in "The Wolf", a two and a half hour play on the same station.'[6]

Photographs of WGY's engineer and the WGY players with a microphone disguised as a lamp to minimise performers' jitters appear in the American publication *The Early Days of Radio Broadcasting*.[7] Since opera is effectively musical theatre, it can be argued that there are earlier licensed and regularly scheduled instances of audio drama transmission. KYW in Chicago began in 1921 as a specialist opera station and did not include time signals, weather bulletins, news and phonograph records. The early pioneering programming concentrated on six days a week broadcasts of the Chicago Civic Opera Company.[8] On 15 March 1922 WJZ in Newark brought the entire touring company of the opera production of Mozart's *Impresario* into a 10 by 40 foot makeshift studio and broadcast the production as a radio/studio based event rather than a remote broadcast.[9] The 27 October 1923 edition of *Radio Digest* disclosed:

> The radio play, a new form of dramatic interest, is increasing rapidly in popularity. Go to a movie and then come home and listen to a Radario and you will have received two exactly opposite theatrical effects. Perhaps, in the near future, you may have both movie and Radio broadcast to you . . .
>
> Of course, scenes and acts from current plays are often broadcast, but many eastern stations now have their own theatrical groups and give plays especially adapted for Radio use. Pretend you are blind and listen to these plays. The better your imagination, the better the play.[10]

Dates for the first transmission of radio drama on BBC Radio depend on what you define as a radio play. It is generally agreed that the first play written for radio was *A Comedy of Danger* by Richard Hughes, which was transmitted on 15 January 1924. Research by Alan Beck has highlighted a personal account of the play's genesis in an edition of *The Listener* magazine in 1956:

> the climax came when we said we wanted an explosion. The engineers had helped all they could, but this was the last straw. Even popping a paper bag would blow every fuse in Savoy Hill. But Playfair was something of a genius, and utterly unscrupulous. Reporters and critics were going to listen in a room specially provided for them, with its own loud-speaker. It would never do for them to hear no more than the diminutive 'phut' like the roaring of a sucking-dove, even if that was all the public would get. So Playfair staged a magnificent 'explosion' in the room next door to the press-room. Our 'explosion' got top marks with the press. They never discovered they had heard it through the wall. And so – presumably for the first time in history, anywhere in the world – some sort of 'listening play' specially written for sound somehow went on the air, thanks to Playfair's ingenuity and the helping hands of all Savoy Hill. Radio drama had emitted its first, faint, infant wail.[11]

The engagement of public relations by the play's director/producer Nigel Playfair resulted in national newspaper coverage in the *Daily Mail* on Wednesday 16 January 1924:

> In a brightly lit room a young woman in evening dress and two men holding sheets of paper in their hands declaimed to a microphone their horror at being imprisoned in the mine. Outside the room a young man sat cross-legged on the floor, with telephone receivers on his ears, and as he heard through the receivers the progress of the piece he signalled to two assistants on a lower landing to make noises to represent the action of the play.

However, Lord Asa Briggs in his formidable history series of the British Broadcasting Corporation states that 16 February 1923 signified the transmission of extracts of Shakespearian classics such as *Julius Caesar*, *Henry VIII* and *Much Ado About Nothing*, while the first abridgement for radio of an entire Shakespeare play was *Twelfth Night*, transmitted on 28 May 1923.[12]

It would appear that the first radio play produced and broadcast in Australia was a melodramatic production of the myth of *Sweeney Todd, The Barbarous Barber*, on the Melbourne station 3LO, which went out on 21 March 1925.[13] About a year earlier the Sydney station 2FC broadcast a direct transmission from Her Majesty's Theatre, Sydney, of the Royal Comic Opera Company staging *A Southern Maid*. This was achieved by placing a microphone near the centre of the footlights with a special speech amplifier under the stage.[14]

I think that radio drama has shared with stage theatre an evanescent art form status. If the script does not survive and there is no permanent recording how are we to evaluate the artistic experience? The title of the first chapter of Lance Sieveking's publication on radio drama *The Stuff of Radio* (1934) is 'Ghastly impermanence of the medium'. Most early radio plays created by the BBC and other international broadcasting organisations have not survived as mechanical records.

Very few mechanical records are made of stage productions. The script has tended to survive for both forms in the same way that manuscript musical scores have preserved the code of historic operas and musical presentations. Without permanent record, radio drama is an ephemeral art form. It exists in the moment of its produced performance. Peter Brook defined the experience of stage theatre as RRA: 'repetition, representation, assistance'.[15] The third ingredient of his definition, 'assistance', is where stage theatre and audio theatre experience their significant differences.

It is interesting that French writers have asserted that film was born in 1895 and became the 'seventh art'. However, it is my belief that rather than audio drama becoming *l'art huitième*, the position of media nascence should be reversed. Sound art or storytelling through recorded and transmitted sound was spawned before the technological gestation of film. Sound drama achieved its artistic independence as a dimension of theatre before film.

A theoretical framework for evaluating radio or audio drama is largely dependent on the physical and psychological relationship between performance/presentation and reception/perception. Is sound drama only a sound phenomenon delineated and separated from image-based narrative? I would argue that it is not. I would argue that it cannot be said that the ear cannot see. Blind people see. I realise that this is an oxymoronic statement but I would additionally argue that their brains construct an imaginative world based on image and fully separated from the eye as camera. Their experience is as rich and fulfilling as those who have the eye as camera. Profoundly deaf people can hear in their minds. The music created by deaf people has narrative, mood, emotion and aesthetics. I have been engaged in an interesting debate with a stage theatre director on the meaning of the word 'theatre'. My position is that 'theatre' as a dramatic etymological concept is not exclusively owned by stage or physical theatre. In Latin theatre is a feminine noun, *theatrum*. In Greek it is a feminine noun, *theatron*. *Theaomai* means 'behold'. The theatre director asserts that *theatron* means 'spectacle'. I disagree. I believe that a more appropriate translation is 'drama'. Sound theatre exists as a dramatic storytelling form communicating action as well as narrative.

I stress these issues because if we are talking about radio or audio drama, the state of listening is linked directly to the technological and psychological experience of hearing radio signals. The same can be applied to audio or sound signals. Can theatre encompass the idea of a staging or amphitheatre in the mind of the individual as much as in the physical auditorium or cinema? I believe that theatre as a concept is not intrinsically linked to and dependent on the spectacle. It is as much about listening as it is about spectating. Inside the mind of the listener we have the conditions of both the spectator and listener. Audio/radio drama shares the imaginative function which is recognised as 'off-stage' in live physical theatre. Hence the confidence in the expression 'the Theatre of the Mind'. I believe this is what Marshall McLuhan meant by 'I live right inside radio when I listen'. Perhaps he should have said 'radio lives right inside me when I listen'.

Is there a seminal theoretical text to accompany an understanding of the social and artistic significance of sound and radio in relation to the human imagination? I would venture to suggest that McLuhan's *Gutenberg Galaxy: The Making of Typographic Man* (1962) is this text.[16] McLuhan parallels the impact of electrical communications technology with the significance of the invention of Johann Gutenberg's printing press in the fifteenth century. Print communication created a psychological perspective which was linear, uniform, connected and continuous and heralded a linear framework of thought which McLuhan went on to assert manifested itself in linear economics, industrial environment and the linear assembly lines of manufacturing. It became a communications root for disseminating the concept of nationalism.

The primary medium of human communication in the preliterate, tribal era was the spoken word and the human ear. The Gutenberg Age introduced the printed word and the human eye as the primary medium of human communication. McLuhan defined the spoken word as 'acoustic space'. This is boundless, directionless, charged with emotion and horizonless. The written page bounded this space with margins, sharply defined letters and edges. The printed page removes the acoustic space for speech, but it then acquires a powerful visual bias.

The significance of the introduction of sound recording and transmission technology is that it marked the onset of the retribalised electronic age. McLuhan argues in his *The Medium is the Message* (1967), that the apparently powerful extension of speech afforded by recording and transmission technology had the effect of reducing the sensory capacity of speech.[17] He asserts that radio is not speech, but like writing, it creates the illusion of containing speech. What is clear is that mechanical and electronic sound communication depends on the single sense of the auditory canal and like writing stimulates a powerful visual perspective. I would suggest that McLuhan's analysis supports my definition of the unique nature of audio/radio drama. It is auditory in the physical dimension but equally powerful as a visual force in the psychological dimension. McLuhan said in 1964: 'Radio provided the first massive experience of electronic implosion, that reversal of the entire direction and meaning of literate Western civilisation.'[18]

McLuhan emphasised in 1971 that radio in contrast to the telephone permits the listener to fill in a good deal of visual imagery. In 1954 McLuhan thought about the spatialisation of media and ascribed to writing the spatialisation of thought. I believe that a significant factor in audio drama is that its literary quality enables the creator of audio/radio drama 'to control space'. When McLuhan wrote in 1954 that the 'power to shape space in writing brings the power to organise space architecturally. And when messages can be transported, then come the road, and armies, and empires. The empires of Alexander and the Caesars were essentially built by paper routes', he could have been defining the potential for the audio/radio dramatist.[19]

McLuhan has classified radio as a 'hot' medium. A hot medium is that which has high definition for senses and gives a lot of information with little to do. He is right in the sense that only the ear as a sense is engaged. But I believe he may well be wrong in the limit he places on the participation of the listener as audience. Lance Sieveking stated that 'a reader of a novel always has to meet the author half way and do half the work. He has to imagine for himself what the people look like and the scenery, creating them out of his own experience. So he has in the radio-play'.[20]

McLuhan was undoubtedly right in his realisation that modern electronic communications were creating a 'global village'. His empirical and philosophical exploration of this notion was certainly predated by the 1936 work of Rudolf Arnheim, who devotes his 'Introduction' to a lyrical description of sitting in the harbour of a southern Italian fishing village. The café proprietor tunes in a large radio set and fishermen watching their catch being brought home hear an English announcer introducing folk songs in German. Then the dial is retuned to an Italian station playing a French chansonette:

> This is the great miracle of wireless. The omnipresence of what people are singing or saying anywhere, the overlapping of frontiers, the conquest of spatial isolation, the importation of culture on the waves of the ether, the same fare for all, sound in silence.[21]

Here is an inspiring definition of the first electronic global village: it was radio. Arnheim mentions that 40 million sets were scattered around the world in 1936. In 1996 it was estimated that 40 million computer users were connected to the Internet. In sixty years the global village was transmogrified into a multi-dimensional nexus of world media. Sound whether by wire or wireless is a communications web that has made our world a village of information and entertaiment. By the year 2000 it has been estimated 300 million people will have been connected to the Internet.

Sieveking's book was written and published at a defining moment in the history of British radio drama. About ten years had elapsed during which transmitted audio drama had had a dominant 'laboratory' period. There had been the curious juxtaposition of sound drama offering words but no physical images, and silent films which offered images but no physical voices. It should not be forgotten that film was presented to audiences with a powerful, dramatic and narrative structured musical accompaniment. This laboratory stage operated in other countries.

In the German Weimar Republic, radio programming had embraced a powerful and experimental period of audio drama production in the context of a non-commercial and state controlled industry. Weimar Republic thinkers had high expectations for radio, believing that it could be used to educate the masses politically and culturally. Radio was to be the medium which brought the fine arts of music and theatre to the common people. Bertolt Brecht was a pioneer practitioner and significant theoretical philosopher on the artistic and social potential of radio. In 1927 his play *Mann is Mann* was adapted for radio broadcast. In his essay 'Der Rundfunk als Kommunikationsapparat' Brecht argued against the passive unidirectional function of radio:

> radio is one-sided when it should be two. It is purely an apparatus for distribution, for mere sharing out. So here is a positive suggestion: change this apparatus over from distribution to communication. The radio would be the finest possible communication apparatus in public life, a vast network of pipes. That is to say, it would be if it knew how to receive as well as to transmit, how to let the listener speak as well as hear.[22]

Brecht argued that there was a risk in radio's technological development surpassing the listeners' ability to appreciate and utilise its value:

> It was not the public that waited for radio but that radio waited for the public; to define the situation of radio more accurately, raw material was not waiting for methods of production based on social needs but means of production were looking anxiously for raw material. It was suddenly possible to say everything to everybody but, thinking about it, there was nothing to say.

Brecht's analysis was intriguingly echoed in 1974 in Marshall McLuhan's comment on radio: 'Radio . . . transforms the relation of everybody to everybody, regardless of programming.'[23] Brecht's apprehension about the power of radio is illustrated by his poetic observation:

> You little box, held to me when escaping
> So that your valves should not break,
> Carried from house to ship from ship to train,
> So that my enemies might go on talking to me
> Near my bed, to my pain
> The last thing at night, the first thing in the morning,
> Of their victories and of my cares,
> Promise me not to go silent all of a sudden.[24]

Between 1933 and 1936 several key texts exploring ontological and conceptual considerations for radio art or sound art were published and provide useful foundation stones for a theoretical radio drama discourse. Sieveking's *The Stuff of Radio* (1934) is predicated from his practitioner status, but he does touch on literary and psychological issues. Rudolf Arnheim's *Radio* (1936) is probably the first extensive philosophical analysis of radio as an art form. Arnheim defined the challenge with his observation:

> The essence of broadcasting consists just in the fact that it alone offers unity by aural means . . . The sensory preponderance of the visual over the aural in our life is so great that it is difficult to get used to considering the aural world as more than just a transition to the visual world.[25]

Chapter 2

Radio drama as modernity

Despite the considerable development of feminist perspectives within media and communications and cultural studies, contemporary scholars appear to have neglected the practical and theoretical contributions of Hilda Matheson (1888–1940), who was the highest achieving woman in British broadcasting before the Second World War. Her book *Broadcasting* (1933) would appear to have been the first single authored text on radio and broadcasting by a woman published in English.[1] Yet in the vast majority of theoretical analyses of radio it would appear that Hilda Matheson did not exist.[2] Matheson founded the separation of an independent News Section at the BBC and fostered the cultural celebration of literature through broadcast talks. It was her championing of the avant-garde writer James Joyce through Harold Nicolson which led to her falling out with Director General Sir John Reith and her departure from the BBC. Her contributions are paradoxical for the period and for the stereotypical assumptions made about gender equality and social hierarchy in Britain at that time.[3]

She was a communist and at the same time patriotic. Her over-exertions in intelligence work during the Second World War probably contributed to her early death. She was a passionate believer in freedom of expression, particularly in the context of culture and literature, yet she had been and continued to be a British intelligence careerist. She was a lesbian and lover of Vita Sackville-West and at the same time and for six years a close working colleague of the allegedly homophobic Sir John Reith. She predates Marshall McLuhan by quoting H. G. Wells on the sociological and cultural significance of radio communication:

The history of mankind down to our own day might be shown, as Mr H. G.

Wells has suggested, in five different stages: (1) Before Speech, (2) Speech, (3) Writing, (4) Print, (5) Mechanical Transport and Electrical Communication . . .

How can we escape from this new noise that is adding to the distractions of an already complex world? Is it to be yet another by-product of man's inventive mind which will get beyond his control before he has learnt its power?[4]

Matheson echoes Brecht in the opening rhetorical section of her book. Chapter 5 of her book, entitled 'Literature and drama', is an articulate and reflective essay on the ontological as well as practical philosophy of radio drama and communication of literature. The questions she posed are as relevant today as they were then:

Drama, throughout the ages, has been presented as an art, a show, in which vision was at least as important as hearing. How far can broadcasting hope to translate the appeal to the eye into the appeal to the ear? How far must it seek for a new literature and a new drama? And how far – to look even deeper – can any form of art, – most of all, perhaps, the intimate art of poetry – hope to make itself understood and appreciated when it is diffused indiscriminately through millions of loud speakers to the whole general public?[5]

Hilda Matheson was at the heart of the British cultural intelligentsia responding to the creative and social impact of new communication technologies. To what extent can this experience account for the emergence of modernity in the contemporary writing of the period? James Joyce embraced the linguistic experimentation of subtext through phonetic irony in a way which challenged the linear framework of the hundreds of years of previous literary expression. Paul Tissien of the Wilfrid Laurier University has recognised this curious dynamic:

In a way, the highly visible new media made strangely appropriate bedfellows for the new literature developing under the modernism of Joyce and Eliot, Richardson and Woolf. The modernists were 'making it new' in their prose fiction and poetry, largely discarding conventional literary allegiance to linear space and time and the objective authority of the omniscient narrator. They were exploring subjectivity, dream, memory, and the unconscious by concentrating on the impressionistic role of the various senses in apprehending experience; to observers as early as 1919 and 1920, the modernists seemed at times to be imitating, or parodying, the new media.[6]

A few years later in 1927 the German philosopher Martin Heidegger was also writing about how radio was transforming the concept of spatiality, and more recently Paddy Scannell has recognised the ontological significance of radio bringing the concerns of the wider world within the range of the listener's sense of being.[7] A key word in Heidegger's *Being and Time* (1917) is *Dasein* – a sense of human life as past, present and future:

> With the 'radio', for example, Dasein has so expanded its everyday environment that it has accomplished a de-severance of the 'world' – a de-severance which, in its meaning for Dasein, cannot yet be visualised.[8]

In 1917 T. S. Eliot was pointing to the capacity of the auditory imagination to renew and retrieve human art through the technological extension of communication:

> What I call the 'auditory imagination' is the feeling for syllable and rhythm, penetrating far below the conscious levels of thought and feeling, invigorating every word: sinking the most primitive and forgotten, returning to the origin, and bringing something back, seeking the beginning and the end. It works through meanings, certainly, or not without meanings in the ordinary sense, and fuses the old and obliterated, and the trite, the current, and the new and the surprising, the most ancient and the most civilized mentality.[9]

Chapter 3

The electrophone or théâtrophone

Broadcasting audio drama before the radio

It is significant that an entire culture of audio transmission of drama entertainment had been established and funded by a subscriber system in the three decades before the advent of radio. In 1881 French engineer Clement Ader had filed a patent for 'improvements of Telephone Equipment in Theatres'. His invention, known in France as the 'Théâtrophone' and marketed elsewhere as the 'electrophone', involved telephonic transmission of live performances from theatres and music halls into domestic households and amplification of the sound through phonograph speakers. The new entertainment was funded by the telephone companies. Ader himself was responsible for the first wired broadcast experiment at the Paris Opera.

Ader's pioneering invention also introduced the technological concept of stereophonic transmission nearly forty years before Edwin H. Armstrong patented the radio transmission of stereo signals on FM. Ader's 'musical telephone' was a major attraction at the International Electrical Exhibition in Paris in 1881 and he presented a stereo transmission by direct telephone from the stages of the Paris Opera House and the Comédie Française. The 'stereo' technology consisted of two transducers picking up signals from two points close to each other. It has been argued that the transmission was nearer to 'two channel mono' than true stereo, since there was a separate channel for left and right with none of the 'phasing' which occurs in real stereo.[1]

From August to November crowds queued up three evenings a week before two rooms, each containing ten pairs of headsets, in the Palais d'Industrie. In one, listeners heard live performances of the opera transmitted through microphones arranged on either side of the prompter's box. In the other, they heard plays from the Théâtre Français through ten microphones placed at the front of the stage near the footlights. Not only were the voices of the actors, actresses and singers heard in this way but also the instruments of the orchestra, the applause, laughter of the audience and the voice of the prompter were heard.

In 1890, the Compagnie du Théâtrophone commercialised the technology by distributing music by telephone from various Paris theatres to coin-in-the-slot telephones installed in hotels and cafés and to domestic subscribers. This demonstrates that the principle of 'pay per view' was predated by 'pay per listen'. Subscribers were offered special hookups to five Paris theatres for live performances. The annual subscription fee was a steep 180 francs, and 15 francs more were charged to subscribers for each use. Between acts and when nothing was happening on stage, the company piped out piano solos from its offices. The market for such acoustic consumption was so strong that it was possible to present several different programmes from various theatres. The Théâtrophone receivers were attractive ornamental boxes with telephone earpieces attached on trailing wires, and connected by the use of a pair of microphones, left and right on the stage, to the home receivers.

The English electrophone had arrived on the scene by 1895. Subscribers were offered 'local' relays from theatres, churches and London's Royal Opera House.[2]

Radio did not kill off the Paris service until 1932. The communication of concerts over longer distances was achieved between Paris and Brussels in 1887 and from Paris to London in 1891, and a mixed service of news, telephone concerts and lectures was developed in Budapest in 1893.

An article in the *Boston Evening Record* in 1891 indicates that electrophone communications were being developed in the USA. Telephone operators sometimes sponsored entertainments in the middle of the night when consumer demand was small. The *Evening Record* reported that a concert was organised by a group of telephone operators in Worcester, Fall River, Boston, Springfield, Providence and New York. The paper stated:

> The operator in Providence plays the banjo, the Worcester operator the harmonica, and gently the others sing. Some tune will be started by the players and the other will sing. To appreciate the effect, one must have a transmitter close to his ear. The music will sound as clear as though it were in the same room.[3]

There are various sources in American newspapers charting the development and potential of electrophone technology. A thousand people were said to have listened to a formal recital presented through the facilities of the Home Telephone Company in Painesville, Ohio, in 1905.

In England in 1889 people in Hastings could hear *The Yeoman of the Guard* nightly at the Tower of London. Religion was a major incentive for the application of the new technology. Carolyn Marvin found evidence of an inauguration in 1890 of a service in Christ Church in Birmingham which was connected to subscribers in London, Manchester, Derby, Coventry, Kidderminster and Hanley.

> When the morning service commenced there was what appeared to be an unseemly clamor to hear the services. The opening prayer was interrupted by cries of 'Hello, there!' 'Are you there?' 'Put me onto Christ Church.' 'No, I don't want the church,' etc. But presently quiet obtained and by the time the Psalms were reached we got almost unbroken connection and could follow the course of the services. We could hear little of the prayers probably from the fact that the officiating minister was not within voice-reach of the transmitter. The organ had a faint, far-away sound, but the singing and the sermon were a distinct success.[4]

From 1895 the Electrophone Company established connections for subscribers and hospital patients to the leading churches of London, including St. Margaret's, Westminster; St. Anne's, Soho; and St. Martin's-in-the-Fields and St. Michael's, Chester Square.

By 1896 well-off people could hear a full programme of live entertainment, musical, operatic and theatrical, for an annual rent of £10 after an installation fee of £5. Queen Victoria was an enthusiast with special lines from her sitting room to the Foreign Office, the Home Office, the Board of Green Cloth, and Marlborough House.[5]

At the beginning of the twentieth century *Daily Mail* reports underlined the historical though as yet under-appreciated significance of this advance in tele-communications. On 5 November 1903 Lord Northcliffe's paper demonstrated how journalists in London could hear a live telephonic broadcast of a speech by a leading politician of the time in Birmingham:

> The electrophone beat the telegraph by one hour and twenty seven minutes . . . In a silent room at the 'Daily Mail' office last evening a dozen men sat at a long table listening to the speech of Mr Chamberlain as the words fell from his lips in the Bingley Hall, Birmingham. To look into the room was to hear nothing. But to take a seat at the table with one of the little Y-shaped electro-phone 'receivers' at one's ears was to be transported instantaneously as by a magic carpet to Bingley Hall, Birmingham about 113 miles away.[6]

During the First World War, when 10,000 telephone users in London cancelled their connections, there was a definite increase in subscriptions to Electrophones connecting people to theatre and music halls. A *Daily Mail* article on 4 April 1916 quoted an official from the Controller's Office stating: 'People do not care so much about going out at night and like to have amusement brought to their fireside.' The headline 'Fireside Music-Halls' predated the communications value of the beginning of licensed radio by six years. Recordings of short plays presented at music halls during this period were also marketed on phonograph discs for domestic entertainment and some of these have survived in private collections and are now available on archive compact discs (CDs).[7]

There is a series of reports published in the London *Times* in January and May 1913 referring to the extent of electrophone consumerism and its potential as a social mechanism for cultural entertainment. Socially and psychologically the communication and the experience by the listener was equal to the relationship between broadcaster and listener in radio. On 15 January 1913, the London *Times* reported the presentation of a paper by J. H. Pattman to the Institution of Post Office Electrical Engineers about 'The Electrophone Service'. The report included valuable information about the technology and problems encountered:

[Pattman described] the apparatus by which subscribers are enabled to listen to the performance in any theatre, music hall and gave an account of the methods by which the service is maintained. The appliances supplied at the subscribers' end, he said, comprised a portable table, four pairs of receivers (or in the case of the limited subscriber 2 pairs) induction coil, cells and c [etc.] and the operation of which was explained. In the theatres the installations varied in accordance with the demands for service and the numbers of transmitters ranged from 12 to 96, 20 to 24 being the general number. The transmitters were fitted in the footlights and the other apparatus was placed in a cupboard under the stage. The transmitter, known as the Angelini and made in Rome, was of the granular type. Its efficiency was greater than that of any pattern tried hitherto. The apparatus employed in churches was similar to that used in the theatres and in this case it was placed in the pulpit, the lectern or the choir stalls. In the exchange situated at no. 36 Gerrard Street, there was equipment sufficient for 1,000 subscribers and at present the total was 850. The author was convinced that there was a future for the service if it could be developed on business lines. There would be considerable improvements to transmission at an early date. The present trouble was connected with the transmitter for although the volume of sound received was satisfactory, the desired clearness of articulation was not secured.[8]

It is in the last sentence that the *Times* report demonstrates that Mr Pattman had defined the essential challenge for verbal communication in the new medium of sound. When a performance using words is projected in a large space, microphones and amplifiers can only pick up an ambient acoustic, whereas the successful future for sound recording required the mastering of a close microphone technique of talking and performance to the microphone. It is intriguing that the BBC in 1995 made this basic mistake when attempting to record and broadcast the West Yorkshire Playhouse production of Wole Soyinka's *The Beatification of Area Boy* on BBC Radio 3.[9] Musical performance did not necessarily suffer from this problem.

The year 1913 also saw intriguing news reports of the electrophone being used for a London and Paris link up and the Royal Family embracing its potential for providing entertainment to the Empress of Russia. On 20 May in London *The Times* published a report headlined 'Paris Opera By Telephone':

> The British Post Master General and the French Minister of Post and Telegraphs have concurred in a proposal for an interesting international exchange by telephone wire. Tomorrow evening an electrophone connection will be made between London and the stage of the Paris Opera House and guests invited to the Electrophone Salon in Gerrard Street, W.C. will listen to the opera and to other Parisian performances. Similar arrangements will simultaneously connect Covent Garden Opera House and other London theatres with Paris.[10]

The Times followed this report with a review of the event, which was published on 22 May 1913.

> It is true that owing to the difficulty of returning possession of the trunk lines only brief snatches of Faust were to be heard and for the most part the instruments repeated strains from London theatres and music halls. But sufficient was heard to prove the practicability of transmitting music from Paris to London and though the sounds were less in volume than those which are from places a few hundreds of yards distant, they were not less distinct. This achievement has been rendered possible by means of technical improvements which have been introduced in the construction of the lines in particular the adoption of loading.[11]

On 30 May *The Times* provided a report which was the ultimate marketing coup for this new technology. Empress Marie of Russia came to London on a state visit and opera by means of electrophone became part of the hospitality:

> By request of Queen Alexandra, the electrophone was installed at Marlborough House and the Empress Marie heard the performance of 'I Grojelli della Madonna' by means of it. The electrophone was placed in the footlights at Covent Garden Theatre.[12]

A *Times* report on 16 December 1914 provided a fascinating dimension to the development of electrophone entertainment in wartime:

As an instance of some of the refinements of active service to which we are being introduced, it may be mentioned that the men in certain front line trenches have been regaling themselves by listening on the telephone to a gramophone concert 8 miles away.[13]

So the electrophone discloses the existence of a sophisticated and extensive delivery of vocal and sound expression through a new technology to a developing audience. Intriguingly it was an audience which satisfied the defining distinction of 'broadcasting' which elevated new technological communication from the one-to-one relationship of wireless telegraph. 'Broadcasting' is derived from the farming metaphor of casting seeds broadly and widely with one sweep of communication. This was the wonder of the invention and development of radio communication by the egotistic and aggressively competing Lee D. Forests, Reginald Fessendons and Edwin H. Armstrongs of the radio age. Yet a source transmission to a multiplicity of telephone subscribers achieved the same purpose. There is evidence that the electrophone technology and style of 'phone broadcasting' was extensively developed in other countries such as Hungary.[14] Entertainment in Budapest was subsidiary to the communication of information such as stocks and shares, but there was a published schedule mainly distributed to the ruling classes which could afford the expensive service. It is right to look at the social hegemony of access based on cost. This was a precursor to the issues raised by access cost in Internet broadcasting which, as in pre-First World War Budapest, is delivered by telephone cable.

Chapter 4

The six ages of audio drama and the Internet epoch

So I have stepped back from 'radio' to highlight an age of communication in audio drama with an established market and a bridge to the world of theatre. I believe we can also step back into another age which overlapped the era of the electrophone and radio and has now considerably widened its tributary into a rapidly flowing river. Experimentations with the phonograph have been studied and referenced with considerable scholarly genuflection since the 1980s. The emphasis has been on the avant-garde and use of sound as art. There certainly has not been any attention paid to traditional dramatic and narrative communication and expression in phonograph technology. I have previously discussed the extent of phonograph usage and penetration of domestic household entertainment and have suggested that it has been significantly underestimated.[1] Millions of phonographs were sold and distributed in Britain, the USA and other European and English-speaking countries. When we consider the trail of the focus of domestic communications through new technology we have the following narrative of replacement, substitution and overlapping from the 1890s onwards. I have cited years when sales began to take on the appearance of mass consumption.

1890	phonograph
1925	radio
1955	television
1960	(transistor radio – portable)
1980	video / satellite receiver
1994	personal computer (PC)

So how many ages can we identify for sound drama or audio drama? It is possible to tentatively advance a breakdown of six epochs or phases.

The First Age: origin time impossible to determine

Oral culture or single voice narratives spring from the earliest beginnings of human storytelling. They have been rooted in the onomatopoetic reliance on rhyme and metrical speech rhythms to preserve storytelling cultures before the development of literature. The oral tradition had been the medium by which various African civilisations had communicated culture and identity from one generation to the next. Archaeological analysis of the Zimbabwe civilisation demonstrates the development of a complex urban society on a parallel time-line with European history. The respect and veneration of elders encompassed the realisation that the death of an elder was equivalent to the destruction of a library. Marshall McLuhan used the maxim 'Look behind you without turning round' to explain the psychological dynamics of acoustic space. McLuhan said in 1954 that human languages are the greatest of all works of art, beside which the works of Homer, Virgil, Dante and Shakespeare are minor variations. He also said in 1972 that 'speech in its subliminal resonance unites us with the most distant ages as well as with the present multitudes'.[2]

The year 1450 introduced McLuhan's Age of the Gutenberg Galaxy. Print enabled 'the translation of auditory into visual terms' and set up 'an inner life in man which separated him from the external world and, in part, from his own senses, as we know from the study of pre-literate societies'.[3] Could this explain the ability of Francis Bacon to imagine the transmission of disembodied voices in his Theory of Sound Houses?[4]

About a hundred years separated the invention of print technology and the imaginative invention of another communications concept not supported at the time by technology but amounting to a prescient prophecy. This is the first evidence of somebody writing about dramatic and narrative communication being amplified by an external agent or mechanism for communication. Throughout this phase the human voice and crude machine components had been used in theatrical presentations to synthesise natural and biological sound. The idea of sound being used imagistically and symbolically in dramatic presentations and narrative entertainment was not an alien experience.

The Second Age: 1878 onwards

The phonograph made possible the first experience of recording and playing back human sound and the sound of natural phenomena, synthesised sound and sound symbolism. In 1877 it has been documented that Thomas Edison recorded the 'Halloo' followed by 'Mary had a little lamb, her fleece was white as snow and everywhere that Mary went, the lamb was sure to go'.[5] This epoch introduces the concept of editing sound communication and recorded sound and the mass marketing of phonographs for entertainment and education. An early sound advertisement for the Edison phonograph (1906) boasts about its potential for helping people to learn languages, and preserve musical performances.[6] This age is still with us. After a period when qualitative delivery of music over the radio nearly extinguished the phonograph industry, musical entertainment was reinvented through the jukebox, the flat disc, improved recording techniques and product promotion through music format radio. From 1986 the USA and Britain have experienced a significant burgeoning of the market for and consumption of spoken word. The Talking Books industry has been embraced by major publishers and some writers now prefer to release their novels as single voice recorded narratives before traditional book publication, e.g. Alan Bennett and *The Clothes They Stood Up In* (BBC Radio Collection 1997).

The Third Age: 1902 onwards

The telephone or cable had become a carrier of broadcast and downloadable sound services. The electrophone was the first device to achieve actual 'broadcasting' by disseminating the same source to a wide number of individuals at the same time. The telephone became critical in the process of networking radio services in the 1920s to remote and distant transmitters. Since the 1970s it has been available as a means of listening to radio stations 'as live' around the world, for specific transmissions of programme items and pieces of information 'on demand' during which the telephone user pays a premium that returns a royalty to the authors of the sound material. Telephone and cable have remained the technical mechanisms for delivering and distributing Internet services, cable television and satellite channels. These are good reasons for giving this period an epochal status. Between 1902 and 1922, the electrophone served as a viable and unique method of communication to listeners without any significant competition from radio.

The Fourth Age: 1908 onwards

Radio or wireless resulted from the development of broadcasting using electromagnetism and the delivery of sound programming to a mass audience, the development of a style of performance and writing which engages with the human ear and imagination. Radio drama was established as a new medium for dramatic expression with plays originally written for the ear. The potential for greater quality of sound transmission has been developed through FM, satellite and digital transmission and reception. The radio drama programming for the Fourth Age is the focus of succeeding chapters and so will not receive detailed treatment here. It is a story characterised by landmarks, some of which continue to have cultural and historical resonance such as the CBS *War of the Worlds* (broadcast on 30 October 1938) and *Under Milk Wood* by Dylan Thomas (1954). Others have receded into obscure and esoteric datelines in radio history such as Archibald MacLeish's *The Fall of the City* (1937), Norman Corwin's *We Hold These Truths* (1941), Giles Cooper's *The Disagreeable Oyster* (1957), or Anthony Minghella's *Cigarettes and Chocolate* (1988). There are the classical dramatisations and popular series. Most of them had powerful cultural resonances when radio was the primary electronic means of mass communication. Some have endured during radio's subsidiary status which followed the ascendancy of television.

It is interesting to highlight that radio drama has succeeded in achieving Brechtian interaction through phone-in participation. The commercial station in London, Capital Radio, began a live 'soap' inviting audience participation to adjust and influence the plot development in 1973. There is a reference to another interactive radio drama project on the London commercial station LBC. In *Radio City*, a study on London radio published in 1989, it was described as 'a project with the drama group Isoceles Triangle, an interactive soap opera which ran for six months and in which people could phone up and take part in the next episode'.[7] A similar experience was successfully undertaken by Finnish Radio Theatre in 1997 with a series called *Diamonds out of a Hat. Call 09/1482822*. Brecht might well have been amused by the idea of a 'programme that cannot be made without listeners, since the listeners devise the plot of the instant radio plays. Anyone can be the script-writer or director'.[8] This was an interactive programme in which listeners were able to influence the outcome not just by saying 'Yes' or 'No' or by expressing their personal opinion on some issue. The drama floated in a phone-in programme in which the listener could order something not prepared in advance. The content was improvised. The programme succeeded in covering the entire range of styles and emotions and fluctuating in a somewhat melodramatic way with the serious being cut short by the ridiculous, horror by romance, satire being transformed into an operetta, and tragedy into an advertisement.

The programme makers claimed that they had removed the gulf between themselves and the listeners. The presenter was not just 'a superfluous dummy'; instead there were four actors and a musician improvising in the studio. The concept had the advantage of asking callers on phone-in shows to provide creative ideas instead of providing opinions. The impetus for this development may have been the fact that improvisation theatre had been popular in Finland in the 1990s. It had also been recorded before a live audience for television, but the transition to live radio took place in March 1997. It has to be realised that radio improvisation is a genre all of its own because the actors do not have eye contact with their audience and all images have to be created through sound, as pure telecontact improvisation.

The process of interactive communication is based on an actor asking the listener to provide three words chosen at random. The actors then make up a story around these words. While the story is in progress, the next caller may alter the style and the plot. The success of the programme depends on the instantaneous inspiration of the actors and callers. The result is a form of radio drama which avoids having to pay for a commissioned writer and limits the costly preproduction process. The adrenalin-charged atmosphere can certainly stimulate powerful performances and links the radio drama of the present with the excitement of live radio drama of the past.[9]

The Fifth Age: symbiosis with film and television from 1926 onwards

The advent of optical recording techniques led to talking pictures and the crosspollination of the artistic experience of sound communication with visual image. Orson Welles in *Citizen Kane* (1943) brought to the film medium a wealth of experience and creative energy in using sound dramatically. Which comes first in the experience of film consumption by the audience? Seeing or hearing? If dramatic development and introduction and development of character are communication through sound then their artistic importance in film should be elevated and consolidated to a degree unacknowledged by most film studies scholars. There is a conceptual resonance between the interplay of sound and vision which is rich and powerful. The Wizard in the film *The Wizard of Oz* (1939), starring Judy Garland, remains as an imaginative engagement through voice/sound stimulation until the end, when the face is revealed for the first time. The same can be said for Hal in Stanley Kubrick's *2001: A Space Odyssey* (1968) and the mother in Alfred Hitchcock's *Psycho* (1960). Francis Ford Coppola's study of obsession *The Conversation* (1974), starring Gene Hackman, is predicated on a sound design which intrigues centrally as a storytelling device. Hackman plays Harry Caul, an industrial spy engaged on a surveillance job using sound recording eavesdropping techniques.

Derek Jarman's film *Blue* (1993), which explores through the dominance of a stereo sound track and a blue screen the film-maker's experience of blindness through his AIDS condition, represents one of the most exciting correlations of this symbiosis. It was premiered simultaneously on UK Channel Four terrestrial television and BBC Radio 3 FM broadcast in September 1993.

One of the world's leading sound designers, Walter Murch, has said: 'We gestate in Sound, and are born into Sight. Cinema gestated in Sight, and was born into sound'.[10] This confirms the theoretical symbiosis between the media and it is supported by the world's leading theorist on cinema sound, Michel Chion, who has asserted:

> We never see the same thing when we also hear; we don't hear the same thing when we see as well. We must therefore get beyond preoccupations such as identifying so-called redundancy between the two domains and debating inter-relations between forces (the famous question asked in the seventies, 'Which is more important, sound or image?')[11]

The Sixth Age: Internet and digital communications from 1994 onwards

The Internet and World Wide Web began to deliver sound services to a mass audience when the multimedia PC became a mass marketed product. The ability to receive sound and pictures from anywhere in the world via the telephone or ISDN line predates terrestrial and satellite digital communications. Established radio stations all over the world began to datastream the live sound of their broadcasting. More imaginative efforts have been made to provide specific audio programmes on demand outside the scheduled framework of daily transmissions that depend on audience and advertising for income and funding. The US Pacifica network was a pioneer in this area. In the field of radio drama the Swedish Radio drama company in Finland discovered the advantage of making radio plays available on demand supported by text and lateral dimensions of information. In 1997 the company was claiming that *Särskilt de primitiva*, or *Particularly Primitive Ones* was (as far as it had been able to ascertain) the first of its kind in the world: 'the first straight audio drama broadcast as radio-on-demand over the Internet'.

Swedish Radio Theatre in Finland took a different approach from its Baltic cousins in Estonia. When the company first started discussing using the Net in 1995, most of its computer addicts insisted that they should start producing interactive, game-like Internet plays. At that time the editors did not feel that such a move made sense because most people were connected to the Net via modem and the bandwidth simply was not big enough for hypertextually constructed Internet plays if they were to be enjoyable. However, audio streaming was in a state of rapid development which evidently meant that the Net could soon be used as a very cheap way of distributing traditional storytelling in a new form: as audio-on-demand. The editors explained their decision to begin with *Particularly Primitive Ones*:

> At the outset we felt that the largest group of people using the Net were

probably young male technofreaks. Consequently our first Internet play is a short science fiction adventure – with lots of Radio play as audio-on-demand explosions and futuristic sound effects.

Nevertheless, *Particularly Primitive Ones* may be a play to be taken seriously (at least according to some science fiction *aficionados*). It can be seen as a play about the roots of xenophobia, or at least about our fear of the unknown. The story is a simple one: a man is rescued from a lifeboat in space. While he is being questioned his interrogators soon find something unexpected about his DNA. He may not be entirely human. They send him back into space and pretend that he never existed.

Of course, the play has a surprise ending. While the scientists have been studying this possibly alien being, they have also been participating in a different study: the whole situation is part of an experiment by the alien anthropologists studying primitive races.[12]

The play was presented in a span of 15 minutes.

Estonian Radio produced a scrolling World Wide Web (WWW) version of the radio play *StrawBully-TarBubble* in 1997. The idea was to present a children's radio play with 'subtitles' and additional information on the Internet. The aim was to make it possible for radio plays to use new channels to win new listeners among children and young people, computer users and Net surfers. The programme makers realised that the interactive presentation of *StrawBully-TarBubble* on Estonian Radio's website gave listeners the following possibilities:

1 Entering Estonian Radio WWW page you can listen to the radio play in real time whenever you want to.
2 You can read the text in three languages (Estonian, Russian, English) synchronously with the sound (in Estonian).
3 You can roll the text on screen and start the play at any point you choose.
4 Clicking on marked words, you can get additional information.
5 See moving pictures that illustrate the radio play.
6 Criticise the play, express your opinion.[13]

Estonian Radio believed that their project presented an image of progressive art for the radio play which could be followed all over Europe and the rest of the world.

Independent Radio Drama Productions (IRDP) in Britain established the first 'UK Internet Play of the Month' and web designer Marja Giejgo has established a unique site providing sound on demand, scrolling scripts and background information to radio drama which can be accessed from anywhere in the world. Surround sound and advanced recording techniques can be appreciated on home and portable PCs while consumers surf the Internet or operate their computers for wordprocessing, databasing and other tasks.

The pioneering communication of audio drama on this website has been recognised by a number of notable British radio critics. Ken Garner of the *Express on Sunday* (a newspaper with a circulation of more than 1 million) and also a lecturer at Glasgow Caledonian University, stated (19 July 1998) that IRDP had 'an acclaimed website (www.irdp.co.uk) with its Internet Play of the Month for July – one neat idea the BBC's website doesn't offer.' Richard Rudin, lecturer in media at Liverpool's John Moores University, reported in his *Radio Magazine* Sound Sites column (3 January 1998):

> IRDP have scored a remarkable first in putting their productions on the Internet so that anyone in the world with access to a computer, modem and 'RealAudio' software can listen to a new play every month. The first 'UK Internet Play of the Month' is a remarkable production of Francis Beckett's satire 'The Sons of Catholic Gentlemen' . . . The play can be downloaded in five files, each of around ten minutes. Well worth a listen! Elsewhere on the IRDP site you can download pages of related information, such as how to write radio drama, details of drama competitions, the background to the prestigious Prix Italia, awards won by IRDP . . . There are also pages about the history of radio, particularly its power and psychological impact. All of this is very well written, researched and presented.

Jerry Stearns on his 'Radio Theatre on the Web' site stated that IRDP was

> One of the biggest and most certainly the best radio drama production companies in the United Kingdom. I've heard a number of their pieces on National Public Radio here. The Web Site has information about their broadcast schedules, tapes available from them, and a few other interesting and useful items and articles about radio drama. I've never met them, but I like them already.

The *Observer*'s Internet critic John Naughton, an author and Cambridge University scholar, observed (14 December 1997):

> It's amazing what people are using real audio for. This week, a British outfit called Independent Radio Drama Productions started broadcasting an 'Internet play of the month' on its site (www.irdp.co.uk/playmonth.htm). The first production stars Tony Booth, the Prime Minister's father-in-law, in Francis Beckett's satire about an oppressive Jesuit public school, The Sons of Catholic Gentlemen. The play consists of five links – each containing a separate episode – on a Web page. Click on an episode, wait a few seconds and out boom Booth and the rest of the cast from one's speakers.

The radio critic for the *Guardian*, Anne Karpf, wrote (13 December 1997):

Is it a bird? Is it a plane? No, it's the first UK Internet Play of the Month, accessible to anyone with a computer and a modem. It even stars the PM's father-in-law, Tony Booth. Modern or what? For the listener, too, though at first it seems perverse to put an aural genre on to what is still primarily a visual medium, there are evident benefits. This is 'radio drama on demand', access-ible (from http://www.irdp.co.uk/playmonth.htm) on Real Audio stereo whenever a listener chooses, for as long as they choose. And of course there's a potentially global audience.

The IRDP site was the first audio drama web service to be recognised by the prestigious UK Radio Academy/British Telecom technical innovation award (16 July 1998) and the first UK audio site to win an award at the International Interactive Media Awards, Washington DC (September 1998).

One of the political and social features of Internet broadcasting is that it can be achieved without any state interference or censorship by regulation. It can be argued that it is a profoundly liberating medium for communities and social groups that are exposed to cultural and political discrimination. In this way the Internet can advance the democracy of communications to a level never experi-enced before.

IRDP has been excluded from the BBC approved list of independent producers, a decision made without any notice or credible process of appeal. Despite its documented track record in developing new writers and innovation in audio drama it has no access to the £18 million monopoly of radio drama funding controlled by the BBC each year.[14] As a non-profit arts company IRDP does not have the economies of scale to capitalise 'tendering bids' for digital and analogue channels. In October 1999 the UK's first national radio drama, comedy and readings channel was expected to start on the DigitalOne multiplex owned by GWR. Political-economic conditions block and exclude the opportunity for free-dom of expression in a wide range of audio delivery systems. The Internet bypasses these mechanisms of cultural discrimination.

All India Radio provides plays on demand in Tamil, Hindi and other Indian languages. This Internet service provides a significant weapon to resist the pres-sure of American and western cultural hegemony. The Internet also provides the power and opportunity to link the present with the past. The American website www.scifi.com/set/ provides the 'Seeing Ear Theatre'. The company offers resources of contemporary audio science fiction production with celebration of significant archive. Sound streaming is directly linked to the scrolling narrative of graphics which offer a new dimension of artistic fusion with sound. The images are not mimetic, nor are they a halfway gesture towards presenting film and video.

Chapter 5

From sound
houses to the
phonograph
sound play

Having set out a theoretical manifesto for defining the separate and overlapping epochs or ages of audio drama, it would now be helpful to discuss the sources which underpin and illustrate the first, second and sixth ages. The fifth age, involving the symbiosis of audio storytelling sound with film sound, is covered in the section on 'sound design' (pp. 70–90).

Our exploration of the first age of radio depends on the preservation of texts and artefacts demonstrating specific techniques of articulating sound to engage with the human imagination and exploring imaginatively the disembodied communication of sound. Little evidence is available to us. In many ways Francis Bacon's enthusiasm for 'sound houses' in his Utopian book *The New Atlantis* (1626) belongs to the genre of contemporary soothsaying. The image is an extraordinary prophecy about the potential of sound communication three centuries before scientific development could reproduce the idea as reality:

> We have also sound-houses, where we practise and demonstrate all sounds and their generation. We have harmony which you have not, of quarter-sounds and lesser slides of sounds. Divers instruments of music likewise to you unknown, some sweeter than any you have; with bells and rings that are dainty and sweet. We represent small sounds as great and deep, likewise great sounds extenuate and sharp; we make divers tremblings and warblings of sounds, which in their original are entire. We represent and imitate all articulate sounds and letters, and the voices and notes of beasts and birds. We have certain helps which, set to the ear, do further the hearing greatly; we have also divers strange and artificial echoes, reflecting the voice many times, and, as it were, tossing it; and

some that give back the voice louder than it came, some shriller and some deeper; yea, some rendering the voice, differing in the letters or articulate sound from that they receive. We have all means to convey sounds in trunks and pipes, in strange lines and distances.[1]

Although his writing would appear to be fantastic, Bacon's prophecies were often derived from an empirical link between observation and theory. Margaret Drabble has said:

he proposed that nature's secrets should be unlocked, so that mankind can acquire power over its circumstances, by means of a mechanical routine of eliminative induction, making a gradual ascent from the level of the observably particular to the ever more general level of theory.[2]

Bacon's thinking could have been placed into the realms of modern science fiction writing. He has something in common with H. G. Wells who, in his novel *When the Sleeper Wakes* (1899), predicted babble machines chattering out news and propaganda into people's homes everywhere. The old man character made this interesting philosophical observation about the cultural limitations of physiologically separating the human voice from the body:

When I was a boy – I'm that old – I used to read printed books. You'd hardly think it. Likely you've seen none – they rot and dust so – and the Sanitary Company burns them to make ashlarite. But they were convenient in their dirty way. Oh I learnt a lot. These new-fangled Babble Machines – they don't seem new-fangled to you, eh? – they're easy to hear, easy to forget.[3]

The central character Graham appreciates the propagandist power of this new medium of communication. Bear in mind that H. G. Wells was writing in 1899, twenty-two years before radio was effectively established as a 'broadcasting' service:

He went off at a tangent to ask for information about these Babble Machines. For the most part, the crowd present had been shabbily or even raggedly dressed, and Graham learnt that so far as the more prosperous classes were concerned, in all the more comfortable private apartments of the city were fixed Babble Machines that would speak directly a lever was pulled. The tenant of the apartment could connect this with the cables of any of the great News Syndicates that he preferred. When he learnt this presently, he demanded the reason of their absence from his own suite of apartments. Asano stared. 'I never thought,' he said. 'Ostrog must have had them removed.'

The second age has the advantage of leaving us a limited though fascinating legacy of recorded artefacts proving and demonstrating communication through sound.

The accident of survival and avoidance of destruction means that we have to be very cautious about making exaggerated claims about a particular recording that was preserved by a private collector and passed into a sound archive.

Shakespeare is an author who seems to have an all-pervasive influence throughout a variety of cultures which transcends centuries in the enduring production, interpretation and publication of his texts through stage performance. It is not surprising that presentation of his plays embraced the new technology of sound recording. Generally this took the form of single voice soliloquy performances of well known speeches by the stage stars of the late Victorian and early Edwardian period. The old adage that actors recreate Shakespeare in the image of their own epoch is more than confirmed by listening to these rare recordings. All the early BBC experiments in live radio drama were centred on Shakespearian text. As John Drakakis confirmed in his book on *British Radio Drama* (1981):

> The early radio adaptations of Shakespeare, carried out by Cathleen Nesbitt under the direction of C. A. Lewis . . . in addition to the quarrel scene from *Julius Caesar*, adaptations included the trial scene from *The Merchant of Venice* (23 May 1923), a recitation by the actress Ellen Terry of the Hubert and Arthur scene from *King John* (31 May 1923), excerpts from *Henry VIII* (7 June 1923) and *Romeo and Juliet* (5 July 1923), and readings from *Macbeth* by John Gielgud and Ben Webster (18 October 1923).[4]

Pavilion Records has published a fascinating compendium of recordings in the CD collection *Great Shakespeareans* (1991) which means that they are now accessible to students. The earliest recording is from 1890, by the American actor Edwin Booth, the brother of John Wilkes Booth, who assassinated President Lincoln in 1865 during a Washington DC performance at the Ford's Theatre of Tom Taylor's play *Our American Cousin*. David Bruce in the accompanying CD sleeve observes:

> Edwin Booth made his debut in Boston in a small part in *King Richard III* and was soon hailed as America's greatest tragic actor. A memorable Othello, he played this part in 1882 at London's Lyceum Theatre. Ellen Terry was the Desdemona and Booth alternated the title role with Henry Irving.[5]

Booth is heard performing Othello's speech which begins 'Most potent, grave and reverend seigniors'. Other early recordings include Sir Herbert Beerbohm Tree (1906), Arthur Bourchier (1909), Lewis Waller (1911) and Ben Greet (1912).

David Bruce observes: 'the actors had no recording technique, and apart from heeding the advice of the recordist to speak loudly and clearly probably did no more than repeat their customary stage performance into the recording horn' with the time honoured professional technique of 'projection' in a large amphitheatre. However, something more important needs to be deduced from these performances. They captured Shakespearian soliloquies which parallel the internal monologue convention of modern radio drama. The late actor Don Henderson, who had a distinguished career in the Royal Shakespeare Company, frequently observed that Shakespeare wrote as if he was serving the sound medium.[6] It was as though Francis Bacon's sound houses were a reality. Contemporary Shakespearian productions engaged the imagination much more extensively than lavish Victorian and twentieth-century productions which sought to reproduce reality with effects and exotic costume and set design. The reliance on imaginative sympathy and the closer link with the oral tradition – reflected in the use of the iambic pentameter and poetic expression in rhyme, metre and metaphor – makes Shakespeare a natural forum for communication through sound alone.

Edwin Booth's performance through the crackle and static of an 1890 wax cylinder suggests a more intimate style of dramatic communication than the clichéd idea of loud rhetorical and declamatory Victorian acting. The CD includes more fluent and romantic performances by John Gielgud and Maurice Evans recorded in the 1930s as radio's 'golden age' became fully established and both performers gesture towards the modernism of radio microphone technique in their interpretation of Shakespeare's famous speeches.

There is little evidence available of attempts to fully record dramatic stage performances for phonograph entertainment. Recording engineers were faced with the problem of ambient communication of different voices in a wide arc of positions. The microphones available at the time had a limited direct sound potential. However, Pavilion Records has included a recording made in 1917 on its CD of *The Great War*; this presents remarkable evidence of an ability to present complex, sophisticated and highly entertaining performance by a large cast with a range of synthesised sound effects that create a clear sound design. 'In the Trenches' by Major A. E. Rees is 3 minutes 28 seconds long. It begins with a background of machine-gun and whiz-bang shelling sounds and a well articulated dialogue. There is clear evidence of the company being directed by Major Rees to bring performances to the foreground of the microphone pick-up field in order to focus on the central dialogue. A balance between the foreground dialogue and background sound of larger numbers of soldiers and atmospheric and spot effects has been clearly arranged. The result is that here is a propagandist and popular drama being communicated with clarity on a wax phonograph and predating production techniques which were to become standard five to six years later.

It is also intriguing that there is clear evidence of writing for the 'mind's eye'. Rees gives his central characters lines such as 'Here Sergeant have a look through this telescope, there's something out there in No Man's Land'. A sound picture of the rescue of the wounded soldier is presented through descriptive language. Historians Tonie and Valmai Holt observe in their notes on the accompanying CD sleeve:

The characters in this 1917 sketch resemble Bruce Bairnfather's loveable creations, Old Bill, Bert and Alf. The dialogue is peppered with WW1 phrases: 'meatless day' (more likely to be declared on the Home Front than in the Front line, when many days were unplanned meatless days); whiz-bangs (a particularly noisy German shell); 'napoo' (which came to equate to 'kaput'); 'over the top'; 'No Man's Land'; a 'dud' (so many British shells failed to explode that it caused the infamous 'shell scandal'); 'the Boches' (Tommy's name for his German counterpart). Our hero, 'Tippy', rescues a wounded comrade, under enemy fire, bringing him to safety on his back.[7]

It is reasonable to argue that this could be the earliest surviving audiophonic play.

Evidence of the use of phonograph technology by the pioneers of acoustic art has been documented by Douglas Kahn in *Wireless Imagination* (1994),[8] and a translation into English of an essay by Klaus Schöning entitled 'The contours of acoustic art' (1991).[9] No doubt there is likely to be a considerable range of texts available in Russian, Italian and German exploring the work of the early pioneers of what is becoming known as 'Ars Acoustica'. But these references are a useful starting point. Kahn explores the metaphorical inspiration of the development of sound technology and communication in literature. I have already mentioned H. G. Wells. Bram Stoker's *Dracula* (1897) also featured the character Doctor Seward using the phonograph as a social recording device to archive his psychiatric observations.[10] Kahn successfully cites more poetic expression of the new technology in the development of early science fiction literature. Villier de l'Isle-Adam's *L'Eve future*, Marcel Schwob's *La Machine a parlier*, Maurice Renard's *La Mort et le coquillage*, Alfred Jarry's *Phonographe* and Raymond Roussel's *Locus Solus* transmogrify the sound-emitting power of modernist machinery into nightmarish, futuristic and supernatural images and contexts. Kahn places great store on the experimental writing of the Italian futurist Marinetti, who covered the Italian-Turkish war in Libya in 1911 and the Balkan war a year later. In his script *Zang-tumb-tuum, Adrianopoli, ottobre 1912*, Marinetti 'takes on the role of the phonograph by enacting an onomatopoetic reportage of the ZANG-TUMB-TUUUMB of the cannon, the taratatata of the machine guns, and other sounds interspersed with musical instructions'.

This work inspired the genre of *parole in liberta*. A stimulating debate ensued with Luigi Russolo publishing a manifesto *The Art of Noises* (1913) and exploring the artistic potential of sound. Schöning gives Russolo's publication more influence and status by suggesting that it inspired Erik Satie's use of noises in his score for Serge Diaghilev's ballet *Parades*, which was premiered in Paris in 1917. Guillaume Apollinaire made the rather self-evident point in his essay 'The new spirit and the poets' (1918) that there did not seem to be much point in verbally imitating 'worldly sounds such as the futurist-like "whirring of an air plane" when auditive reality will always be superior'.[11]

At the same time the Russian futurists were seeking an emancipation of the sounds of language. The publication of *A Slap in the Face of Public Taste* (1912) included contributions from Velimir Khlebnikov and Vladimir Mayakovsky. Schöning has also unearthed earlier examples of 'sound poems' from the German genre of literature. They include Paul Scheerbart's *Kikakoku* (1897) and Christian Morgenstern's *Das grosse Lalula* (1890). While these literary references to debates about the phonic dimension of poetry are interesting, they are not backed up with any evidence of contemporary experimentation with the technology available.

So far text references appear to cite only one concrete incidence of applying the new ideas and theories in a practical way during the second age of audio drama. In Petrograd in 1916 Dziga Vertov founded the 'laboratory of hearing' and experimented by editing shorthand records and gramophone records. He was using a Pathephone wax disc recorder and attempted documentary recordings of a waterfall and the sounds of a sawmill. It would appear he gave up rather quickly when he realised that the existing technology could not enable him to montage and edit with precision. He documented, 'I must get a piece of equipment that won't describe, but will record, photograph these sounds. Otherwise it's impossible to organise, edit them.' These technical difficulties were also experienced by Laszlo Moholy-Nagy.

In his *De Stijl* article 'Production-reproduction' (1922) Moholy-Nagy sought to fuse writing and sound into a new synthesis. German acoustic artist Walther Ruttman experienced a similar frustration; he would progress towards a successful expression of sound montage with the flexible editing potential of optical film strip. Ruttman's *Weekend* broadcast on Radio Berlin (13 June 1930) appears to be the earliest example of sound art to have been preserved. But this was in the middle of the radio age and the mechanism for communication was the radio medium. Vertov was working in Soviet radio after the October Revolution and in 1925 he was writing about the concept of radio-film. During this period Radio Berlin's director Alfred Braun was seeking a filmic visual montage approach to sound. Schöning quotes him as saying:

> Acoustical film was the term we used in Berlin . . . for a radio play that through its dream-like, quickly moving sequence of images gliding, jumping, overlapping each other, alternating between close-ups and distance shots blending in and out deliberately transferred the techniques of moving pictures to the radio.[12]

Douglas Kahn has researched the impact of sound technology and radio as an artistic inspiration to poets and novelists. Again we have evidence of this creative dynamic breaking open the reliance of creative writers on the linear narrative framework of communication. Kahn makes the point:

Although projects such as this may seem to bear little relevance to 'practical' work, often the best art resides in idea alone, unencumbered by inhibiting pressures bound to time and place. This is especially so when these ideas are about radio, which is by its nature at least two places at once.[13]

This simple though noble conclusion supports my earlier contention that the space for radio/audio drama lies in the physicality of aural experience and the psychological space of the mind's imagination which is, of course, visual and aural.

It is conceivable that sound artists not documented by existing texts or surviving evidence may well have succeeded in advancing the art of sound expression. The phonograph offered the opportunity to mix a multiplicity of sounds from different machines. 'In the Trenches' by Major Rees in 1917 demonstrated the potential for phonography. Major Rees seems to have been a writer and director with more determination and persistence. It was not beyond the technological initiative and creative ingenuity of sound artists to attempt something more ambitious. Whether documented or undocumented sound artists achieved anything significant will remain a mystery. The second age of audio drama spanned the last twenty years of the nineteenth century and the first twenty years of the twentieth. This was a time when the value of writing and archiving sound production was limited.

Chapter 6

A technological
time-line

Key dates in the technological development of recorded sound are listed here.

1877 Thomas Edison recorded the word 'Halloo' onto a paper version of his cylinder phonograph in July and then succeeded in preserving the expression 'Mary had a little lamb' on 6 December. His engineer John Kruesi is said to have replied 'Gott im Himmel!' The machine was patented in February 1878.

1885 Alexander Bell and Charles Tainter patented the rival technology of the 'Graphophone', which used vertical cut grooves on wax cylinders. They were working with Columbia Phonograph Company.

1888 Emile Berliner patented the 'Gramophone' using 7-inch flat discs with grooves cut laterally, which ran at 70 revolutions per minute and had a 2 minute capacity. Edison increased the cylinder duration capacity to 4 minutes in 1908. This period onwards saw the development and marketing of cylinder and disc machines.

1889 W. K. L. Dickson demonstrated the 'Kinetophonograph', a device which synchronised sound by phonograph with images projected from film, to Thomas Edison, but they failed to develop the system effectively.

1898 Valdemar Poulsen patented the first magnetic recorder, called the 'Telegraphone', which used steel wire.

1921 Record sales began to fall from a peak of $106 million a year due to the expansion of live music transmission on radio, which offered better quality with no charge.

1925 AT&T achieved the first electrically recorded disc.

1926 Warner Bros signed a contract with the AT&T subsidiary Western Electric to use a new machine described as the 'Vitaphone', which used 20 inch acetate-coated aluminium transcription discs which could record in synchrony with film reel. It was introduced in August during a presentation of *Don Juan* in a theatre on 51st Street, off Broadway, New York City. Music and sound effects and an introduction by William Hayes were all pre-recorded on 'Vitaphone'. Hayes later gave his name to the 'Hayes Code', which became a strict censorship policy determining severe limits on the depiction of sex or human passion on screen.

1927 Warner Bros inserted Vitaphone recorded sequences into the *Jazz Singer* (1927), which was premiered in New York City, and along with *Lights of New York* (1928), which was the first all dialogue film, heralded the advance of 'the talkies'. Fox Film began to advance an alternative sound recording technology which used light beams or 'optical' transfer from film image rather than a mechanical transfer by way of a needle cutting into a disc or cylinder. William Fox leased the method from AT&T for newsreels in April 1927, five months before the opening of *The Jazz Singer*. Fox presented the only sound footage of Charles Lindbergh's take-off and triumphal return across the Atlantic. This was also the year when the juke-box was invented by Automatic Music Instrument in Grand Rapids, Michigan, but it was not built in large quantities until 1934.

1928 Dr Fritz Pfleumeer patented the application of magnetic powders to strips of paper or film in Germany. AT&T licensed optical film/sound recording to Paramount, MGM and United Artists and it became the standard method of delivering sound to cinema audiences.

1931 Alan Blumlain patented the stereo or 'binaural' recording method.

1932 BASF of I. G. Farben developed magnetic tape recording in partnership with AEG of Telefunken.

1933 Jukeboxes were sold to distributors for installation of music systems in drinking taverns.

1936 First tape recording of a live concert by Sir Thomas Beecham in Germany.

1939 Wire Recorders were invented by Marvin Camras in the USA and sold in large quantities to the US Navy.

1940 RCA/NBC's David Sarnoff installed secret recording technology in the US White House and used the film optical recording technology.

1945 US Signal Corps Captain John Mullin discovered German magnetophones at Radio Frankfurt in Germany with half-inch ferric oxide coated tape on 20 minute reels. BBC engineers also sent machines back to Britain, but the Americans seized the potential and Bing Crosby liaised with Mullin and Ampex on the manufacturing of US tape recorders, which were introduced in 1948.

1948 First 12 inch LP vinyl with playback at thirty-three and a third revolutions per second marketed by Columbia. Magnecord manufactured the first open-reel stereo tape recorder.

1949 RCA Victor introduced the 7 inch vinyl record that could play back at forty-five revolutions per second.

1951 Stefan Kudelski built the first portable, self-contained sound recorder and marketed it under the trade name 'Nagra'. Experiments with video tape recording began.

1954 Manufacture of the first portable transistor radio in Indianapolis.

1964 Introduction of the audio cassette for domestic consumption.

1969 Dolby Laboratories introduced Dolby Noise reduction for pre-recorded tapes. The first telephone line link was made between two US defence computers, which is regarded as an important moment in the development of the Internet.

1979 Sony introduced the Walkman portable audio cassette player.

1987 Digital Audio Tape (DAT) players and recorders were introduced to the domestic market.

1989 Britain's first public Internet service was started by Demon Internet.

1991 HTML by Tim Berners-Lee at CERN was released under the name 'World Wide Web'.

1992 Mosaic was developed by Marc Anderson at the National Center for Super-computer Activity, University of Illinois, a navigational programme displaying graphics and hyperlinks for windows. During the US presidential campaign Senator Al Gore spoke about the 'Information Superhighway' and heralded the use of the Web as a business strategy.

1994 The BBC and major commercial broadcasting groups decided to invest in the development of Digital Audio Broadcasting. Over 200 Internet service providers were now in business in the UK.

1996 One estimate asserted that 40 million people were connected to the Internet with a rate of 10 per cent increase per quarter.

The personal computer, Internet and World Wide Web time-line of dates is tentative. Between 1969 and 1974 the original networks were military and academic: ARPAnet connected US universities, MILnet connected military bases and JANET connected UK universities.[1] What started as a defence establishment and university network of communication has expanded into a new 'galaxy' of media experience and has further enriched the McLuhan 'bath immersion' definition of the individual's relationship to the global village of world communication. The language of web communication is Hyper Text Markup Language (HTML), which was developed by Tim Berners-Lee and his research team at CERN, the European Organisation for Nuclear Research in Geneva. The objective was to enable researchers in high-energy physics to share their research with one another. The development of Mosaic by Marc Anderson at the University of Illinois interfaced text as well as graphics, and introduced navigating with hyperlinks that could be activated with the click of the mouse. The World Wide Web has seen unprecedented growth since 1992.[2]

Chapter 7

A culturalist approach to Internet audio drama

At this point it would be useful to set out the interactive and precise social and psychological factors which extend the body of the human individual's communication capacity through Internet audio drama broadcasting and reception. The theorist Mark Poster identifies the introduction of the new media of the Internet as *The Second Media Age*.[1] Poster posits a communications environment which is decentralised, multidirectional and interactive:

> the mode of information indicates communication practices that constitute subjects as unstable, multiple and diffuse . . . if that is done the questions of the mass media are seen not simply as that of sender/receiver, producer/consumer, ruler/ruled. The shift to a decentralised network of communications makes senders receivers, producers consumers, rulers ruled, upsetting the logic of understanding the first media age.[2]

It can be argued that the Internet expands the democratic potential of freedom of expression in writing and art in broadcasting. It clearly extends public access to mass communication and participation in the public sphere. Young writers who have experienced the brunt of exclusion and denial of opportunity in BBC licence-funded radio drama since the late 1980s have been given an opportunity to send and receive communication on a level not seen since the introduction of the telephone. The Internet depends on participation in the political economy of the technology, but compared with terrestrial analogue economies of scale in broadcasting, the Internet is remarkably cost-effective.

The delivery system, which is vast and a veritable electronic galaxy of penetration, is not a significant charge for the communicator. It is there like space or air.

As a comparison with the telephone, only the production and the telephone itself have to be funded. Connection charges are no more than those associated with telephone communication. Yet the transmission is not one to one but a broadcasting distribution. The transmission of the sound as in waves through FM, AM or short-wave broadcasting is not the communicator's responsibility.

Another important factor from the point of view of democracy is the absence of state regulation. There are no top-down agencies of control. Broadcasting on the Internet is not restricted to oligopolies that operate in so many national broadcasting systems.[3]

The IRDP audio drama website produced by Marja Giejgo provides a global and convergence outlet to satisfy a demand to produce and experience new writing, and share in cultural expression by young people in a medium which has been dominated by BBC Radio 4 in the UK and Old Time Radio in the USA. The audiences for both are dominated by a 55-plus age-group profile. The existence of demand is indicated by the fact that by March 1998, IRDP had received and evaluated 4,287 scripts from young writers. All received critiques and 114 scripts were professionally remunerated and produced for radio broadcast. Ten writers had their radio scripts developed and produced for professional stage theatre production. The writers had been drawn from all areas of the UK and reflected the multicultural profile of contemporary society. Twenty-three of the young people produced have gone on to develop professional writing careers with repeat commissions and productions in other media. They include Simon Beaufoy, screenwriter of *The Full Monty*, one of Britain's most successful films; Jane Duncan, winner of a Channel Four screen writing competition, Scottish theatre playwright; Anna Hashmi, who had a production on BBC Radio 4, film screen writing and membership of the Royal Court Theatre writers' group; James Payne, a BBC Radio 1 and Carlton Television writer; Emma Howell, of the BBC Radio and Theatre Royal Stratford East writers' group, and William George Q, the Edinburgh Festival and BAC playwright.

A March 1998 evaluation of IRDP's performance on equal opportunities disclosed that professional production of writers demonstrated the following balance:

- Women writers: 52 per cent
- Men writers: 48 per cent
- Non-white writers: 7 per cent
- Writers under the age of 30: 72 per cent.

The large percentage of writers under 30 can be explained by the fact that the company's national young writers' scheme created an output of more new writers than any of its other projects. In 1996 the UK's ethnic communities comprised 3 million of a total population of 55 million, a proportion of 5.5 per cent.[4] IRDP's output of writers from ethnic minority communities was better than many arts organisations.

By March 1998, the BBC had closed its script development units for television and radio and did not have any consistent policy on providing training, education and encouragement for young writers. It can be argued that the cultural value of British dramatic writing and expression is dependent on sustained infrastructures for writing encouragement and development. IRDP's modest expansion of the provision of this public service on UK commercial radio between 1988 and 1998 took place while the BBC retreated. The independent radio expansion clearly demonstrated that young people demanded this opportunity and responded with a reviewed track record of creativity and success. The main outlet for radio drama broadcasting in the UK was the national network BBC Radio 4 with an average listener age of 53. Out of 11 million listeners every month, only 2.6 million were under the age of 45.[5] In the absence of a national outlet for terrestrial transmission the Internet and World Wide Web offered an alternative medium which younger people were more in tune with as a communications medium.

By March 1998 there were clear indications that people aged 21 and under were being guaranteed their introduction to the Internet and World Wide Web through education. About 18,400 of the UK's 34,300 schools were connected by the end of 1997. The National Grid for Learning and UK NetYear was seeking to achieve full connection for all state-funded schools, particularly those which were small, rural and disadvantaged. The Teacher Training Agency was developing a strategy for teaching information technology to British teachers. Multimedia computers were the fastest selling electronics communications product in the UK. By the middle of 1997 about 2 million people owned a personal computer and 750,000 had a link to an Internet Service provider. This market was growing rapidly. British Interactive Broadcasting (BT and BSkyB) was working on a convergence technology between computer and television to achieve Internet access for the 22 million households with a television set.

The development of the IRDP website was appropriately timed to coincide with the project to ensure Internet connection for the UK's 9 million school pupils. By March 1998 all UK universities and further education colleges had a provision for Internet access, which involved around 2 million people aged 18 and above.

In March 1998 IRDP surveyed a sample of fifty young writers (aged 30 or under) to seek their views and opinions on the potential of Internet audio drama. The sample was drawn from writers who had previously been produced by the company for radio. The subjects were asked three questions:

1 What are the advantages of writing audio/radio drama for the Internet?
2 What are the advantages of hearing audio/radio drama on the Internet?
3 How does it compare with terrestrial radio broadcasting?

The following is a summary of what they defined as the advantageous characteristics:

1   Workshopping and script development create a training and educational interaction that is personal and on demand for anyone with access to a personal computer and the Internet.

2   The harnessing and development of young British writers offer national and international exposure and presentation not currently available through the old technologies.

3   The training and production of new writing is superefficient from the point of view of economies of scale in training and production. More qualitative plays can be produced and transmitted through sound than through other media such as book publication and distribution, stage theatre, film and television.

4   The Internet provides a fully interactive and personal teaching relationship through email and the provision of sound, video, graphics and text material. No other teaching environment can reach so many people with this level of intensity and depth of interaction.

5   Dramaturgical development with new writers is far more instant and efficient through the rapid changes that can be achieved through digital text editing and emailing. Submission of completed scripts is highly efficient through email and this interactive relationship continues with the writer's involvement in casting, direction and production.

6   The production and broadcast represents a major transformation of the relationship between writer and audience. The writer can provide a lateral framework of information through text, pictures and video to accompany the transmission of the sound play. The writer can establish lateral dimensions and options in the presentation of plot and offer the listener choices in the content of the storytelling. A story can diverge into parallel directions of narrative which can be experienced at different times by the listener.

7   The listener can choose when and how long to listen to the play. The listener has access to the play 24 hours a day and this empowerment enables the listener to experience a less ephemeral relationship with the writer. In fact this dimension of communication provides a more defining and tangible literary quality to the author's work. The script can be published and scrolled on screen at the same time as the sound play is transmitted on demand. Background and cultural context and critical review can be provided and exchanged with the audience. The listener can return to the work and deepen the experience of listening by repeating the process or choosing to select sequences exciting further interest.

8   The Web becomes an all-encompassing promotion of the identity of the writer through autobiographical information, individual promotion and links to other aspects of the writer's contribution to the community. The position and value of the writer is therefore enhanced through the use of this new technology.

9   The promotion and transmission of the writer's work continues to use the existing technology of terrestrial radio transmission on LBC 1152 AM in London and distribution to other radio services interested in transmitting drama so that the experience of writing development and production is a symbiotic partnership of old and new technology.

10 The dedicated commitment of schools, colleges and universities to investment in PC and Internet resourcing for students of all ages means that radio writing dramaturgy on the World Wide Web could be providing a comprehensive educational Internet service which is of value to teachers and students at all levels.

This limited though enlightening survey, combined with the development of the IRDP, Swedish Radio Theatre in Finland and Estonian Radio websites for audio drama, highlights the convergence of radio drama broadcasting with the Internet and the creation of a new medium embracing the capabilities of both. Text, pictures and additional data accompanying the audio mean that interactivity is central to the listener's experience. This is more so than the multilateral development of Digital Audio Broadcasting which retains the point to point, master–servant, sender–receiver relationship inherent in terrestrial broadcasting to listeners. Email and live on-site chat groups move interactivity further. It is perhaps here that Marshall McLuhan can provide a significant observation on the implications of this development:

> Archimedes once said, 'Give me a place to stand and I will move the world.' Today he would have pointed to our electric media and said, 'I will stand on your eyes, your ears, your nerves, and your brain, and the world will move in any tempo or pattern I choose'.[6]

Personal computers are also introducing through advanced sound technology as well as three-dimensional visual technology a 'virtual reality' experience which raises questions investigated by the French philosopher Jean Baudrillard on the difference between the real and the represented. But in relation to audio drama, the principle of simulacra is not, I would argue at the moment, a relevant issue with regard to culture, literature and society. Its concern has more to do with politics and economics. The bizarre 'BBC Experience' exhibition on radio history demands a box office entry fee at Broadcasting House in London and has become a commercial celebration of a programming heritage funded by public taxation.

I think that this funfair of broadcasting offers a disturbing study of Baudrillard's simulacrum. The hyperreality of this absurd exhibition is plain to an independent thinker, but would appear to be rather seductive for the majority of participants with its distorted misrepresentations of history and strange interactions for visitors. The subject of 'the experience' has become dominated by objects of fascination, in other words the perceived value and significance of BBC cultural history. When opposites in integrity and dishonesty, quality and poor production values, beauty and ugliness begin to collapse the essential purpose and cultural value of radio drama implodes into a flawed and vacuous hyperreality with the difference between what is real and what is imagined utterly effaced. As Baudrillard said:

> There is in this conformity a force of seduction in the literal sense of the word, a force of diversion, capture and ironic fascination. There is a kind of fatal strategy of conformity.[7]

The Internet dimension of technological communication, with its surround sound delivery and three-dimensional visual interaction, recasts and retrieves McLuhan's pre-Gutenberg Galaxy acoustic space. Hearing is now from all directions at once on a 360 degree axis. McLuhan asserted in 1988 that:

> Much of the confusion of our present age stems naturally from the divergent experience of Western literate man, on the one hand, and his new surround of simultaneous or acoustic knowledge, on the other. Western man is torn between the claims of visual and auditory cultures or structures.[8]

At this stage it would be interesting to refer again to the complex though interesting analysis by Paddy Scannell of Martin Heidegger's *Being and Time* (1927).[9] Here is a brave attempt to root the dailiness and time perspective of contemporary terrestrial broadcasting with a philosophical text that was pre-occupied with the meaning and significance of daily life. You could not have a more divergent position in relation to evaluating the purpose and value of electronic media. McLuhan posed questions to inspire us to seek to see things that are there. His system of explanation, such as it is, rests on an interactive tetrad of questions: What does it extend? What does it make obsolete? What does it retrieve? What does it reverse into? Heidegger struggles to define the purpose of existence in an existential tradition. The media and radio are an extension of the human function and existence for McLuhan. For Heidegger the modernity of electronic media communication desensitises people and cloaks them in artificial ways of being. Scannell stretches Heidegger's definition of *Dasein* with a positive and encouraging discussion about the caring inclination and sociological motivation of programme makers and the dailiness of existence being supported by the past and present heritage of regular time structures such as the breakfast reality of the *Today* programme on BBC Radio 4, *Desert Island Discs* and the longest running 'soap' in radio history, *The Archers*.

Scannell's discourse is both intellectual and rather romantic and excludes acknowledgement of the tendency to promiscuousness by radio listeners in a more competitive and fragmented radio market. The introduction and potential convergence of everyday broadcasting with digital Internet consumption and interactivity challenge Scannell's optimistic restoration of the magic of everyday existence through Heidegger. The interactivity of the Internet means that daili-ness as an existence framework determined by the traditions of terrestrial broadcasting is largely broken up by the independence of the listener determin-ing the structure and style of consumption. This runs laterally along the world timeline as well as the past and present time-line of chronological programmes, particularly if the previous programmes are held on an 'on demand' audio archive.

Scannell's romantic argument therefore becomes an intriguing ontological symbol of media history rather than a helpful 'media law' which can be used to explain the rapid technological, cultural and sociological changes in media com-munication. He links the conditions of rather controlled and limited state broad-casting in radio (e.g. the BBC) with Martin Heidegger's writing. Unfortunately Heidegger's views and activities moved on from 'Sein und Zeit' (Being and Time) in 1927 to explore the notion of nothing and then embrace the cultural politics of the Third Reich in the 1930s. While any move to challenge the Marxist concept of alienation by Scannell is reassuring, there are too many intervening variables. I would respectfully argue that one cannot rely on a media interpretation that depends on sociability being linked to schedule.

The introduction of mass domestic video recording technology destabilised this link in a significant way in relation to television. As time patterns between the private and public worlds for the individual began to shift significantly, video technology was utilised to determine a more self-empowering schedule for tele-vision consumers. The same did not happen in radio. But the choice for listeners in Britain exploded from 1973 (introduction of independent radio) and 1989 (substantial deregulation) onwards. Neither was there a mass marketing demand for programme recording audio equipment. Why? I believe this has more to do with the fundamental change in the nature of listening with the advent of popular television, which radio drama producers for all their care and dedication failed to recognise and have continued to fail to recognise in the UK state broadcasting sector. Radio became more of an accompaniment medium rather than 'must hear or must see' medium. From about 1988 onwards the expanding 'spoken word' market in cassettes and CDs has enabled media consumers to revisit their favour-ite programmes or enhance the source of listening entertainment when travelling by car.

It can be argued that *The Archers* is a cultural anachronism despite the loyalty of a substantial part of the BBC Radio 4 audience. It is sustained not by commercial imperatives but by a public taxation on people who want to watch television and have no interest in it. It has been struggling to reinvent its target audience. It is arguable whether radio and television ever constituted a social horizon determining the meaning of the world for their listeners and viewers. *The Archers* would have been an unreliable model 'to disclose the everyday historicality of the world every day',[10] since it took the series twenty-five years to recognise that there was a substantial and significant Asian community in the Midlands, which, although primarily urban and not rural, had been established between 1973 and 1994. Between its inception on Whit Sunday 1950 and the introduction of the British Asian solicitor Usha Gupta in 1994, there had not been any representation of non-white characterisation in the series. In fact the actress playing Usha, Souad Faress, is half Syrian, half Irish. I would suggest that McLuhan has set up a more reliable system of explanation by asking questions rather than deriving answers from a German neo-Existentialist.

The Internet has rendered obsolete state regulation and the top-down systems of control and access for radio drama writing and production. It has taken the message of audio drama art into a medium which is being accelerated by the younger generation in terms of consumption. It has extended the physical and imaginative participation of the listener and created interactive and lateral dimensions of experience for the listener, author and producer. The new medium has therefore created a new message in audio drama and a new relationship between sound play and listener which extends its artistic, social and political potential while at the same time consolidating its cultural and literary status.

There has been some new research which supports my argument. In March 1999, *The Times* reported that Internet/World Wide Web usage had a subtracting impact on traditional media apart from radio. A surveying organisation, Continental Research, found that more than one-third of people surveyed (34 per cent) spent less time watching television since they had gone on-line. *The Times* reported: 'Not all media have been hit in this way, however: radio appears to be complementary to surfing the Web, with 25 per cent of people claiming to listen to more radio since they started using the Net.'[11]

If there has been a consistent pattern in the history of mass media in the twentieth century it has been the decline of the dominant prominence of media that are overlapped by technological younger brothers and sisters. It does not mean the inevitable death of a communications medium. There are still Queen's Scribes producing calligraphical manuscripts despite the onset of the Gutenberg Galaxy from 1450. Print has survived radio and film as radio and film have survived television and television has survived the Internet and multimedia. The world of communication has become more complex because of the growing extension of communicating artefacts.

Audio drama had a short period when it floated in the luxury of radio as an electronic medium that was dominant for about thirty years (1922–52), but with the overlapping dynamics of McLuhan's tretrad, 'the tribal drum of storytelling' has to recognise what it extends, makes obsolete, retrieves and reverses into. The phonograph reinvented its technical characteristics and cultural purpose to survive in the present age as the CD, cassette and mini-disc machine with an expanding and profitable market of 'programming' to appreciate. The electrophone or cable message system (telegraph) has reinvented itself as the delivery technology of digital electronic language and now exists as the medium for the new media of Internet and World Wide Web virtual reality. The dynamic pattern of electronic effects and purposes is remarkable and inspiring. The development of mass telephone one-to-one communication seemed to have diminished the social custom of handwritten letters. Yet the Internet with email communications facilities has revived the social habit of written though electronic correspondence. Forums and mailbases lead to instant correspondent broadcasts within specific interest areas. Written electronic communication is faster and more efficient, but the technological delivery system is by telephone cable. The principle is no different from that of the telegraph, which in the nineteenth century based its communication language on a plus/minus, on/off, 1/0 or dash/dot contrast in signalling, similar to the smoke communication language of Native American Indians, and the semaphore concept of signalling developed by the Romans and redeveloped by Claude Chappe in late-eighteenth-century France. The binary code of communication has been rooted in the past and is the foundation of the essential code of contemporary digital audio transmission.

The concept of using electricity to convey messages was being written about as early as 1267 by the English philosopher and Oxford-educated monk Roger Bacon. The sixteenth to early-seventeenth-century Neapolitan philosopher Giovanni Battista della Porta discussed the potential for transmitting information through magnetism as well as predicting and demonstrating optical experiments which defined the technical foundation of film and television.

Bacon and della Porta were distinct from their contemporaries because they advanced the horizon of human knowledge by reflecting on observation, which is probably the first law of media by Marshall McLuhan. I would therefore conclude this chapter with a self-evident truth about the dynamic between theory and practice in audio drama. There can be no effective theoretical discourse without a rigorous ontological reflection on the observation of practice. This is what I believe binds all the writers mentioned so far from Roger Bacon to Francis Bacon, Scannell to Heidegger, Sieveking and Matheson to Arnheim, Baudrillard to McLuhan and Beck to Crook. The bridging between theory and practice continues.

Part II

Sound theory
and practice

Chapter 8

Radio drama is *not* a blind medium

We begin to hear before we are born, four and a half months after conception. From then on, we develop in a continuous and luxurious bath of sounds: the song of our mother's voice, the swash of her breathing, the trumpeting of her intestines, the timpani of her heart.

Walter Murch[1]

An unborn child may be startled at the sound of a door slamming shut. The rich warm cacophony of the womb has been recorded: the mother's heartbeat and breathing are among the earliest indications babies have of the existence of a world beyond their own skin.

David Burrows[2]

The audio artist or sound dramatist should have an assured understanding of the philosophical source and practical application of sound. By 'sound' in Part II I mean the crafting of sound in its pure sense. This includes the sound of words and music as much as 'pure' sound effects. So attention will be given to the aesthetic use of words and music as sound rather than its narrative content. I have grounded my debate by studying the writing of these writers and scholars: Rudolf Arnheim, Lance Sieveking, Hilda Matheson, John Drakakis, Donald McWhinnie, Louis MacNeice, Michel Chion, Andrew Crisell and Alan Beck.[3] T. H. Pear did an early study of the psychology of radio listening in 1931 entitled *Voice and Personality*.[4] I also humbly submit some of my own observations and apologise for neglecting other writers who may have explored more fruitfully and extensively before me.

I started this section with Walter Murch's physiological challenge to the assumed hierarchy of the senses. He challenges the assumption of visual hierarchy by reminding us that all human beings first hear before they see. I think there is something inherently depressing about the human inclination to establish the concept of hierarchy in any context. Is it necessarily right to define radio as a 'blind medium'? What is the philosophical difference between seeing physically with the eye and seeing with the mind? How can vision be placed ahead of sound from the point of view of sensory hierarchy when numerically the organs are equal? Is the blind person more disabled than the deaf one? Andrew Crisell raised the curious question of whether sound communication is based on the fictional dimension of the image as seen in the mind's eye.[5] I believe this question merits considerable exploration, which I attempt in Chapter 12 on radio panics and the psychology of audio drama. Leaving these questions aside, are there artistic and philosophical truths about the use of sound in communication that we can define, understand and apply? I seek to find and discuss these and in this way the other questions may be answered or at the very least debated.

To what extent is the journey from auditory stimulation to imaginative image a truly fictional phenomenon? When the personality or character of the person speaking in sound is well known through still or moving image then there is perhaps more imaginative representation from memory rather than pure fictional-isation of the image from the voice of an unknown person. There would appear to be three levels of signposting:

1 Where there has been visual familiarity or identification.
2 Where the communication is based on words.
3 Where a constructed communication based on non-word sounds has been introduced or indicated by title. For example listeners are given a substantial clue if they are introduced to a sound story without words called 'Chase'.

Because we are debating the mechanics of a self-styled art form I would argue that consideration of this issue should be more aesthetic than scientific. Edwin Brys, Head of Features and Drama at Belgium's public radio service, BRTN, made the compelling point:

> Writers, poets and composers reconstitute feeling. There may be years between the moment when intense feeling is experienced and moment of creation. In fact that postponed emotion often results in better poems than the impulsive record of recent turbulent emotion.[6]

The BBC's experimentation with the all sound radio play, written by Andrew Sachs, inspired by Tom Stoppard and called *Revenge*, was heavily signposted with an introductory discussion and an historically resonant exhortation to listen in complete darkness and without distraction. Here the BBC was covering all the angles. I listened to a cassette of *Revenge* in the car travelling to London on a busy dual carriageway and despite my commitment to the art of radio drama I personally did not find it demanding listening.

Experimentation in workshops has established some interesting conclusions about the fluid dividing line between fiction and reality in imaginative stimulation. In writing workshops during 1992, 1993 and 1994, I played sound actuality of the mother of a 19-year-old girl who drowned in the *Marchioness* River Thames disaster of 1989.[7] She was distraught after the master of a heavy dredger which collided with the pleasure boat had been acquitted at the Central Criminal Court for a navigational misdemeanour. During the recording she builds up an impassioned speech of injustice which ends in her breaking down in tears.[8] The workshop participants were told that this was a recorded soliloquy or speech from a character in a radio play. No other information about the source of her grief apart from clues in the recording were provided.

Transcript:

[*Two deep intakes of breath*] I'm . . . I'm overwhelmed. Really. I can't. I just can't believe that, th' th' that [*sharp intake of breath*] that British Law allows this to happen. [*Deep intake of breath*] There's something very, very wrong with the law [*breath*] that doesn't allow all the evidence to be examined in a case like this. [*breath*] And . . . for the true . . . ugh . . . things to be put to the jury for them to [*short pause*] consider. The true facts and to . . . to . . . to reach a verdict. [*Pause*] It's . . . It's a waste of public money [*deep intake of breath*] and it's . . . [*pause*] yet again after now nearly twenty months has left us [*deep intake of breath*] without a public enquiry, without an inquest, [*deep intake of breath*] with no right of redress to anybody. [*Quick breath*] Here we are silenced again. [*Quick breath*] And the psychological [*pause*] effect that this is having [*quick breath*] on all of us [*quick breath*] is . . . iehhhhs . . . ieeeeeehs overwhelming. I . . . I just can't tell you how we feel. I'm lost for words. [*Quick breath*] It's . . . [*quick breath*] We need a Royal Commission to look into what's wrong with the law [*quick breath*] that allows what's happened in there to happen today. [*Breath*] We need the MPs in Parliament to get up and look at the laws. [*Volume increasing in strength and voice beginning to slightly echo as sound waves bounce from walls*]. We elected these damn people into Parliament to represent us [*sharp intake of breath*] and make sure they represent us. [*Beginning to sound upset*] [*rasping almost sobbing intake of breath*] They've got to see what's happened to all of us in that court today. [*Now crying through her words*] [*Sniff*] And bring these people to justice. We only want justice. [*A friend says 'come on'.*] We don't want anything else. [*Sniff as intake of breath is blocked by the running of tears*] We want justice. [*Another loud sob*] That is all we want. [*Moving away from the microphone.*]

Having presented the piece as an extract of drama I asked the workshop participants to assess the performance, writing and direction as well as their imaginative view of the 'character'. On 14 July 1994 at a workshop with twenty participants I made the following notes. The participants had attended the workshop on the basis of being interested in writing radio plays. There were twelve women and eight men (fifteen white and five non-white).

Ages: under 18: 3; 21–30: 8; 31–40: 6; 41–50: 3

To begin with not one of the participants challenged my presentation of the actuality as a piece of audio drama. Retrospectively none of them said they guessed it might be 'real', which seems to indicate that signposting is an effective contextualisation in radio or sound communication. I asked them to assess the 'sound design' of the recording, which was 1 minute 37 seconds in length. Was the 'performance' recorded in the studio with an atmospheric effect added or recorded outside 'on location'? Twelve said it was recorded outside while eight thought it was recorded in the studio. The following observations from different participants were noted:

The city atmosphere was more real.

Traffic seems to have more texture.

People walking by had a different pace and wore different shoes. You can't do that in the studio.

Her voice seems to exist in a space with buildings.

It had to be outside because the noises around were so complicated you never hear that on the radio. Producers are too lazy to spend so much time mocking it up.

The event was actually recorded on a pavement outside the Central Criminal Court in the City of London using a stereo microphone set up with a 120 degree ratio field of pick-up. It was sobering that a marginal majority of the participants who were 'committed' listeners without distraction had appreciated the dynamic of the recording, but intriguing that eight out of twenty had not.

I next asked the question about performance and the quality of acting. Again each of these twenty comments is from a different participant:

It was OK. I think she went over the top. She seemed to be struggling with the journey from control to breaking down. Sounded a bit false in places.

Melodramatic. Awful. I would turn off.

Very poor radio acting. I hear it all the time when listening to Radio 4. They sound like they've plucked a voice. You know. Voice number 5 from acting school. Upset relative breaks down at press conference sort of thing.

I thought you were playing take one or take two. Sounds like an out-take. She keeps fluffing her lines.

I didn't like it. I couldn't sympathise with her. Not very naturalistic. Slightly Charles Dickensish. Little Nell and all that.

Typical direction by a man. The portrayal of the hysterical woman again. Tiresome and clichéd. It's time women actors moved away from this straitjacket.

Very moving. It was unpredictable and raw. There was something truthful about it, but I thought the actress did not have full control of the piece.

It was excellent. I liked the way she was hesitant at the beginning and began to gain her strength and kind of choked with emotion. She's thought about the character.

It was all right. Maybe seven out of ten. I'm sure I've heard this actress before but I can't quite put a name to her.

I'd ask her to do it again and pull back on the volume and tears at the end.

This is the way radio actors should be performing. She sounded real rather than performing something. She didn't overdo it. You know 'I'm getting upset and angry and I'm going to make sure everybody knows that'. Her timing was pretty good.

I'm convinced. I think it was a lousy script to work with. It's a bit much having to go through so many hoops and hurdles in so short a time. Is this from one of your short story dramas? You know birth to death in five minutes and two minutes of the after-life? (*Laughter from other participants*)

Very effective. I was captivated and wanted to hear more. She's a good actress.

Is this an audition speech? She sounds a bit desperate. A bit like: 'I'm an unemployed actress please, please give me the part even though it's profit share.'

Very honest performance I think. She captures the nature of the breathing of people in that situation. You hear her breathing first. That's bloody good business in terms of theatre acting. I didn't think you could have such good 'sound business' in radio.

A good performance but it doesn't sound anything like I am used to hearing.

I thought she was struggling. It makes you think how difficult some actors find performing badly written scripts.

I think you've played us an extract from an improvisation class. This is because the actress is switching whenever a thought comes into her head. That's how she surprises us with the quick switches from not being articulate. You know she says 'I'm lost for words' to a kind of agitprop soap box opera and then breakdown. I would expect that from actresses.

Over-acted. She needs to pull back. She needs to make it more simple.

It's a bit like Gloria Swanson in *Sunset Boulevard*. Derivative and copying. I do wish actors could be a little more original.

The majority viewpoint was rather negative on authenticity in performance. I was surprised by this reaction because the purpose of the exercise was to emphasise the need for 'naturalistic integrity' in writing and performance in radio drama. I thought this extract of genuine actuality had honesty, raw, truthful emotion, dignity and nobility in expression, and was moving. It worried me that with a fictional signpost most of the participants reacted negatively to the extract as a piece of sound drama. Sixteen of the participants thought it had been written very badly. The four who were impressed recognised that the 'script' had more of a spoken word feel about it and they realised that starting a sentence and not finishing it and punctuating words with breathing and repetition to reflect natural speech could be adopted as part of the writing craft as much as the acting craft.

The question about how each of the twenty participants visualised the woman was equally unexpected. I as the producer had my own 'real image' of the person concerned and to have this challenged so powerfully by the power of other people's imagination was enormously intriguing:

Small, squat with an angry face. Jet black hair. Suburban.

Tall and gaunt. Dressed in black. White hair. She was attractive but her good looks have been broken by grief.

A beautiful middle-aged woman. Dressed in dark but elegant clothes. Ear rings. She's wearing ear rings. And gold rings on her wrists. I see her as brunette with a white streak going through the middle.

An old woman. 60 plus. Overweight. Panting because she has so much weight to carry. Large fat cheeks. Always looking up to the sky. Middle height. She's carrying a small handbag.

A very tall and noble lady. Eva Perón. I see Eva Perón. Blonde but now needs to use a dye. I think she's 45. Very well educated. Not quite aristocracy but there's something foreign about her. Don't know what.

Pinched features. Bitter. She looks very bitter. Black and bloodshot eyes. I think she's rather small. I think she's Cockney gone out to Chigwell. She's got some airs and graces but she looks very tired because she sounds tired.

I think she's New Age. You know ex-hippie but now draped in crystal and long cotton and silky multicoloured clothes. I think she looks much older than she is. I think she looks something like 55 but she's only 40 maybe.

I see her in a scarf, with dark glasses, very sad looking. I think she was a young mother. I see her as 41 or 42. Very beautiful. Dressed in black.

Old. Maybe in her 60s. Tall. Very blue stockinged and stiff upper lip, but obsessive. A broken woman physically and mentally. Carrying a handkerchief.

I see a very, very strong woman with a determined face. I think she's 50 years old. For some reason I see her limping. Probably because she has lost something inside her and she doesn't have the balance to walk easily. I think she's physically small, but very large in terms of personality. She would dominate in terms of presence. She would stand out in a crowd.

Grey and pale. Middle aged and still wearing her grief. I see her in dark grey colours. She's wealthy. Well dressed. Court shoes. Scarf. A long coat. Grey. I think she's dressing more than the climate requires her to because she's cold inside.

The first thing I see are her eyes. They are haunting. Blue. Deep laser sharp blue eyes that pierce you when they look at you. Physically she's rather tall for a woman. I see her wearing dark blue, but not black. Elegantly dressed. There's a feeling of 'Harrods' about her. I think she's affluent but powerless and angry.

A plain woman. The sort of woman who would be an assistant bank manager or a supervisor in Boots. I think she looks rather drab and old even though she might still be in her 40s. I see her face contorting with anger. A bit of a Madame Defarge when she screams 'Justice'. Quite terrifying really.

I think of her as somebody who was really happy, fulfilled and somebody who perhaps lived through the person she has lost, but has been crushed by anger and frustration. I think she's disillusioned and this means she doesn't follow fashion. Perhaps she's wearing the same clothes she would have worn when her loved one was killed. I'm sure she's lost a loved one. I see a tired, serious almost Gothic face. Her speech reminds me of Dickens. Victorian. Yes a Victorian image. She could be a spinster. She could be Miss Haversham in black.

A very determined face. Not as strong as Mrs Thatcher. But very stern and angry. I do see her in black. She's still in mourning. I think she would have an obsessive stare because she's haunted by this terrible sense of injustice. For some reason I see her as having very long hands.

I see a radio actress going into a radio studio and playing a part with a script before a microphone. For some reason I can't visualise the character. I know this sounds ridiculous but I see a Juliet Stevenson type person in sweater and jeans with no make up playing this role and putting too much into it. That's very unfair on Juliet Stevenson. She could be any actress really.

Tired and haggard face. Eyes sparkling with tears and anger. She has a long bent nose. She's medium height. She's a teacher perhaps. Her hair is done up in a bun and suddenly she's old. She's become an old woman even though she's probably only 46 or I don't know maybe 50.

I feel this was a very beautiful woman when she was young but she has been hit very hard and I think it must show. Small with a large face, but it's lined and she's wearing brown. Dark brown which matches her brown eyes.

I see an athletic and energetic woman who is perhaps no more than 35. I don't know the real reason for her anger but I think somebody close to her has died. A husband. She sounds like a widow, but a young and angry one.

I think she would be an intimidating figure. She might not be very tall but she feels very tall. She would have a matronly type of face. Very severe. I think she's wearing dark glasses. I know it sounds very Mafioso, but I have this idea that she cries so much she's determined to hide that by wearing shades.

The conclusion that can be drawn from this limited survey is that without accurate signposting the fictionalisation of the mind's eye or imagination has full reign. It proves that the degree of signification in radio or sound goes beyond the superficial and subtextural layers of the sound itself and must encompass the interaction with memory, other media and contextualisation. A very disturbing conclusion that can be drawn is the fact that perception of integrity and honesty is not an assured effect. In 1931 the professor of psychology at Manchester University, T. H. Pear, identified that radio listening was a process of thinking. He confirmed that listening to a radio play was an individual as opposed to group activity. He subjected himself to a study of his own reactions to radio plays being broadcast by the BBC in the late 1920s and early 1930s. He concluded that quite apart from the filtering of sounds to establish mind images based on his own personality and experience the radio play itself had its own 'rhetorical structure':

> Dream-images are often, perhaps usually, symbols of complexes which have been aroused inside the listener's mind, and therefore, from his standpoint, are important. In radio-drama, on the other hand, the experiences evoking the images are sprung upon the listener. His personal complexes may not be ready to leap out, receive them and immediately illustrate them by vivid images.[9]

He was perhaps pointing to the fault lines in radio play construction and the over-reliance by writers and dramaturgists on assuming that every sound, montage or performance that intended an image engendered an image. Professor Pear hinted that the real strength in audio drama was to be found in fantasy and supernatural cadences. 'Continuous stream of consciousness' was becoming a fashionable concept in literature and art at the time. Dramatising that which has never been seen physically would be more effective than attempting a representation or illusion of reality. There is no doubt that he was pre-empting a definition of the special quality of the hit 1978 BBC sci fi series *Hitch-Hiker's Guide to the Galaxy* written by Douglas Adams.

I believe that an essential ingredient is missing in the definitions that have been advanced to try to explain the psychological bond between sound and being: the 'sense of feeling'. So much stress has been placed on the mind's eye or the image generated by the mind, that an essential feature of human experience in drama – 'emotion' and 'feeling' – has been overlooked. Feeling and emotion is often determined by music. Accompanying music appears to make a substantial contribution to 'focusing' intended aspects of characterisation. This conclusion is supported by a complex qualitative research study by the UK Radio Advertising Bureau (RAB) in 1993 which sought to investigate radio 'as the theatre of the mind'. The focus groups were asked to visualise the content of radio advertisements. Participants had difficulty describing what they 'saw' when listening. The RAB concluded that the theatre of the mind was in fact 'the theatre of the gut': 'the theatre of the mind is an emotional theatre, where feelings are the primary currency, mixed with mood, memories and imagination'.[10]

Professor Pear published his findings in the early 1930s when British radio drama producers, editors and early thinkers were beginning to grapple with the first decade of radio empiricism. Americans were ruminating as well and artists such as Orson Welles and Norman Corwin continued to ruminate well into the later part of their lives. Orson Welles described radio as 'an abandoned mine'. He said that radio like the silent movies had become 'a victim of technological restlessness. Radio still functions in a way of course; but the silents are wiped out. That's like giving up all water-colours because somebody invented oil paint.'[11] In 1939 Norman Corwin expressed his creative philosophy of radio drama through audio verse in a production commissioned by the National Association of Broadcasters to make people more 'radio conscious'. As an antidote to the somewhat negative retrospection of Orson Welles in 1969, Corwin's title was called *Seems Radio is Here to Stay*.

> Do we come on you unaware,
> Your set untended?
> Do you put down your paper to lift an ear,

Suspend what you were just about to say,
Or stay the finger tip that could snap shut
The traps of night between us? . . .

We wish a thousand words with you
Concerning magics that would make a Merlin turn pistachio with envy:
The miracle, worn ordinary now, of just such business as this
between your ears and us, and oceantides of ether.
We mean the genii of radio,
Kow-towing to Aladdins everywhere,
As flashy on the run as Light, and full of services to ships at sea and
planes in air and people in their living rooms, resembling you.[12]

Lance Sieveking advanced a modus operandi for the use of sound effect in audio drama in 1934 as opposed to the use of music and speech.[13] A common theme in analysis between the writers cited in Part II is the interweaving and relationship between music, speech and sound effect. In the discussion on the theory and practice of writing audio drama I have argued that the dramatist can anticipate an intention with regard to the 'fifth dimension' – the imagination of the listener.

I have defined the fourth dimension as previously recorded archive which I believe has a special psychological resonance in the way it engages images and feelings of culture and memory both public and private.

The fifth dimension I define as the 'imaginative spectacle'. It is the video or film camera of the listener which is also a sound recorder and production house and personal movie theatre. This dimension can create anything. It has visual spatialisation in the imagination of the listener. The imaginative spectacle has the power to recreate a full sensory spectrum of experience:

- colour and visual depth
- olfactory perception
- touch and texture
- imaginary sound and taste.

There is a major risk in attempting to sustain this metaphor of 'radio's blindness'. It implies that the radio medium is handicapped by some kind of limited or disabled method of communication. The radio communicator and listener are in danger of being marginalised by the medium's perceived limitations.

Very few people find themselves in conditions where radio is determined and experienced by being blind. Even though the BBC exhorted people listening to the first play written for radio (*The Comedy of Danger*, 1924) to turn out the lights, the reality of listening for most people is communication while seeing and doing something else. Ian Rodger observed that the patronising direction to listeners in 1924 arose because 'It was somehow believed that this new drama for an audience which had no eyes could only be appreciated by simulating blindness.'[14] The mythology of radio's 'blindness' is further confirmed by Rosemary Horstmann's observation that radio is 'for all practical purposes blind'.[15] Jonathan Raban realised the danger of diminishing radio in terms of its blindness:

> The 'blindness' of radio is not necessarily a disease or an affliction at all; and it should certainly not be thought of as the one quality distinguishing radio from all other media. If we do accept that argument, then radio turns into the beggar of drama.[16]

The visual spatialisation in radio drama is also supported by Elissa Guralnik in her detailed study of Beckett, Pinter, Stoppard and other contemporary dramatists on radio:

> The blind must assemble their world, as an ever-emerging unproven hypothesis, from such small information as comes to them piecemeal. Trees are inferred from the rustle of leaves; a lawn, from the spring of the sod or the scent of mown grass; apples or pears, from their contours and textures, their tastes and perfumes. A world so discerned – that is conceptualised, not witnessed – is patently constructed as an act of the mind. Nothing is there, for the blind or blindfolded, except what they sense (or contrive to be told about) and then visualise in approximate images: ideas of things, not things in themselves.[17]

Guralnik is in fact searching for a third dimension of radio meaning which goes beyond what Roland Barthes defined as informational and symbolic levels. It is a meaning which is embedded in the psychological experience of aesthetics. She continued:

> Clearly radio is fertile field for dramatists bent on exploring the mind in relation to objective reality. Especially for those who would objectify the mind in order to see how reality responds. On film or on stage, we know what we see, even when the spectacle is called into question. On radio, conversely, we know only what we know, because what constitutes spectacle is purely imaginary. As a consequence, radio inclines us to favour the action of the mind above the actuality of matter. This, without denying that the mind has its limits, insofar as the world may refuse to conform to the mind's impression of it. Merely thinking does not make things so . . . Nonetheless, by a paradox central to cognition, things can only be as thinking makes them – a fact that the radio is peculiarly suited to demonstrate.[18]

When blind himself the writer John M. Hull embodied his daily existence and experience by explaining that he met his own mind where the world ought to be:

> Sighted people live in the world. The blind person lives in consciousness.[19]

In radio the sighted listener bridges the perception of the real world with existence in imagination and consciousness.

What is it that the listener experiences when realising an idea in imagined consciousness which is aesthetic and goes beyond the obvious intended meaning, the 'truth' which the authorial sender wishes to communicate, didactically, explicitly or through a lexicon of symbols? Barthes called it the 'obtuse meaning'. It is both an emotional and an intellectual experience. It is indifferent to the obvious story, it is discontinuous. It is a form of 'meta-language'. It is metaphonic:

> If it could be described (a contradiction in terms), it would have exactly the nature of the Japanese Haiku – anaphoric gesture without significant content.[20]

It has all the illogicality of John Cage's silent musical composition $4'$ $33''$.

Marshall McLuhan has indicated that the technological breakthrough of radio/sound communications retribalised the acoustic space of storytelling prior to the invention of the printing press which he described as the 'Gutenberg Galaxy'. But as explained in Chapter 7 McLuhan realised that radio extended and subtracted advantages and disadvantages of acoustic space and the engagement of the imaginative spectacle through 'reading'. Radio extends the range of the casual speaking voice, but it forbids that many should speak. And when what is said has such range of control it is forbidden to speak any but the most acceptable words and notions. Power and control are in all cases paid for by loss of freedom and flexibility.[21]

The auditory codes of radio exist physically as speech, music, sounds and silence which are framed by time, so the experience is ephemeral. The other important factor is the listening situation. But radio cannot be defined as a purely 'blind medium'. It is not only psychologically visual but also experienced by most people in physical visual space as well as acoustic space.

David Mamet in his essay on 'Radio drama: writing in restaurants' confirmed the physical geography of radio's consumption as storytelling art and the reality of its status and function when competing with other media:

> Sunday nights we would go visiting. Coming home we'd play the car radio. It was dark and we'd be rolling through the prairies outside of Chicago. CBS 'Suspense' would be on the air, or 'Yours Truly', 'Johny Dollar – the man with the Million-Dollar Expense Account'. And the trip home always ended too soon; we'd stay in the car until my dad kicked us out – we wanted to hear how the story ended; we wanted the trip to be endless – rolling through the prairies and listening to the intimate voices. But we went into the house. It never occurred to us to turn on the radio when we got in. We were the very first television generation. My dad was proud of the television, and we grew up considering the radio déclassé – it was used for information or background but not for entertainment.[22]

As Tyrone Guthrie observed: 'Everyone will provide his own particular brand of moonshine'.[23] The individuality of that internalised perception compensates for the disadvantage of not depending on visual language which Michel Chion and Rudolf Arnheim have conceded to be rooted in the sense we mostly rely on.

A further advantage of radio is that it persists and stays with the individual in a greater variety of physical environments compared to other media. This means that in the changing priorities of physical, imaginative and acoustic experience the message has a bigger space in which it can be absorbed and evaluated. Furthermore the spatialisation of radio and sound has been substantially expanded through the digitalisation of sound and the challenge to its ephemeral status through a greater opportunity for repetition and the physical reproduction of live and pre-recorded communication on cassette, compact disc, computer hard disk and mini-disc.

The experience of listening depends on either a choice or manipulation of the hierarchy of perception. Our sense of the world through hearing is a continuous spatial environment. There are two listening perspectives: elliptical listening and parabolic listening.

1 Elliptical listening: based on a metaphorical representation of an elliptical section in a cone. The summit of listening consciousness is high but tilted towards the basal orientation of physical listening environment and aural hearing field.

   • Physical position: static and controlled to concentrate on sound broadcast; blacked out environment.
   • Imaginative spectacle: fully engaged and without physical interruption by light, sound and movement.
   • Acoustic space: specifically arranged to appreciate the full potential of programme maker's sound design. In some circumstances virtual reality listening is attempted through binaural or surround sound arrangement of speakers and headphones.

2 Parabolic listening: focus of imaginative spectacle in the metaphorical representation of the conic section is parabolic with field of concentration drawn down to the basal root of physical position and acoustic interference.

   • Physical position: mobile or active; senses fully engaged in instinctive or mechanically demanding interaction requiring cognitive decisions responding to evaluation of space and geographical location.
   • Imaginative spectacle: partly engaged, but the quality and concentration of 'day dreaming' is adjusted to give priority to the process of cognitive and physical interaction with the outside world.

- Acoustic space: competing with other sounds and attempts by other agents and sources to communicate through sound. These could amount to noise pollution, ambient sound continually changing through movement, or the presence of alternative electronic media such as television and personal computer.

The radio listening experience is very much a variation between physical position, imaginative spectacle and acoustic space. Michel Chion wrote about the dynamic of 'synchresis', which he defined as 'the forging of an immediate and necessary relationship between something one sees and something one hears at the same time'.[24] Since the relationship is psychological, there is a justifiable synchresis between imaginative spectacle and acoustic space and physical position or environment.

Andrew Crisell explained that the variety of listening situations determined the differing ranges of attention given to any particular message: 'From hearing through "overhearing" to listening, from those who want unobtrusive background noise – acoustic wallpaper – to those who seek an object of concentration.'[25]

The balance between the physical and the psychological existence through the experience of 'the imaginative spectacle' has been defined by Maurice Merleau-Ponty in this way: 'We have said that space is existential; we might just as well have said that existence is spatial.'[26]

Notions of radio's 'blindness' therefore need to be abandoned as a gesture of intellectual and philosophical insecurity. Radio's imaginative spectacle presents a powerful dynamic which is rarely prioritised by alternative electronic media. By giving the listener the opportunity to create an individual filmic narrative and experience through the imaginative spectacle the listener becomes an active participant and 'dramaturgist' in the process of communication and listening. This participation is physical, intellectual and emotional.

The British radio drama director and producer Donald McWhinnie, who produced Samuel Beckett's first play for radio *All That Fall* in 1957, explained that 'Nothing is duller than to make imagination redundant'.[27] The common language of radio listening throughout the world is that it remains a universal mixture of physical texture, colour and detail and cognitive emotions and ideas through the varied hierarchy of perception determined by both the physical and psychological engagement of the listener. The intensity of that experience is usually dependent on the quality of programme. McWhinnie said:

> The radio performance works on the mind in the same way as poetry does; it liberates and evokes. It does not act as stimulus to direct scenic representation; that would be narrow and fruitless. It makes possible a universe of shape, detail, emotion and idea, which is bound by no inhibiting limitations of space and capacity. In a way it is a bridge between poetry or music and reality; a

means of apprehending what is artistically incalculable with one's feet several inches off the ground.[28]

One of the more experimental explorations of this issue was the unusual collaboration between myself and theatre director Tom Morris in a virtual sound, completely blacked out stage presentation of Samuel Beckett's *All That Fall* at the BAC theatre in March 1996. Morris rehearsed blindfold actors who would perform to an audience which was rendered physically blind within the theatre space. I constructed probably the most ambitious virtual reality listening experience in the history of British theatre. Throughout the 55 minute production, with the assistance of Indira Sengupta, a sound design operated for every second of the performance from seventeen speakers, two surround sound fields of transmission and three stereophonic fields of reproduction. Two computers, a sub-woofer to enhance base frequency and a substantial array of digital technology were deployed to provide near 'virtual reality' acoustic space to operate in time to the actors' script cues.

The tensions that radio's advantages and disadvantages bring to the listening experience mean that the avant-garde programme makers sometimes arrogantly jettison the reality of the medium's relationship with its audience in order to more fully challenge the nature of sound and radio artistically. As Mark Ensign Cory wrote:

> The potential of the new medium could never be tapped as long as the main effort was spent on compensating for a handicap. Somehow the lack of visual stimuli had to be turned into an advantage . . . Action was internalised, realistic physical dimensions suspended, and time telescoped – all in the interest of new artistic, symbolic and increasingly lyric (as opposed to drama) effects.[29]

Culturally the most common programming feature of radio throughout the world is music and not speech. It is the most widely used aural code. This is largely due to the fact it is a universal though generally non verbal language. Andrew Crisell has written:

> for while music may allow us to use our imagination it does not 'refer to' anything in the way that speech does and so does not require us to use it: it therefore makes ideal background listening.[30]

However, it may well be a mistake to exclude the potential for referral by way of the listener's imaginative spectacle. Most popular forms of music are structured by lyrics and these verbal 'stories' are not completely bereft of narrative codes. It is accepted that the singing is sometimes inarticulate and more surrealistic in its impact. In an experiment I conducted with participants at a radio drama workshop, I discovered that there was the same variation in the structuring of the imaginative spectacle whether a character was defined by voice or music. If anything, playing a sound sequence from the 'Dance of the Sugarplum Fairy' seemed to determine a greater consistency of imaginative description of character rather than simply playing the voice of an individual.[31] Quantitatively and qualitatively these experiments are not conclusive, but I think they are unique enough to support my argument and can, of course, be repeated in other educational fields as confirmation of my original work in this area.

The original characterisation in a play I was developing in script and sound design was:

> Small, but very overweight man in his middle forties. Much wider in the middle than at the top or bottom. Profession: Dance choreographer. Sexuality: bi-sexual with something of a camp voice. In the text he is described as somebody who 'minces petulantly when unsuccessfully presenting his authority within the school' but when in a leotard and tights 'presents a picture of comic grace as he leaps and pirouettes across the studio floor with his arms flapping like an obese sparrow struggling to stay in the air.'

To a workshop of fifteen participants I played a short sequence of monologue performed by an actor who was a close approximation in real life to the physical description in the narrative text. The transcript contained the following words:

> Whatever I do, however hard I try, however much pain I go through, whatever my sacrifice which is immense, whatever the cost which is the most intense human suffering imaginable, it is always the same. Nothing. I am the eternal fleck of what people forget or never thought of. Invisible. I am the lapse of thought when people say 'What was it that I was going to say?' or that feeling 'I know I came here to do something, but I can't quite remember'. When they retrace their steps it is futile. To be lost and never found is hell in purgatory or should I say purgatory in hell. I'm not even a Catholic.

There is nothing physically referential about this passage. The interior speech is a combination of explicit characterisation with implicit subtextual spatialisation. Having heard the passage without any location background or musical backdrop, the presentation of imaginative spectacle by listening workshop participants was divergent and as complex as the observations concerning the mother of the *Marchioness* victim. These observations illustrate the wide range of appreciation:

PARTICIPANT A I saw a kind of tall middle-aged grumpy man with a grubby rain-coat, lumbering sloth, chain-smoking fags and looking really sorry for himself.

PARTICIPANT F Sallow and monkish. Almost bent double. Twitching and neurotic looking. Wiry and gaunt.

When I then played 40 seconds from the 'Dance of the Sugarplum Fairy' as the character's 'signature tune' or 'anthem' these two participants provided the following descriptions.

> PARTICIPANT A   A gay dancer or somebody involved in the theatre. His voice sounds a little middle-aged so could he be a director or choreographer in ballet or musicals? I see him as being squat, roly-poly, bald – a sort of Hampstead Joe Pecci.
>
> PARTICIPANT B   He becomes more comic-tragic now. The guy I can see is a kind of ballet-dancing Micawber. Do you remember that character in *Dad's Army* who played the pompous bank manager. Mainwaring. That's it. Captain Mainwaring in tights. But he's a lot more camp. A cross between the late Arthur Lowe and Julian Clary. But definitely in a gold . . . what do those dancers wear . . . leotard and lime green leggings (*laughter from the rest of the workshop*).

I accept that there was a grave risk of stereotyping dance choreographers and 'bisexual' or 'homosexual' campness in this experiment. This was undoubtedly reinforced by the selection of style of music, and the language used in the verbal characterisation. Out of fifteen workshop participants, twelve were able to match 80 per cent of the character's textual description after being provided with the musical coda.

It was also necessary to introduce a control sample so in another workshop with fifteen different participants as we discussed characterisation through music with limited verbal signposting I asked for word descriptions based on the engagement of the music with individual imaginative spectacle: 80 per cent of the responses matched at least 70 per cent of the physical features of the character by imaginative speculation based on hearing the music. In the earlier workshop I had given the title 'Dance of the Sugarplum Fairy' which became more symbolic for the people being tested. 'Fairy' suggested effeminacy. 'Dance' provided a precise verbal syntax for the music's representation and 'sugarplum' rather like 'Spoon-face' in the BBC Radio 4 play title served to symbolise shape and imply a penchant for sugary foods on the part of the main character.

Chapter 9

Sound design
vocabulary

Michel Chion extends the philosophical and practical analysis of constructing sound as communication in the context of film. But he goes much further for the sound designer in all fields including radio and 'audio art'. Combined with the observations of other writers such as Andrew Crisell and Lance Sieveking, we can begin to construct a reliable vocabulary for critical values and concepts in sound design.

Sieveking's laws

Lance Sieveking appears to have been the first radio producer who attempted to define rules of sound production in audio drama. These are what I call Sieveking's laws.[1] I do not think he intended any hierarchy in the ordering.

The realistic, confirmatory effect

This is a sound which amplifies a signpost rooted in the dialogue. Sieveking means by this that if a character has introduced the idea of a storm, the sound of 'a ship labouring in a storm' will confirm the idea. The practice of radio drama production reinforces the need to provide textual pointing for many sounds. Roland Barthes described this signposting as 'anchorage'. It is the same as captioning photographic images. As Barthes said in *Image – Music – Text* (1977), words 'fix the floating chain of signifieds in such a way as to counter the terror of uncertain signs'.[2] But the realistic, confirmatory effect also does the same for words. How interesting it would be if the anticipated 'realistic, confirmatory effect' was designed to do the exact opposite. This concept has not been explored enough in audio drama largely because writers and producers have not had the courage to represent alienation, dislocation and the loneliness of the human condition by using sound to 'cast the anchor' and deliberately render the listener 'adrift'. This notion has its equivalence in what Michel Chion defined as 'anempathetic sound'. He said 'this seems to exhibit conspicuous indifference to what is going on in the film's plot, creating a strong sense of the tragic. For example a radio continues to play a happy tune even as the character who first turned it on has died'.[3] A good example of anempathetic sound in audio drama would be a widow whistling 'Happy Days are Here Again' within seconds of learning of her husband's death. To carry my definition further, anempathetic sound would also be a narrative character being heard to describe a storm which is represented by a warm embrace of dawn chorus, or indicate a wedding when Chopin's *Death March* is played. The dissonance in confirmation is a substantial pointer to a disruption in the perception of the character which the listener fully identifies with because the listener is located with a focus on the perception of this character.

The realistic, evocative effect

Here the sound does not depend on a signposting location through word. Sieveking explains an evocative effect by suggesting that Morse Code represents ships in the distance. He describes a rural, rustic atmosphere of church bells, bees buzzing and a mowing machine as creating a sense of peacefulness. Here we have the beginnings of the semiotics of sound. Sign, signifier and signified are well illustrated by these examples.

The symbolic, evocative effect

Sieveking called this an 'abstract rhythm of a churning and insistent nature', not music. The purpose is to represent or express confusion in the character's mind, so we could describe this as a symbol of mood or feeling. This is a sound symbol of mind state or being. It is the sound equivalent of an artist's abstract brush or pencil stroke on canvas. It is the sound equivalent of an indecipherable mark chiselled into limestone or granite.

The conventionalised effect

Sieveking described these as 'average sounds', easily identifiable. They represent objects and phenomena such as cars, trains or horses. It is a sound sign that is immediately recognisable. A good example would be the notorious BBC seagull that has had more appearances and fewer royalties than any other item in the history of human dramatic communication. I think Sieveking makes a mistake when he supposes that no mood, idea or feeling is necessarily being symbolised by the use of such sound. When it becomes stereotypical and clichéd it is almost inevitable that the sound conveys by way of cultural codification a mood, idea or feeling. It could be a feeling of nostalgia, patriotism, nationalism or 'sense of belonging'. The sound of Big Ben is unmistakable. It gives us a stereotypical mind image of London. But it also signifies other ideas depending on the overall context. There are jokes among sound designers now about the ubiquitous use of the BBC baby from a certain sound effect CD.[4] Lazy sound designers mistakenly use this effect to represent babies who are much older or younger than the subject originally recorded. The same can be said for the sound of a tawny owl, which is overused in innumerable night-time scenes for television, film and audio drama.[5]

However, Sieveking observes that the listener 'knows subconsciously' that the conventionalised sound effect being heard is 'very far from the real thing'. In relation to Big Ben or the seagull the listener knows subconsciously that a sound effect is being used. Professor Pear reported that two psychologists listening to radio drama could not come to terms with their knowledge that effects were fakes. Pear asserted that radio drama had failed in its attempt to establish visualisation when a listener would say 'I can see the man knocking the coconut shells together'.[6] Sieveking rightly ripostes that strong visualisation has been achieved even though it has knocked out the intended images. This interesting debate in *The Stuff of Radio* predates issues raised by Bertolt Brecht and Roland Barthes. The use of sound effects in radio drama requires Samuel Taylor Coleridge's willing suspension of disbelief in order to constitute the necessary poetic faith in the radio play. Radio drama, like stage theatre and film, needs the essential paradox of human consciousness: that unrelenting and vulnerable desire and willingness to be intensely moved by something that does not exist, never has existed, and never could exist. Curiously in radio the imagination of the listener has to fictionalise the idea of performers attempting to prevent an audience from forgetting that the play is all an illusion. How can the distancing or *Verfremdung* effect of Brecht's Berliner Ensemble bridge the dynamic of audio drama communication when it is so dependent on individual fictionalisation in the imagination of the listener? The answer to this question is remarkable and should reverse the cultural hierarchy of the preconceived notion that stage theatre determines the new direction and philosophical agenda of radio theatre. Bertolt Brecht was introduced to non-English theatre audiences as a result of translation and radio production by BBC Radio in the 1950s. Radio drama advanced the cause of the writers of the Theatre of the Absurd, not the other way round.[7]

Impressionistic effect

In modern language we would now call this the surrealistic effect. At the time Sieveking wrote his book, surrealism was not the centre of consciousness from the point of view of artistic expression or vocabulary. Sieveking relates this type of effect to the world of dream. A character's entrance or exit is marked by comic fanfares. Artificial voices or echoes indicate the end of temporalism and mortality. Sieveking also talks about 'choral shouting of repeated phrases' that mark a crisis within the character's mind.

Music as an effect

Sieveking may well be making the case for the use of music as characterisation but he does not go that far. He cites the example of fading a Beethoven symphony against jazz to symbolise 'sacred and profane love forces' in one of his plays. Loss of memory in another play is symbolised by an insistent and repeated unfinished musical phrase. Certain musical pieces can have dangerous, divergent cultural resonances. 'Amazing Grace' played on bagpipes in Britain would strike up a beautiful feeling about Scotland, its glorious and spectacular Highland landscape, and the romantic notions of a Highland world now lost to history. In the American South, 'Amazing Grace' is an anthem for the white terrorist movement, the Ku Klux Klan.

Sieveking somewhat axiomatically states that every sound effect must register in the listener's mind instantaneously. He also observes that every sound effect can be given additional coloration through dialogue and narration. For example the sound of water becomes hot when associated with somebody stating an intention to have a hot bath. The sound of water becomes threatening and freezing when identified as the rush of water from a broken river bank near the Arctic Circle as an injured man thrown from his horse and disabled for days struggles to crawl on to a small hillock for safety. Will he die by drowning or will he die by exposure? As snow falls and he tastes a snow drop on the tip of his tongue this might momentarily quench his thirst, but he realises that the water he craves is also the water that could kill him.

The very practicality of creating sound has been somewhat neglected by the theoretical writers. Sieveking acknowledges that the creation of sound effects in drama needs the agency of the lively imagination and a rhythmic sense of timing. The sound people were very much the creative wizards of their time. At the BBC they were called studio and assistant studio managers. Elsewhere they were called 'sound men' although the most brilliant and invaluable sound creator for CBS in the 1930s was a woman called Ora Nichols. In the modern world of film and in much audio dramatic production, the creative contribution and work of the 'sound designer' is now being recognised. The idea that sound is being 'designed' rather like graphic art or as a set for theatre is designed visually is now confirmed and consolidated by the use of the 'graphics interface' in multi-track computer sound programs.

Again as a result of the human propensity for snobbery and hierarchy, the value and contribution of the sound person has been remarkably underestimated. Very few people are prepared to acknowledge that equal creativity and strength comes from sound design as from writing, performance and direction. I certainly experienced this when agreeing to sound design a modern musical in the West End of London. The design of the sound effects and their participation in the production was equally critical. Timing and style were fundamental. The work was artistic, scientific, mathematical and highly disciplined even with the advantages of modern technology. From the point of view of the sound designer, the director and his team did not seem to appreciate this. Orson Welles knew differently. After the success of the *War of the Worlds* (broadcast on 30 October 1938) Orson Welles handwrote a tribute to his sound creator Ora Nichols: 'Dearest Ora: Thanks for the best job anybody could ever do for anybody, All my love, Orson'.[8]

Matheson's laws and fine art

Hilda Matheson's analysis of radio drama in her 1933 book is more in the nature of observations than laws of production.[9] She was not the enthusiastic evangelising radio dramatist and director that Lance Sieveking was. However, her much more reserved and measured conclusions about the success and failures of certain types and styles of radio plays are pertinent. She attempted one of the first classifications of audio drama. Low on her list of successful broadcasting was the theatre play either by way of 'slung microphones in theatre wings' or by bringing the cast into the studio with shouting declamatory actors. But she had recognised notable exceptions. These were the great plays which are also great poetry, in particular the plays of William Shakespeare, and including plays of discussion such as those by George Bernard Shaw, who was a dominant icon in drama when her book was published. Matheson concluded that the listener needs powerful subject matter and context to maintain engagement. She stressed the human element in bringing the listener close to the feeling and emotions of characters interpreted by actors.

Her appreciation of the link between dramatic poetry and the powerful success of radio drama has been confirmed and consolidated by the observations of Martin Esslin, who took over from Val Gielgud as BBC Head of Radio Drama in 1963. He left the BBC in 1977. The revolution in English-speaking theatre from the middle of the 1950s through the 1960s is defined by Esslin as being a focus on inner consciousness as opposed to a fixation on a portrayal of external reality.[10] Shakespeare's dramatic poetry was successful because he articulates through accessible, popular and beautiful poetic verse the human essence of feelings, emotions and existence. Though the vocabulary is centuries old the orientation towards 'inner perspective' can resonate with the contemporary audience. The success is wholly dependent on the quality of casting, direction, performance and production values. The bridge in theoretical definition between Matheson and Esslin is more significant than has hitherto been realised.

Matheson identified the similarity of the depth and spatial awareness of the sound microphone with that of the camera. The microphone can pick up rapid changes in aural scene, suggestions of 'infinite distance as well as infinite closeness as well as the general fluidity of time and space'.[11] Matheson was critical of radio drama directors who indulged in sound and ethereal concepts which had more to do with style than with content. This is a criticism which is somewhat timeless and relevant. One can speculate about whether she was directing her observation towards producers like Lance Sieveking. She warns about 'wearisome preoccupa-tion with sound'. She states rather eloquently:

> The end of the world, the transition from life to death, from the earth to space, living backwards in time – all such speculative or fantastic scenes offer scope to the radio-dramatist; but if their expression depends too much upon the hum-ming of super-dynamos, on the beat of railway engines, or submarine engines, a certain monotony may easily supervene.[12]

Matheson's prescience on radio drama's weaknesses extended to the risks of 'plays of incident' which depend on action. She so rightly judges that 'adventure, excitement, fights and quarrels, are all apt to involve a confusion of noises and of voices which is exasperating to a listener'. She recognised that sound plays needed as much precise 'blocking' in the sound stage before the microphones as any stage play. Principal characters needed to stand out clearly from their background. Overwrought and emphasised realism confuses the story and distracts the focus of the ear. It is astonishing that these basic mistakes are a common feature of con-temporary BBC radio drama production. They highlight the failure to maintain the traditions of 'a radio drama guild' where the more experienced train and guide and the oracles of the past are made available and respected.

It is through the correlation between filmic and television concepts and radio or sound concepts that the new generation of audio dramatic artists can learn their craft. The camera operates in long shot and close shot. So does the microphone. The long shot in sound extends the spatialisation of the listener's position. It is a panoramic perspective. To strike its dynamic properly, great subtlety and skill is needed. The long shot in sound very often needs a narrative voice to create the architecture and primary colours in sound imagery. The close shot needs the intimate voice of character whether internal or external. 'Long shot' and 'close shot' are terms which are not etymologically exclusive to film. The 'firing' of a perspective is more of a sonic experience than a visual one. Matheson is saying in her neglected and much forgotten book that action adventure in sound is difficult but not impossible. The art of balancing focus and close shot with long shot background could be described as choreophony.

It is the design of sound. It is basic to the art of direction. Just as the fine artist needs to know the techniques of colour, colour mixing and perspective, so does the sound artist. The analysis given to fine art is relevant to any analysis of sound art or radio drama. When a painting is appreciated attention is given to function, context and meaning both at the time of its production and in subsequent periods. Fine artists use technical elements in describing the 'language' of painting. I believe there is a close correlation in the adoption and use of visual 'vocabulary' to enable radio drama artists to communicate in a language of choreophony. The next transition in correlation should embrace the 'language' of music which over hundreds of years has had to develop and establish a vocabulary able to explain and critique the artistic design of sound.

Fine artists work with colour. Sound artists work with a similar system of elements – sound. All sounds have a hue – a spectrum of nature. They can be defined scientifically, e.g. oscillation, reverberation, pitch, decibels in terms of level, or equalisation. In fine art, colour is spoken of in terms of primary colours: blue, red and yellow. Secondary colours are produced by mixing equal proportions of two primary colours. Thus blue and yellow produce green, yellow and red produce orange. A complementary colour is a primary colour which when placed beside the secondary colour produced by the other two primaries appears brighter and stronger. Here we have a visual system to correlate and determine a fundamental choreophonic principle in radio drama. Contrasts in intensity and mixing succeed in highlighting a single stream of communication that the writer and director wish to dominate the sound picture.

Intensity or saturation refer to the degree of brilliance or purity of a colour. A pure, vivid colour is said to have a high chromatic value. *Chroma* in Greek means colour. We have a long established notion of chromatic sound: a chromatic sound is saturated with intensity. It is a pure hue. It is voice alone, enunciated and articulated with intensity. It is a sound effect alone – definite and single and not mixed. It is the crying of a dog rather than the idling of a motor car, which is a mixture of sound, i.e. the rattle and vibrations of the car chassis as well as the complex mechanical combination of noises from the internal combustion engine and exhaust system.

When fine artists talk about local colour – colour inherent in a particular object – it is not difficult to find a choreophonic equivalent. Do a table or a chair have local colour? Only when it is a word. But then from the point of view of semiotics the word 'table' encompasses the concept of sign, interpretant, object and signified. The word 'table' does exist in isolation. It is part of a code of language, just as local colour is part of a visual code of communication. Swiss linguist Ferdinand de Saussure would therefore say that uttering the word 'table' is producing an acoustic image and a concept.[13] The word is a sign which describes an object (i.e. table) and creates in the mind of the person hearing the word an interpretant or signified (i.e. a table as an inanimate piece of furniture with four legs and a flat surface which is used to hold up things). For the purposes of comparing visual artistic vocabulary with sonic artistic vocabulary a table can be said to have local colour in sound. Bear in mind that American philosopher and logician C. S. Peirce asserted that spoken language creates a range of different signs which include icons, indexes and symbols.[14] Another semiotician, Raymond Firth, defined a further verbal sign which he called 'signal'.[15]

Icon is a representation or resemblance to an object. So a photograph of a statue or a person is an icon. A map is an icon of a country. What is the equivalent in sound? The dramatised performance of a historical figure? A sound poem about something or some person? Can it not be argued that objects and beings that can produce sound are creating sounds which are always iconic? The sound of wind rustling through the trees is iconic of wind and other metereological phenomena.

Index is a sign connected or associated with an object. Smoke is an index of fire. Blood is an index of circulation. Water is an index of flooding. The concept exists as a sound as well as being signposted by contextual verbal language. You cannot hear smoke. You can smell it. You can see it. It can be described for the blind person. It can be felt, because it has temperature and gaseous texture. Water is more indexal in terms of sound because it has its own intrinsic sonic quality.

Symbol is a communication sign which is abstract because it has no connection with the object or idea in terms of resemblance. It has a meaning beyond its object. Sounds both verbal and non-verbal will have this quality in the context of programme and culture.

Firth's 'signal' is defined as a sign which stimulates a consequential response.[16] A fire alarm whether electronic or by handbell indicates danger and culturally stimulates an action which is either to seek safety by evacuation or seek help by way of fire-fighting.

Modulated colour is colour affected and adjusted by light, shadow or reflections of colour from adjacent objects. Sound has its equivalence. Modulated sound is influenced, affected and adjusted by atmosphere, climatic conditions, by the presence of other sounds and physical objects in the environment.

Colour has tone. So does sound. Colour has lightness and darkness. Tone has often been used in the context of musical and sound description. Sound production equipment often has a tone control which adjusts for treble, middle and bass frequencies. Sound engineers and artists often say that you brighten or lighten a sound signal by increasing the treble. You darken or lower the tone by increasing the low base frequency sometimes in direct proportion to the high treble frequency. So as in fine art, it can be argued that sound and sound drama can have tonal value.

Fine artists also talk about the temperature of colours. The attribution of warmth or coolness to a colour is well established in critical language. Reddish-yellows are warmer like fire. Blue-greens are cooler like ice. Can sounds have temperature? Words, communication of words and sounds, and the context of sounds can certainly describe explicitly and implicitly notions of temperature. The word 'ice' denotes frozen water and connotes coldness. The sound of fire has temperature. The sound of hailstones connotes coldness as does the sound of footsteps on snow. The concept of temperature in sound can be utilised as a critical and aesthetic term.

Chiaroscuro is Italian for 'light-dark'. I have heard this term used as an applied critical observation in audio drama. Rembrandt and Caravaggio spawned this adjective in critical appreciation because of the balance of light and shade in their pictures. In literature the term is used to describe the balance of contrasts. Semi-focus in sound or voice establishes the notion of shadow in sound drama. If in Rembrandt's *The Young Haaring* light seems to shine into areas of the canvas rather than emanating from or through the object it depicts, what is the equivalent in audio drama? The resonant echo of a condemned man's cry elevates the background or spatial environment of spectators, observers and the society which has executed the subject of the scene. The sonic illumination is rippling through the social and physical environment more than through the author of the sound and the subject of play. Is this not chiaroscuro which is particular to audio drama?

A common critical term in fine art is the notion of texture. This applies to the quality of the paint surface of the picture, the imagined quality of the surfaces of the objects depicted, and the rhythm of the brushstrokes. Texture unites the visual with the tactile. You can feel the surface of the painting or the sculpture as well as imagine the surface of the object represented. The notion of texture is fundamental in sound drama. Sound drama in all its technical, literary and performance elements builds to create a phonic texture that depends on rhythm, imagination and the physical impact of the sound via the listener's auditory perception.

Does sound have line or contour? Linearity depends on a boundary of any two- or three-dimensional shape. Or does sound have a 'masses' quality? Does it communicate in indeterminate patches of colour or sound rather than delineated and drawn shapes with clear contours and outlines? Does time determine the linearity of sound? Timing is fundamental to rhythm. The language of music is determined by time. It depends on a value of so many sounds to a second. So sound does have linearity and contour. Does it have mass? Yes. Sound can be expressed very effectively in indeterminate splashes and effusions of noise. Speech can be expressed without regular, patterned timing. It does not have to be under-scored by metre or rhythm. Shakespearian drama has linearity and contour in the iambic pentameter. Modern drama has a 'masses' quality.

Sound also has a dynamic in stereo and Dolby Pro-logic surround sound that is in addition to the spatial perspective of the recording of sound in front of a monophonic microphone. This dynamic has movement (kinesics) as well as presence and position (proxemics).

Sound can be lateral as well as linear. It can come from both sides or all sides. In surround sound there are four points in a spatially physical spectrum. Far left, far right, far centre and far behind if the speaker arrangement for reception as well as production has been set with this perspective. The dynamic of movement is from far left to far right, or far right to far left, far centre to far behind or far behind to far centre. Four different signals can move in those directions at the same time. In stereo two different signals can move far left to far right or far right to far left at the same time.

In this way choreophonic design can establish for the listener's imagination different picture planes, establish picture space because the dynamic of stimulation is by the mechanism of sound perspective. Perspective is the visual representation of three-dimensional objects and volumes of space. The sound artist has the capacity and ability to create and determine three-dimensional sound perspective both from the point of view of the listener's imagination and the listener's phys-ical experience in stereo, in binaural and in surround sound. The potential is therefore imaginary as well as physical sound texture. Dolby development now serves a digital surround system where the rear 'behind' point of the spatial sound spectrum has a stereo movement rear and sound can be phased in a circular dynamic through all speakers.

Composition is the effective combination of the elements in a painting to create meaning. It is the combination and arrangement of colour, light, shape, figures and objects. Critics look for the linear perspective, the scale, tonal range of colours, organisation of the picture space in terms of depth, the balance of foreground with background. In fine art these arrangements determine and influence the way the viewer's eye is led into or across the canvas. The same can be said for the listener's ear in relation to the overall composition of a sound drama.

What are we looking for in sound composition? We are looking for the reason for balancing foreground sounds and background sounds. We are looking and searching for the reason to combine and arrange words, music, sound effects, environmental atmosphere, and the determination of rhythm and sound texture.

The arrangement of sounds in plane, space, perspective, tone, hues and texture determines the quality of the image and moving picture experienced in the mind of the listener as well as what the listener is feeling emotionally.

Crisell's semiotics of radio drama

Based on the semiological writing of American linguist C. S. Peirce, Andrew Crisell was the first writer to seek a definition of radio's semiotic codes and signs. He established a hierarchy with words dominating the code of understanding and sound, silence and music shuffling for position underneath:

1 Words: symbolic. They have no resemblance to and causal connection with what they represent in language apart from sound resembling words known as onomatopoeia in poetry and prose. The voice that articulates the words used in radio is an index or clue to the character of the speaker/presenter. Words retain the primary semiotic code because they have the power to signpost and contextualise. As Crisell says, 'The ear will believe what it is led to believe'.[17] Words help to define a clear meaning from the polysemic nature of various sounds.

2 Sounds: indexal. There is a causal connection to the object represented, though they often need to be symbolised by words. Sounds in live stage theatre have ostension or a physical display. In radio they have a proxemic (location) and kinesic (movement) dynamic in suggesting distance to and from the microphone, and the notion of movement through the monophonic, stereophonic or surround sound stages. Despite existing as sound icons, sounds in radio still need rooting through words to avoid ambiguity. Words are effectively the focus mechanism and lens for the radio camera. As Crisell said: 'The difference between conventional drama and radio drama is merely one of degree: in the former there is likely to be a greater proportion of ostension and in the latter a greater proportion of description.'[18]

3 Silence: indexal. The absence of sound communicates that there are now no objects making sound. Mark Ensign Cory has suggested that silence is also symbolic when it has meaning in relation to action.[19]

4 Music: symbolic, indexal and iconic. Music is indexal when the sound of Chopin's Death March is played in a church acoustic: it means there is a funeral being held. Some music is iconic when it mimics rhythmically and in terms of tonality a natural sound. Music which communicates sentiment or emotion is often symbolic.

Esslin's radio drama signs

Martin Esslin referred to radio drama in terms of its signs in his text *The Field of Drama: How the Signs of Drama Create Meaning on Stage and Screen* (1987).[20] He recognised, largely because of his distinguished radio drama background, that radio drama is both paradoxical and complex in its semiotic codes.

1 Radio drama is mimetic action with acting ability at a higher standard than in film, theatre and television. Esslin was probably alluding to the quality of characterisation through voice and the concentration and commitment which this demands of the actor.

2 Radio drama unfolds in both time and space. The spatialisation is communicated physically through the perspectives established by different angles and distances from the microphone. This dynamic is also determined by the relative strength or volume of an actor's performance. This equates with Crisell's proxemics and kinesics – location and movement. Velocity might be a good term to offer as a definition of both the volume and strength of a performing sound. Esslin contends that in radio drama there is always a strong suggestion of space through sound perspective.

3 Radio drama is visual presence. Esslin does not regard the visual signs as having to be physically present. He says: 'performance in time and space very strongly conjures up visual images.' He says it is arguable that the quality of radio drama's visual images is higher than in television, film and theatre because superlatives translate into the choice and preferred consciousness of each individual listener. The most beautiful woman or the ugliest man so signposted will be conjured personally rather than by the selection of a director, casting director and performer.

Chion's vocabulary for sound design

This is really a matter of adapting Michel Chion's vocabulary on sound design from cinema to the art of radio drama production.

Speech sound

Chion helpfully divided filmic speech (narration and/or dialogue) into three categories which I have adapted for the purposes of radio drama:

1 Theatrical speech: the most common use of speech in radio drama. It is the exchange of language in dialogue or the performance of action by a character.

2 Textual speech: also rather common and intrinsically powerful in audio drama. In film it has the power to make visible the images that it evokes on the screen. In audio/radio drama it has the power to conjure like the lens of a film camera the images both moving and still in the 'imaginative

spectacle'. As Chion says, 'unlike theatrical speech it acts upon the images'. It even controls and determines spatial and temporal continuity. In cinema textual speech is limited in order to preserve its power for certain privileged characters and protect the integrity and primacy of the audiovisual scene. Chion refers the narrative role to 'an archaic power' of transforming the world through language and 'ruling over one's creation by naming it'. In support of my assertion that the imaginative spectacle is one of the most pervasive and powerful concepts in human communication, Chion observes: 'Such an intoxication has been observed in people deaf since birth, when language allows them suddenly to understand the meaning of abstraction.'[21]

The value of narration or textual speech in radio drama is the way it can protect the credibility of characters while providing the visual landscape to enable the listener to perceive the environment in the imaginative spectacle. The narrative or textual voice does not have to be located within the scene (though it can be) and serves to paint or film the spatial and chronological topography without fragmenting the plot and diminishing the credibility of characterisation. Time transitions can be achieved with simple elegance by shifting tense and grammatical sructure in the narrator's voice. Flashbacks and flashforwards are omnipotent mechanisms of storytelling which can be achieved in radio drama deftly and without self-consciousness. This time-honoured definition of the value of narration was challenged by Nick McCarty in his dramatisation of Charles Dickens's *Tale of Two Cities* for BBC Radio 4 in 1989. I would argue that investing separate characters mise en scène with the narrative voice of Charles Dickens was risking their credibility. Madame Defarge and Sydney Carton were not intended manifestations of authorial voice. However, experienced radio drama writers such as McCarty have enough background in script writing to know the rules before breaking them. Some critics have regarded his dramatisation as significant and would disagree with the point of view that by breaking the primary paradigm of radio drama McCarty contributed to a heroic failure in dramatisation rather than a success.

There is one textual speech technique which has been explored with greater artistry in film than in radio. Widening the gulf and striking up the binary opposition between textual and theatrical speech generates a mysterious contradiction or discord. The power of this technique is evident in Orson Welles's *The Magnificent Ambersons* (1942) and Michelle Deville's *La Lectrice, voyage en douce* (1988).

3 Emanation speech: this is a technique rarely used in radio drama but it does have its interesting uses when combined with textual and theatrical speech. The words are not completely heard or understood. The sound represents an emanation from the characters: it is antiliterary and antitheatrical. It is a

fair question to ask why characters should be thus delineated by sonic or choreophonic silhouette rather than direct framing? There could be merit in striking up an enigma or mystery. Furthermore the technique could be used to symbolise another character's emotional and intellectual myopia in relation to the other characters in the story. Jacques Tati used emanation speech very effectively for comic characterisation in his cinematic farces. The British comedian Rowan Atkinson employed a similar communication cypher in relation to his character 'Mr Bean'. When speech became synchronised with film it would appear that the pressure on visual storytelling began to axis the theatrical speech model of the linear verbal continuum. Chion talks about the reaction which relativised speech in terms of a synchresis with vision, and also in terms of the swell of overall sound design – music, noise and conversation. Further developing the critical notion in fine art of chiaroscuro, Chion coins the expression 'verbal chiaroscuro'.

There is evidence of a more filmic orientation in recent BBC radio drama productions, which has been caused by political economies making location recording and performance cheaper than using studios, the discrimination of commissioning in favour of larger television and film independent production houses as opposed to radio specialist units, and a fashion for equating audio drama with film because of film's higher aesthetic and cultural cachet. Verbal chiaroscuro has been amply experimented and the results have been both exhilarating and disastrous. I would classify the 1998 production of the Charles Dickens novel *Bleak House* as another heroic failure. The production failed to respect basic values of audio-dramatic narrative construction. There was clustering in casting and the right balance between choreophonic ambiguity and clear sound indexing was not struck. Whereas the film viewer can always be focused through a visual cue, in audio drama this is not the case and if verbal chiaroscuro fails in its dramatic purpose the loss of the listener's attention is terminal rather than transitory.

Rarefaction in speech emanation is nearly absolute in plays such as *Revenge* (BBC Radio 3 1978) where the presence of human voice is apparent only through breathing and non-verbal expression of pain, emotion and ecstasy.

Proliferation and ad-libs

Originating verbal communication through ad-libbing is not a firmly established tradition or experimental technique in radio drama. It has potential riches. BBC radio came near to it in simulating locations such as the Notting Hill Carnival riot of 1976 – *The Hot Summer of '76* (BBC Radio 3, 28 August 1993, written by Gabriel Gbadamosi) – and news-related plays in which final scenes were recorded on location and sometimes in the context of actual news events such as public demonstrations. Experiments in the USA and France have been bolder, but very poorly documented. The collective hubbub or proliferation of speech around an event has limited temporal value in radio drama although it can have a very intense place in a play's structure.

Multilingualism and use of a foreign language

Chion observes that a few films have relativised speech by using a foreign language that is not understood by the majority of the audience. The instances of the technique being used in audio drama are rare. Having judged many radio plays in their original languages and been given a varied standard of translation, I have tried an individual psychological experiment.

I listened to a play in a language I did not understand, without a translation, and sought to write down the plot and its themes. I was intrigued to judge the extent to which verbal performance and musical codes could communicate the essence of the play. The intriguing result was that in relation to the four plays listened to in this way I was able to establish 65–70 per cent of the theme and story line. The languages were Serbo-Croat, Japanese, Norwegian and Italian. I had no previous knowledge of these languages. Multilingualism has been used in the following films:

- *Anatahan* (1954) directed by Josef von Sternberg: Japanese actors.
- *Et la lumière fut* (1989) directed by Otar Iosseliani: African actors.
- *Death in Venice* (1971) directed by Luchino Visconti: actors in a multiplicity of Hungarian, French, English and Italian.

Submerged speech

Used extensively in Francis Ford Coppola's *The Conversation* (1974), submerged speech is another filmic technique rarely utilised with much dramatic purpose in radio drama. Chion calls it a 'sound bath'. The radio drama listener would be repeatedly submerged and brought back to the surface so that words were deliberately revealed and concealed.

Loss of intelligibility

This is a very brave and unusual technique that places verbal communication in a state of flux and reflux. Alfred Hitchcock used it in his first film *Blackmail* (1929) where a rape victim who had stabbed her attacker to death with a knife found only specific words or sounds around her intelligible. In a way the audio drama is seeking to present to the audience the central character's warped perception. There is a 'word close-up' on key expressions. Chion emphasises that Hitchcock used the technique in only one other film. Unlike out-of-focus visual shots to symbolise lack of consciousness, the aural medium cannot play so fast and loose with the listener's attention. The director Max Ophuls prefers to use verbal chiaroscuro with more control and subtlety rather than using it as a blunt dramatic storytelling device.[22]

Rendering

The use of sounds to communicate feeling or emotions and thoughts integral to the plot. These sounds are an 'illustration of reality' rather than a faithful reproduction of the stated reality. Chion talks about rendering, translating as 'an agglomerate of sensations'. Digital sound processors can often bend or distort sounds to evoke a psychological impact in radio plays. Gunshots often need rendering. Another example of rendering in radio drama is exaggerating certain natural characteristics in a sound and then slowing them down. The same effect is sometimes attempted in film, particularly in military action shots. Rendering is a process of adding value to sound for creative emphasis.

Listening

Chion defines three kinds of listening in his attempt to define the aural relationship of audience to film:

1 Causal listening: listening for the purpose of obtaining information and understanding about the source of sound.
2 Reduced listening: listening for the purpose of appreciating the qualities of the sound itself.
3 Semantic listening: listening for the purpose of obtaining information about the content of communication by the sound. This is usually based on the use of language and appreciating its content.

Acousmatic use of sound

Chion defined this term as sound which the film viewer hears without seeing its source. This means that radio and talking on the telephone are examples of acousmatic media. It is the off-screen sound in cinema. It is also the off-stage sound in theatre. A good example of this was the voice of the taxi driver in the theatrical presentation of the play *Hello?* by Dale Smith at the Cambridge Theatre in the West End of London in 1994 followed by a two week run at the Old Red Lion in Islington in the same year. In the exploration of the shared creative dynamics of theatre and radio the power of presenting an entire character's involvement as an acousmatic source for 35 minutes of visual theatre proved to be enormously effective. In the climactic scene at the end when the taxi driver is revealed but frozen in his distant location and unable to prevent the rape scene which had then become acousmatic, the audience were presented with a powerful and emotionally demanding refraction of location which proved to be enormously compelling.

Is there something truly acousmatic in the sound and radio medium alone? I believe that an acousmatic presence is established in radio drama in a production and script which has not defined the character visually. If visual signposts have been stripped from the construction of the imaginative spectacle, I believe this becomes a truly acousmatic representation of character. The potential for intrigue and 'listener guessing' is still there. This then moves on to Chion's term **acousmêtre**, which is further consolidation of his terminology for cinematic narratives that are heard and not seen. The equivalence in radio is the central narrative voice which has no visual characterisation.

Back voice and frontal voice

Chion defines sound perspective in relation to the character's presence in a film in terms of us hearing the voice as a frontal perspective or in terms of a reverse perspective with the character's back turned. Very few radio drama directors have been courageous or imaginative enough to experiment with the **back voice**. Chion observes that this effect can be attempted in post-production with the removal of treble. I think that the top middle frequencies should come out as well to make this adjustment more equivalent to losing the direct sound perspective.

On-the-air sound

A very straightforward definition of sound which is transmitted by telephone, television, radio or other electronic propagation. These sounds have a completely different frequency response which is directly affected by the motorised structure of the machine's sound production system. Telephones have inferior carbon microphones and the telephone exchange also layers in other forms of filtering and reverberation. A common mistake made in BBC radio drama productions is to use a console filter to simulate the sound of a telephone. The result for decades was that all telephone communication in BBC radio drama productions sounded the same. At Independent Radio Drama Productions we always used real telephones and the resonances were much more authentic, even down to the gripping sound of the actor's hand on the plastic handpiece.

Chion describes this effect as **materialising sound indices**. These are the concrete sonic details that inform the listener that music or sound is being made and expressed. It could be the nervous breathing of a pianist and then the sound of the pianist's physical presence creaking on the piano stool and a wedding ring 'clacking' against the mahogany veneer of the piano itself. The effect of materialising sound indices is to mortalise the creation of sound. It makes it a human production in contrast to a perfected, ethereal abstraction.

An excellent example of authentic telephonic sound quality is demonstrated in the award-winning short story drama *One Thousand to One* by the London African Caribbean writer Gella Richards. There has been an occasion when the BBC departed from its clichéd use of telephonic soundscape. This was in the production of *Burn Your Phone* (1995) by Andrew Wallace, in which a phone operator's working day became a living nightmare.[23] There was evidence of this production being sound designed using multi-track digital technology and it reached standards rarely achieved by BBC producers.

In my opinion **on-the-air** sound has to be transmitted from authentic or near equivalent mechanisms. I know it is somewhat difficult to persuade Waterloo station to allow an actor to make a station announcement for the purposes of a radio play, but there are potential compromises. Combining the real sound of Waterloo station at the time the scene in the drama is supposed to take place with a public announcement in another location or digitally sound processed programme could produce a near authentic result.

Extension, in-the-wings and superfield

These terms are concerned with the geographical plotting of sound in relation to reception and purposeful communication of spatialisation. **Extension** involves opening up the space by sounds, using a wider ratio of stereo recording and transmission and at its ultimate point using surround sound or even a combination of surround sound and stereo fields. In the 'virtual reality' production of *All That Fall* at the BAC (March 1996), I designed an extension which involved the interaction of two surround sound fields, and three stereo fields each with 190 degree dynamic or ostension. Such a reproduction of sound is impossible in radio broadcasting since the bandwidth of transmission can currently accommodate only a surround sound analogue or digital imprint (decoding/encoding). Multiple surround sound fields mixed with additional stereo perspectives are beyond the capability of storage in one medium and the same problem applies to transmission. Surround sound reception depends on the setting up of a surround sound listening perspective by the listener. The quality of stereo reception depends on the position of the listener and the setting of the 'balance' mechanism.

In-the-wings was defined by Chion as the lingering of sound in lateral speakers after the exit of a character, car or train. It is also interesting and useful as indicating the process of arrival before we hear the voice of a character. This effective off-screen presence does have potential uses in audio drama. It has a limited use in monophonic productions, but if the listener is placed in the centre of a two or three speaker sound system, then it can enrich kinesics and proxemics in radio drama sound design.

The **superfield** relates to the full potentiameter of a sound play's reproduction in any context. Chion defines this specifically as the placement of 'multi-speaker' systems in the movie theatre. I would also like to transfer the nature of the superfield into the imaginative spectacle. This is because I have found that surround sound multi-track productions transcoding the texture of these rich and complex dynamic arrangements of sound movements and perspectives are still decoded or transmogrified in the imaginative spectacle of listeners.

Territorial sounds

This is a helpful term to define 'ambient' atmospheric sounds which provide a pervasive definition of space and environmental landscape, townscape or topography. Echoing church bells will evoke in the imaginative spectacle a large space around a church or cathedral. If the bells' sounds are reverberating they evoke a cathedral or city location whereas if they are muffled or absorbed and combined with bird sounds the imaginative spectacle moves to a more rustic location. Sound designers need to be very cautious about persistent and pervasive bird sound which has a presence that is psychologically greater in its impact than its sound. It certainly needs to be substantially reduced as an ambient territorial sound in relation to voice.

Empathetic sound and anempathetic sound

These terms relate more appropriately to music, which tends to be used more as a mood determinant. Empathetic music or sound is introduced to match and enhance the emotions, feelings and mood of the drama scene. Anempathetic is usually diegetic music. There is an emotionally discordant and indifferent playing of sound in the context of the scene or action. An example would be the playing of a joyful, Christmas time Viennese Waltz as a Jewish mother weeps over the arbitrary arrest and execution of her teenage son. I would venture to suggest there is a further category to be included in the context of these definitions: sympathetic sound and ansympathetic sound. This would provide space for not a mimetic matching of mood and emotion on the part of music, ambient or specially constructed sound, but a setting of mood which fluctuates between a halfway point of anempathetic and empathetic sound. By its etymological origin empathetic sound should be virtually vicarious. I believe there are other nuances of music or sound which are sympathetic without fully grounding themselves within the core of narrative feeling or a character's experience.

External and internal logic

These terms have excellent application in the context of radio drama production. The internal logic is a metaphysical or philosophical/aesthetic parallelling of music and sound design to the narrative flow of drama and communication. The internal logic of a stream of sound direction is agreeing and matching the story and direction of parallel sound multi-tracks such as dialogue, acousmatic narrative or even the fifth dimension of characterisation and story development within the imaginative spectacle of the listener. Chion's concept of external logic is the introduction of a sound direction which is discontinuous and nondiegitic as an intervention. This has the potential to strike up irony or tragedy, or herald the potential of conflict and tension in the story.

Phantom/negative sound

Chion uses the French expression *en creux* which means 'negative space'. The equivalent in sculpture is the mould. In terms of our debate, phantom/negative sound exists fully in the imaginative spectacle of the listener. It can be a psychological expectation or anticipation. As a further extension of Chion's struggle to define the dynamic relationship between sound and film he tries to apply a concept of 'magnetisation' which is the mental spatialisation of movement on the screen in terms of locating a sound's source in monophonic reproduction. He argues that if a cinema audience hears only in mono when a train or character approaches from the extreme right of the screen the kinesics of the sound's movement is magnetised in the imagination of the audience. I would argue that proxemics and kinesics in sound are also magnetised by the visual spatialisation of narration and dialogue. I repeat my point that there is therefore a superfield in monophonic drama as much as in stereo or surround sound drama.

Chapter 10

The cinematic
and musical
inspiration

A fundamental mistake made in analysing the divergent histories of cinema and radio drama is to assume that the cinema was silent before the inauguration of the talkies. Nothing could be further from the truth. Cinema may have been born mute but there were plenty of ventriloquists around to give it voice before the start of the 'talkies'. Cinematic presentation of film was accompanied by the sophisticated paraphernalia of vaudeville and mainstream theatre sound simulation and anything from the pianist with a 'Joanna' upright piano to the engagement of entire orchestras. The account by Richard Hughes on the production of the first play specifically written for BBC radio in 1924 confirms that sound production expertise came from the cinema:

> With rehearsals and production, however, a cold awakening! I had spread myself on sound effects without considering how they were to be done. Someone ran round the corner and enlisted the effects man from a cinema in the Strand – wind machine and all. But still we could make nothing sound as it was meant to sound; even in the studio.[1]

Asa Briggs writes in his exhaustive BBC history *The Birth of Broadcasting 1896–1927* that the first drama director R. E. Jeffrey

> wished to signal his debut by introducing greater realism into radio sounds. He began with the sound of a gun, and to the dismay of the staff spent his first few hours firing a shotgun over the banisters into the well of the staircase. He did not succeed: the noise sounded like flat champagne.[2]

In the USA the skills of sound recordists or 'sound designers' enjoyed a parallel development in radio and film, particularly after optical recording substantially improved the quality of the sound imprint for reproduction in the picture houses. The quality of synthesised 'studio sound' could be high. The reference to the phonographic recording of 'In the Trenches' (see pp. 33–4) is an illustration of the sound potential in action sequences. Off-stage sounds for more than a century had been created using the thunder sheet, door bells, telephone rings and 'incidental effects' on glass, metal, sandpaper and wood. A key function in the orchestra pit was the percussionist whose ratchets, cowbells and wood blocks would often punctuate vaudeville, cinematic and theatrical performances. The demand for sonic punctuation in live shows created the demand for a versatile, all-performing sound effects machine. In a way it was the 'one man band sound caboodle'. A highly experienced sound effects man, Arthur W. Nichols, set about building such a machine in the late 1920s. He reported that he would set up a microphone in the kitchen to confirm if he could identify the synthesised sound as the intended effect. Although the advent of the talkies in the cinema reduced the demand for his invention, Arthur Nichols and his wife Ora found a ready demand from the golden age of radio. They became the resident sound team at the CBS New York flagship station, WABC. Ora Nichols continued the work after Arthur's death in 1931.

There is an argument that the introduction of music and spot effects in picture palaces was also an attempt to mask the loud mechanical whirring of the projectors. Bringing in actors, pianos, orchestras and sound technicians and dropping them into the orchestra pits or putting them at the back of the audience provided a welcome distraction. These added components were inevitably expensive for the cinema owners and some must have come to the conclusion that far from reducing the costs of live performance, moving film probably increased the overheads. Since it has been said that money is the imprimatur of technological progress, the introduction of amplification and higher quality, synchronised sound offered the opportunity to save on inflationary costs of live sound performing artists.

It is quite clear that the craft of sound design began to enjoy a parallel importance in both radio and film. Ora Nichols demonstrated that impressive sound effects could be achieved with small-sized yet intelligent application of mechanical technology. She discovered that whirring an egg beater close to a microphone made the sound of a lawn-mower. Decapitation could be represented with the chopping of a red cabbage into a wicker basket. A Martian spaceship could be opened with the twist of a cast iron pan lid. The sewers of Paris could be heard with a microphone in a leaky men's room. Alien beings who turned themselves inside out could be represented with the removal of a tight-fitting rubber glove covered in jelly from a human hand. Movement through thick undergrowth or long grass could be achieved by filling the studio floor with strips of thin paper, or later discarded reel-to-reel tape. Walking on snow could be achieved by sticking cotton wool to the soles of actors' shoes and placing the cotton wool on the carpet as well. Muddy trenches could be achieved by mixing mashed newspapers and water in large floor trays with the actors in bare feet.

I do not believe you can embark on an exploration of sound theory for audio drama without returning to a basic question in music theory. What is the difference between noise and music? Having found an answer to this question, what is the difference between music and audio drama? I think music theory is fundamental to providing a critical and aesthetic vocabulary for the application of sound in audio drama. It also provides a scientific foundation and explanation for the materialistic dimension of the craft. Rudolf Arnheim was conscious of this approach in the 1930s.

Music is fundamental to the successful blending of sounds in cinema. It has become more relevant in UK audio drama since 1988. IRDP at LBC in London revived its value and stylistic use in classical radio drama, a trend which I believe was imitated by the BBC, which was closely listening and monitoring this new challenger to its monopolistic field. It was a fundamental component of successful audio drama during America's golden age of radio in the 1930s and 1940s. Bernard Hermann, one of the giants in cinematic musical composition, developed his early talent and reputation in radio. Hilda Matheson cited music as an equivalent value of importance to actors' performance.[3] She described it as the first fundamental. Early BBC radio drama seemed to have made great use of it at a time when all the radio drama elements were created live in a multi-studio complex at Broadcasting House mixed by a 'Dramatic Control Panel'.[4] This would be recognised in the present day as the sound mixer or console.

Matheson said that music provides printed programme background, scenery and 'something of the emotion which the mass psychology of an audience supplies'. She stressed its 'associative' function. She suggested that music evokes 'epoch, fashion, place, company, and individual'. She was decades ahead of experiment and practice by speculating that music can provide the appearance of a particular character. Music was the means to create atmosphere and emotion and to change scene mellifluously. She said choice of music should be as much a part of the writer's craft as making decisions about theme, plot and characters.

The composer John Cage wrote a 'musical composition' called 4′ 33″. It would appear to be 4 minutes 33 seconds of silence. How can music be silence? Is there such a thing as total silence? Probably not. Scientists will say that there are no sounds in space. It is an inert environment where sounds cannot exist. But John Cage does not set his composition in space. It is set within the atmosphere, in the cultural environment of our society. He as the composer sits silently for this duration. His idea raises a debate about the nature of music. He explains that the composition lasts for 273 seconds, and that minus 273° Celsius is absolute zero, the temperature at which all molecules stop movement.[5] When Mr Cage presents or performs his piece the world of the listener is not silent, but filled with the view offered by this performance and the background sounds of the location of the performance. Is this not potentially a radio play, albeit an abstract one? Is it not that extreme of abstract expression in audio art or 'ars acoustica' that we associate with a rectangle of white paint? Aesthetically the form and the content can be justified but not presented as a regular and popular form of communication.

For John Cage music is the tapestry of sounds heard around us whether we are in the concert hall or not. He wished to celebrate the point that there is no such thing as an empty time. There is always something being heard whether in the imagination or in the physical environment of the earth's atmosphere.

Music for John Cage was sounds occurring in any combination and in any continuity.[6] The rock musician Jimi Hendrix defined music as 'messing with people's heads'.[7] The Russian composer Igor Stravinsky defined music as a 'phenomenon of speculation'.[8] Sound and time are the critical elements. They converge to a definite point and that point is a Wordsworthian emotion recollected in tranquillity. The French philosopher Jean-Jacques Rousseau defined the composition of music as the painting of pictures in sound.[9] The musician as artist makes the very silence speak and expresses ideas by feelings 'and feelings by accents and the passions that he voices move us to the very depths of our hearts'. An eighteenth-century definition for music offers an eloquent and accurate definition for audio drama in the twentieth and twenty-first centuries. The theorists of classical Greece and Rome linked music to mathematics in *musica mundana* and the framework of counting in time has been a feature of musical definition since then. The German philosopher Gottfried Wilhelm Leibniz defined music 'as the pleasure the human soul experiences from counting without being aware that it is counting'.[10]

Discussion about the nature of music is common to all cultures and stresses effects, function and genesis. Like language, music and audio drama is a construction of individual or multiplicities of culture. There has to be a recognition of relativism. It varies from one culture to another, but the common feature in all the definitions is the reliance on sound. The Italian scholar Gino Stefani defined music as any human activity centred around any type of event using sound.[11] This wide definition encompasses all forms of drama, which leads on to the question of whether it can be asserted that drama and music are synonymous? Sometimes they are. However, the precision of meaning achieves greater focus when music encompasses a word based cultural codification. Can a popular tune of music and lyrics be defined as radio/audio drama? If the lyrics communicate a narrative surely the fact that they are synchronised with music is merely an enhancement of the storytelling? Opera is stage theatrical storytelling through music and libretto. The difference with stage theatre can only be defined as the presence or absence of musical accompaniment. The narrative and dramatic elements are synonymous. I believe music and musical forms can be embraced in a landscape of storytelling through sound. The acquisition of 'audio dramatic' quality must surely depend on the presence of action and/or narrative in the communication. I am joined in this view by Rudolf Arnheim, who said in 1936 that:

> music is the purest and most noble art of all. In the other aural arts, the art of speech and of sounds, the terms used by theoreticians of music are applicable. Tempo, intensity, dynamics, harmony and counterpoint, are here too the fundamentally effective elements. [12]

Audio/radio drama has the same material qualities as music. Sound, music and words share the fact that they exist as a numerical value of vibrations in the air. The speed or frequency of a regular pattern of vibrations produces a sense of pitch. The faster the vibrations the higher the sound appears to be. We can scientifically distinguish music from noise on the basis that music has a regular pattern of vibration or oscillation. The human voice when not singing always has pitch. Music has determined a mathematical truth about doubling regular patterns of vibrations. Doubling a steady vibration of 440 Hertz will create the curious quality of a sound which sounds the same but has twice the pitch. It would appear that men and women can sing the same tune but at different pitches. Here we have the concept of the octave and the division of the octave creates a scale which appears to be fundamental to most musical cultures. It is also fundamental to the casting, designing and choreophonic direction of audio/radio drama.

Rudolf Arnheim demonstrates this parallel with a compelling analysis of a German radio play from the 1930s by Leo Mathias called *The Ape Wun*. Musical underpinning defines the differentiation of the characters and their dramatic functions. The fundamental types of bass, tenor, alto and soprano offer a sound canvas for dramatic composition. He was stressing the advantage of the 'compositional function of sounds' rather than the action and the meaning of the words. In *The Ape Wun* there is a struggle between Buddha and the Ape Wun represented by a contrast between tenor and baritone: 'The baritone Wun, at first almighty and invincible, gradually succumbs to the tenor Buddha: clumsy brute force to the physically weak intellectual.' [13] Arnheim convincingly analyses the plot of this play from the point of view of choral composition and concludes that the victory of the tenor over the baritone is a victory of light over darkness. He established a relationship of the sound contrasts and similarities with those of the content. We have here an effective demonstration of sound chiaroscuro. Audio/radio drama is as much about sound tonality as about anything else. He also makes the intriguing observation that subsidiary plots have a limited and restricted range in tonality. They do not rival the dominant struggle. Soprano is pitched against alto. Counterpoint is fundamental to music. It is also fundamental to drama. Spiritual strife is enacted by acoustic tonal opposition.

University lecturer and UK radio critic Ken Garner has emphasised that music and radio storytelling, particularly through audio drama, have more in common in their narrative codes than stage theatre and written prose. He has engaged the attempt by Leonard B. Meyer to link the emotional experiences and responses of listeners to formal structures of music. Meyer contends that music does have two kinds of music – absolute and referential. The absolute meanings relate to the patterns and relationships within music. As Garner writes:

> 'Referential' meaning comes when the music is perceived to relate to – or, most obviously represent – something else in the non musical world (examples might include the opening of Smetana's *Ma Vlast* with its declared attempt to portray musically the progress of the Vlatva river; or Jimi Hendrix's chopped, wah-wah guitar opening to 'Machine Gun').[14]

Music shares with radio the solitary, listening-alone experience. The mnemonic device of repetition, a legacy of the oral tradition, is present in both radio storytelling (commercials, journalism, drama and continuity) and music. It serves as a resonant echo and seeks to connect with the memory of the listener as well as the listener's consciousness. The binary tension in dialogue and conflict is mirrored in the musical device of varying tension and relaxation. As a plot device storytelling revels in deferring and modifying expectations. Such a technique is used by composers to surprise an audience. Musical composition employs a hierarchy of absolute codes in the transcodification of meaning. Aural ostension and the prioritising of sound icons are critical to constructing a framework of meaning for the radio audience.

Ken Garner is correct about the parallels between audio drama and music. Both are organised for the listener in a time frame with tempo, rhythm, meaningful sequences of pitches, otherwise known as tunes, and musical form. The two significant and easily identifiable features of form are undoubtedly contrast and repetition, which reflect the semiotician's key interpretation of language constructed by binary code.

The musical principle of organisation of 'syntax' and 'information' can again be equated with audio drama construction. The less predictable the pattern of sound, the more information is communicated. The more predictable the sound, the less information is imparted. Past, present and future appear to be inextricably linked with a musical system of expectation, frustration and fulfilment. The creative radio drama producer knows that too much information causes frustration and consternation and that too little information induces boredom. Radio drama is an art of striking a balance or equilibrium within in its directions of narrative. As Richard Middleton writes in relation to music: 'there is a widespread feeling that pieces either make sense or do not. So, without wanting to stretch an analogy with verbal language too far, I think there is some point to a comparison between the expectation – structure . . . and the structure of verbal syntax.'[15]

As a conclusion I think it can be shown that the critical language of radio drama shares with music and other art forms the tension between formalist and referentialist interpretation. There is the understandable desire to objectively deconstruct the sound components of audio drama programming and regard its materials and processes as absolutely specific and autonomous to the radio drama form. There is also a strong inclination to link the building blocks and processes of production and communication to other areas of human experience, social structure or cultural practice. They can be expressionistic and highly subjective. That is I believe the privilege of the aesthete. They can also be structural, causative and analogical.

I believe that radio theory and intellectual analysis of sound drama could divide between objectivism and referentialism or combine into what I would call a hybrid approach. The scientific objectivists may seek to show that the meaning of sound drama resides in deep linguistic and syntactical structures which reflect the laws of sound drama. They may seek to show that sound drama patterns draw on conventions and structures of expectation which are uniquely sound based or musical. Furthermore they could argue that sound drama rhythms and 'euphony' arise from and are specific to the nature of sound and the binary relationship of sound communication in radio drama is a fundamental process specific to sound entertainment and music.

The referentialists may hold on to an explanation of radio drama syntax in terms of making choices within a culturally mediated system governed by degrees of predictability. They are in a position to argue that the construction of audio drama with its various sound components is intrinsically linked to the communication and expression of feeling, meaning and emotion. Choices and decisions in the balance of the various 'sound streams' of narrative communication are structured by rhythm because human experience is predicated on the basis of a cultural conditioning of rhythm. Here audio drama equates with a referentialist approach to music. The pattern of repetition and change in the construction of audio drama is inspired by and derived from the wider patterns of human experience in culture and society.

1: Eva Stenman-Rotstein, Director/script editor, Sveriges Radio AB (Swedish Radio Broadcasting Corporation). Pioneered the development of a modern short episodic soap and realignment of drama for young people in publicly funded radio. Her production of the play *The Kangaroo Girl* by Gunilla Boethius for Sveriges Radio AB won a special commendation for Radio Drama at Prix Europa 1998 in Berlin.

2: Christine Bernard-Sugy, Prix Italia winning head of radio drama at Radio France. In charge of a public broadcaster which sustains support of new writing and production of cultural and classical texts. Unlike the BBC, up until 1997 Radio France radio drama producers retained their editorial independence and there had been no pattern of funding reduction.

3: Kate Rowland, BBC. Steered BBC Radio Drama through stormy politico-economic waters. Maintains an exceptionally high aesthetic and creative standard of personal direction and production. However, from 1997 BBC Radio Drama producers have been subjugated into a pitching relationship with commissioning editors.

4: *Losing Paradise* in the CBC studio. Written by Dave Carley, Rob Gittens and Paige Gibb. A three-country co-production between Canada, Australia and Wales. Directed by (far left) James Roy, with (left to right) Rober Bockstael as Jon, Dixie Seatle as Gina and Stephen Ouimette as Andrew.

5: *A Dream Play* by August Strindberg in the CBC studio. Produced by James Roy and Lynda Hill. Actors shown (left to right): Karen Clave as Agnas, Alison Sealy-Smith as Alice and Ken Kramer as Axel.

6: *Beo's Bedroom* by Ned Dickens. Directed by Gregory J. Sinclair. Actors shown (left to right): Yanna McIntosh as Death and Juan Chioran as Bard to Bear.

7: *The Trojan Women* by Euripides. Translated by Brendan Kennelly. CBC/BBC co-production. Directed by Martin Jenkins. Performers shown (left to right): Alison Sealy-Smith as Hecuba and the score composer Colin Linden.

8: Location recording has the advantage of constructing direction and performance within 'realistic' locations. In this narrow, rubbish strewn alleyway studio manager Keith Waghorn (left) is helping to 'block' a scene with Anthony Ofoegbu and Sheelagh Ferrell.

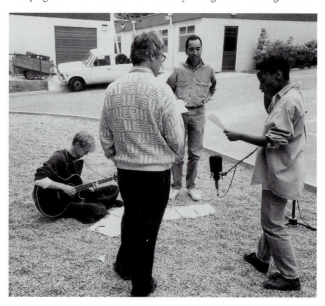

9: Another location scene which is the equivalent of a shingle beach in Los Angeles 'looking out to the Pacific Ocean'. Writer/composer William George Q is performing the blues guitar riffs.

10: The enjoyment of working on location where performers are not constrained by the walls of a studio. Recording *The Great Los Angeles Opportunity* by William George Q. Director Tim Crook (seated with headphones), Peter Guinness (with script) and Cornell John.

Part III

The new radio drama form

Skits and live improvisations

Chapter 11

Blurring fiction
with reality

I didn't do anything. I just kept listening. I thought if this is the real thing you only die once: why get excited?

(A listener to Mercury Theatre's *War of the Worlds* 30 October 1938)[1]

When you consider the history of the twentieth century, broadcasting skits or hoaxes are more associated with radio than with television. This is because radio was the first electronic medium of mass entertainment and radio is a more psychological medium. Its relationship with its audience is based on an emotional and imaginative bond. In 1999 radio has not lost its importance as a huge and significant source for news and entertainment and the opportunity to hoodwink the audience is as strong as it has ever been. Radio dramatists have been highly skilled at demonstrating radio's power to deceive. Art and dramatic narrative sometimes seek to offer the audience a representation of reality. The power to suspend disbelief is a potent weapon of communication and radio dramatists and storytellers have been the most effective. There is evidence that young dramatists largely denied any context for audio dramatic entertainment are using live talk programming to construct their own improvised radio plays. The process is self-reflexive and satirical.

This exciting, dynamic and growing area of creative radio communication offers a considerable amount of scope for linking with theoretical concerns. Theorists have been trying to define 'models of communication' to explain the potency of media broadcasting. A critical development occurred in 1940, two years after *War of the Worlds*, when Paul Lazarsfeld and others studied the 1940 US presidential election.[2] The authors of *The People's Choice* (1944) found no significant evidence that the media had a direct influence on people's electoral choices. Interviewing disclosed that physical campaigning had greater influence. A two-step model of communication flow became more useful as a way of explaining the dynamics of media–audience interaction. The importance of the social context of the audience when receiving and interpreting radio and other mass media communication seemed more relevant. The mass audience is not an immense flock of sheep comprising socially isolated and passive lambs all going 'baaah' when Orson Welles goes 'Booo'. At this stage theorists began to realise that the mass audience is a society of responsive and interacting individuals. Further research and reflection led to the concept of the 'multi-step model' which became a more realistic approach to understanding the complexity of mass communications, particularly in relation to radio.

As contemporary practitioners realise when talking to listeners and attempting to garner statistical evidence from tracking and audience surveys society is now made up of different communication situations and there is a multiplicity of variables. So the 'multi-step model' is helpful by taking into account five factors:

1 the intentions of the source/broadcaster
2 access to and availability of the mass media, i.e. radio
3 the style and nature of the communication
4 the importance of the message to the listeners
5 the extent of audience exposure to agencies of communication.

There are few people who are unaware of the panic created by the Mercury Theatre On The Air on Hallowe'en night 1938. The radio adaptation of H. G. Wells's *War of the Worlds* had been transformed into a close representation of an American entertainment programme interrupted by urgent news bulletins. Orson Welles is credited with the idea. He had been impressed with the interruption of his live broadcast of Sherlock Holmes on 25 September 1938 with a news bulletin on the Munich crisis. Howard Koch is credited with writing the script and the outstanding, realistic acting of the cast is credited with convincing hundreds of thousands of people that the Martians were invading New Jersey.

Professor Hadley Cantrill at Princeton University researched and published the only study into the relationship between the power and effectiveness of a broadcast of this kind and the reaction of the audience. *The Invasion from Mars: A Study in the Psychology of Panic* (1940) remains one of the most significant sociological and psychological studies of radio. It was conducted before the television age of mass communications and so isolates the specific social and psychological dynamics of radio. We now live in a communications age which is much more complicated. Katz, Gurevitch and Hass in their 'On the uses of the mass media for important things', published in *American Sociological Review* in 1973, outlined a circular model of interaction between books, newspapers, cinema, radio and television and sought to indicate why people had a preference for some over others.[3] As a conclusion the authors asserted that people tended to use newspapers, radio and television to connect themselves to society, but used books and films to escape from reality for a while. The better educated orientated themselves towards print media and the less well educated relied more on electronic and visual media. Books were identified as the medium for engineering self-improvement and understanding of the self. This study would now merit reinvestigation in the light of Internet and World Wide Web communications and the widespread distribution of video recording technology.

Cantrill and his team cited 'a lack of critical ability' on the part of a large proportion of the population as a major contributing factor in the spread of panic. He and his researchers became convinced that personality characteristics made 'some people especially susceptible to belief and fright'. They were also certain that the strong reaction of certain individuals 'infected' or caused other listeners to react inappropriately.[4]

Cantrill was curious to try to understand why so many people did not do something to verify the information coming from their loudspeakers. The USA at this time had experienced prolonged economic unrest and the ten year long Great Depression had created a general social condition of widespread insecurity. Cantrill makes the excellent point that the developing details of a Martian invasion created the notion of yet another 'phenomenon in the outside world which was beyond the control and comprehension of the individual'. The threat of war in Europe was very present, particularly as the broadcast quickly followed the Munich conference that had condemned the independent state of Czechoslovakia to partition and military subjugation. The critic Heywood Broun said in the *New York World-Telegram*:

> I doubt if anything of the sort would have happened four or five months ago. The course of world history has affected national psychology. Jitters have come to roost. We have just gone through a laboratory demonstration of the fact that the peace of Munich hangs heavy over our heads, like a thundercloud.[5]

Were the Martians a social symbol for the militaristic and aggressive Nazis under Adolf Hitler? Cantrill offers the interesting diagnosis that 'a panic occurs when some highly cherished, rather commonly accepted value is threatened and when no certain elimination of the threat is in sight'. So he places the panic in the context of prolonged bewilderment combined with lack of training to seek the basic causes of maladjustment. More fundamentally Professor Cantrill draws an interesting comparison between the *War of the Worlds* panic and the hold that Hitler's propaganda was developing over a nation devastated by social and economic insecurity.

The highly persuasive ranting of a demagogue offering simple and nationalistic solutions took on a power that would not have the same force at another time and in different circumstances. Cantrill advocates a critical education as the antidote to social panic behaviour. Given the historical time of the broadcast and his special study, another of Cantrill's observations has intense poignancy:

> Even though the rape of a Southern white woman by a Negro is still a possibility, increased education regarding the frustrations that lead to lynchings may encourage potential mob members to investigate charges more thoroughly before taking their antisocial action.[6]

Two other factors need to be taken into account. The cultural framework of modernity was beginning to take hold in literature, science and popular culture. The idea of life on another planet in the solar system was credible and not fantastic. The competition in news coverage home and abroad by the US radio networks NBC and CBS inculcated an expectation of 'exclusive' news reporting which would not be verifiable by duplication on other channels.

I think we can now say that the panic was authored by someone with a mischievous determination to shock and confuse. The culprit was undoubtedly Orson Welles and there were other unusual circumstances concerning the period and the actual day of the broadcast not covered by Cantrill. I think the evidence available to us indicates quite strongly that Orson Welles deliberately sought to create alarm, although he did not anticipate the scale of the panic. He told Peter Bogdanovich in later years:

> The kind of response, yes – that was merrily anticipated by us all. The size of it, of course, was flabbergasting. Six minutes after we'd gone on the air, the switchboards in radio stations right across the country were lighting up like Christmas trees. Houses were emptying, churches were filling up; from Nashville to Minneapolis there was wailing in the street and the rending of garments. Twenty minutes in, and we had a control room full of very bewildered cops. They didn't know who to arrest or for what, but they did lend a certain tone to the remainder of the broadcast. We began to realise, as we ploughed on with the destruction of New Jersey, that the extent of our American lunatic fringe had been underestimated.[7]

Welles explained that his protestation of innocence afterwards was based on the beginning of lawsuits, with the newspapers quoting claims of compensation amounting to $12 million. At the CBS conference when asked if he was aware of the terror that such a broadcast could stir up, he replied: 'Definitely not. The technique I used was not original with me. It was not even new. I anticipated nothing unusual.' The actual lawsuits that followed amounted to the not inconsiderable sum of $750,000. Listeners claimed to have suffered injuries caused by the panic such as falling down stairs and breaking bones. Orson Welles's lawyer had sensibly restricted the Mercury Theatre's indemnity to libel and plagiarism. CBS settled the claims out of court for a few thousand dollars.

There is the apocryphal story that when Orson Welles was live on the radio reading from Walt Whitman on the day the Japanese attacked Pearl Harbor, the breathless newsman's desire to interrupt the programming with a news flash was challenged sceptically by the producer's refrain: 'Oh Orson, there he goes again.' Orson Welles explained the motive for the skit in a British television interview with Michael Parkinson and stated that he wanted to challenge the public's unquestioning trust of the medium of radio and demonstrate how people could be deceived. He also told Peter Bogdanovich:

> Well, it put me in the movies. Was that lucky? I don't know. Anyway, thanks to the Martians, we got us a radio sponsor, and suddenly we were a great big commercial program, right up there with Benny, Burns, and Allen, and the Lux Radio Theatre with C. B. De Mille. The next step was Hollywood . . . Now there's a station-break, if I ever heard one.[8]

CBS was aware of the risks of listeners being taken in by the realism of the writing and performance. Documentary evidence shows that producers insisted on changing real place names to fictitious ones, but the ersatz place names still had a ring of authenticity. CBS executive Davidson Taylor and the network's team of attorneys insisted on twenty-eight changes to the working script. They feared the drama would be too believable. They were worried that the Museum of Natural History might sue if it was convinced that the use of the institution's name reflected badly on it. The changes to place names were not particularly radical. Langley Field became Langham Field. Princeton University Observatory became the Princeton Observatory and the New Jersey National Guard became the State Militia. Orson Welles also agreed to the deletion of the image of crazed, starving people bolting and trampling on each other, and it seemed the Network's 'suits' were rather concerned that the cries of the advancing Martians, 'Ulia, Ulia, Ulia', were so horrific, they should be excised on the grounds of taste and decency.[9]

Orson Welles was conscious of the psychological impact of Herbert Morrison's emotional ad-libbed radio description of the destruction of the *Hindenberg* just over a year before. In fact the actor playing the reporter in the production was directed to listen to and study the broadcast in a CBS booth during the rehearsals. An attempt was made to mimic the voice of President Roosevelt, and the production successfully pastiched the texture of contemporary networks which were continually interrupting music and soap opera broadcasts to bring the latest news developments from European crises such as Munich and the expansionist designs of the German, Italian and Japanese dictatorships. Cantrill's interviews with listeners proved that the production succeeded in its aim.

The effectiveness of the confusion can be attributed to the fact that the CBS Mercury Theatre On The Air series had an intelligent audience that could engage powerfully with the skilful imaginative and emotional manipulation of the Mercury company. Cantrill and sociologists have stressed that listeners with less education were more susceptible and it was these listeners who were the engine for panic. They may be wrong. The audience would have been classed as an ABC1 audience nowadays. Walter Beaupre, in his Internet essay posted on the Voyager-.com website 'When Mars invaded radio: the broadcast of the century', reminds us that Cantrill's research studies demonstrate that the enlightened listener attempted to verify what was going on by checking other stations on the dial, the newspaper programme guides and public safety organisations. Beaupre says: 'It was not the "unwashed masses" who tuned into dramatisations of works of literature on a Sunday evening in 1938.'

Following the Cantrill study a number of academics particularly from the scientific and mathematical disciplines began to explore the process of mass communication. In 1949 Shannon and Weaver's ground-breaking *The Mathematical Theory of Communication* was published.[10] The three-tier problems of communication raised critical questions. Technical problems begged the question how accurately can the symbols of communication be transmitted, semantic problems raised the question of how precisely do the transmitted symbols convey the desired meaning, and effectiveness problems precipitated the question of how effectively does the received meaning affect behaviour in a desired way.

Radio had revolutionised the dynamics of mass media. Before the age of radio the democracy of participation in mass communications culture depended on literacy. Prior to educational reform in European nation-states during the nineteenth century history had been marked by the existence of educated minorities who controlled the flow of information to the uneducated majority. Social hierarchy and dominance was exerted through the control of information and the power of information acquisition depended on the ability to read. It can be argued that computer literacy presents a similar prognosis for social control between the connected superclass of Internet users and the economically disadvantaged underclass who do not have access to the global network and community of cyber-communications. Apocalyptic predictions about this risk have been challenged by proactive government policy in Britain and elsewhere to connect educational institutions to the Internet and the capitalist dynamics of the market appear to be creating the social and economic conditions for acquisition and consumption of PC/Internet entertainment on a par with television.

Wider literacy became a significant engine for the development of mass newspaper circulation. Radio became the first medium to provide information to people who were non-literate. Radio was and still is a low cost medium of transmission and reception. The scientific engagement with media theory is philosophically interesting. The Internet and World Wide Web is a digital scientific concept based on the binary code of 'bit' information. This is a pattern of 1/0 or on/off. It is a contrast translated in terms of human communication into the tension or conflict of 'Yes/No'. Socio-psychologists assert that the human brain is predicated on an operation of positive and negative. The binary choice codification appears to be central to the semiological writing of Saussure and Lévi-Strauss. The *War of the Worlds* saga is replete with the positive/negative, good/evil dynamics of binary code communications theory. It is a story of survival/destruction, and a war between Humans/Martians. The ultimate skill in the deception, however, was the clever mixing and disguise of entropic and redundant codes of communication.

The Mercury Theatre exploited the conventions of radio communication which are of course saturated with redundancy or high predictability. However, the overall objective of the entire play was entropic. The purpose was not easy to understand. The process of deception was easy communication through the representation of appropriate radio conventions: the big band music, the urgent punctuation of news bulletins, the presidential fireside-chat style of political communication, the realistic ad-libbed description of a dramatic event. The art in the deception was entropic at the time because the convention of integrity and honesty of intent had been challenged by conveying a fiction as reality. But it can now be argued that the radio skit has established its unique conventions and increased the scope for redundancy in communication.

The Princeton University survey was not the only investigation into the nature of the audience on that evening. The Hooper rating company measured that the most popular radio programme on that night was Edgar Bergen's *Charlie McCarthy* show which commanded 34.7 per cent of the audience at 8 p.m. It may seem strange to listeners today that the show's popularity depended on a ventriloquist act. Charlie McCarthy was a dummy animated and articulated by Edgar Bergen in front of a live audience; this act had been previously established in vaudeville. It seemed to transfer rather well to radio.

The Mercury Theatre On The Air had a minority audience of 3.6 per cent. But on this particular night the Hooper rating company discovered a sizeable shift in the audience. Twelve minutes into the hour, Bergen and his dummy finished their popular act and there followed a light operatic piece sung by Nelson Eddy. The Neapolitan Love Song is not what many regular Charlie McCarthy listeners would expect to hear if they tuned in late. This programme continued with an unrelenting diet of dramatic monologue and songs. Hooper concluded that 12 per cent of the Charlie McCarthy audience switched to the CBS networked offering of the Martian invaders in New Jersey. It was reaching its most dramatic mini-climax with Carl Phillips describing in realistic style the crashed Martian space-ship at the Wilmuth Farm in Grovers Mill. With the national audience share now above 15 per cent, it has been assumed that word of mouth and telephone calls to relatives continued to increase the programme's audience share. The tinder dry brushfire of panic spread across the USA.

The rest, as they say, is interesting history. The power of radio was established, Orson Welles's name reverberated around the world, Campbell's Soups decided to sponsor the programme, and Orson Welles's plan to 'make a radio splash' propelled him to Hollywood to make *Citizen Kane*. In fact his entrée to Hollywood was exceptional in the degree of artistic freedom given him. By dramatising death and destruction so realistically he had substantially enhanced the commodification of his value as an international artist. In the process he had invested the Mercury CBS drama programme with sponsorship appeal.

The hysteria and controversy surrounding the *War of the Worlds* broadcast was also accentuated by the hostility of the newspaper media which had seen the infant and now adolescent radio medium aggressively competing for advertising revenue. Here was an opportunity to exaggerate the degree of the panic. It does not appear that anyone died as a result, but listeners were treated for shock, hysteria and even heart attacks. Somewhat suspiciously there were more newspaper offices than police stations swamped with frantic queries: 'What is happening? Where's the nearest bomb shelter? What must we do?'

The author of the original novel, H. G. Wells, was not particularly impressed. On the following day he is reported as saying 'the dramatisation was made with a liberty that amounts to a complete rewriting and made the novel an entirely different story. It's a total unwarranted liberty'. Two years later his attitude had somewhat mellowed because he was happy to meet and be interviewed by Orson Welles on live American radio on 28 October 1940. Why had his early antipathy evaporated? It might have something to do with the fact that the broadcast and publicity had boosted sales of one of his more obscure novels. In the live interview on KTSA, a San Antonio radio station, H. G. Wells referred to the famous broadcast as 'this sensational Hallowe'en panic spree' by his 'delightful little namesake'.

Orson displayed an uncharacteristic humility with repeated utterances of the expression 'you're very kind, sir'. They also talked about the fact that Adolf Hitler had made a specific reference to the event in his 'great Munich speech' and had mocked the Americans for being so gullible. H. G. Wells, travelling from a country at war against a Nazi-dominated Europe, made the point 'You aren't quite as serious in America yet. You haven't the war underneath your chins. You can still play with ideas of terror and conflict'.

Orson Welles's partner in the Mercury Theatre was the actor and producer John Houseman, who somewhat prophetically first worked with Orson in a theatre production of Archibald MacLeish's play *Panic*. Houseman has been considered the kingpin component in the success of the Mercury Theatre by providing the structure and organised channels for Orson Welles's 'gushing burst water main' talent. Houseman has made a unique observation about the success of the *War of the Worlds* which has not been touched on by the myriad of writers, biographers and analysts who have picked over every second of this legendary broadcast. While acknowledging the quality of Orson's acting and directing, he felt that his real genius was to be found in his talent as a magician:

> First and last he was a magician. If you examine all his best work including *Citizen Kane*, you'll find that what he was really doing was a magic act . . . He was at his best when he had very strong material which he could develop and enrich as a magician.[11]

Howard Koch held on to the credit and the royalties for the special adaptation of the *War of the Worlds*. There has not been much focus on his sweat-shop experience as the writer on the project. He had only six days; in fact he was still writing the final pages on the very day of the live transmission. His acute observation on the aftermath of the 'contrite and remorseful press conference' confirms the company's true and original intentions:

> Later that morning I was in the theatre where the press conference had just been held when I saw Orson coming out of one door and Houseman another, exchanging a congratulatory gesture which spoke volumes.[12]

The influential newspaper columnist Dorothy Thompson conferred a seal of legitimacy on the Mercury Theatre's stunt when she explained that the broadcast had alerted people to the dangers of panic should a real enemy ever attack.

Attempts have been made to imitate the *War of the Worlds* scam within regulatory controls. Not surprisingly the US Federal Communications Commission launched an urgent inquiry and Congress passed a raft of laws for US broadcasters to guard against deception of this kind again. Regulators in other countries followed suit. Howard Koch acknowledged a dramatic example of imitation being the sincerest and most dangerous form of flattery. In the rare 1970 publication *The Panic Broadcast: The Whole Story of Orson Welles' Legendary Radio Show*, Koch describes the story of a radio production group in Lima, Peru, who appropriated the play, translated it into Spanish and broadcast it a year later. The transmission caused a panic albeit on a smaller scale because there were fewer radio sets in Peru per head of population than the USA. But the reaction was much more drastic. Koch reports: 'When the Peruvians found out that they had been tricked, and the world was not coming to an end, they decided to put an end at least to the offending radio station, burning it to the ground.'[13] Further research reveals that this incident took place in Quito, Ecuador, and not Peru.

A broadcast of the *War of the Worlds* script in Santiago, Chile, on 12 November 1944 is alleged to have caused many listeners to run into the streets, barricade themselves in their homes and make at least one provincial governor mobilise his troops and artillery to repel invasion from outer space.

The arson story that Howard Koch was referring to appears to have taken place on 12 February 1949 when thousands of listeners in Quito, Ecuador, fled into the streets to escape deadly Martian gas raids. The *New York Times* (14 February 1949) claimed that a mob burned down the radio station broadcasting the Orson Welles style skit, killing fifteen people inside. According to the *New York Times* report the play broadcast on Radio Quito in Spanish was realistic and contained impersonations of well-known local politicians and journalists, and terrifying eyewitness descriptions. The broadcast used real place names, even stating that the Martians had destroyed Latacunga, a town twenty miles south of the Ecuadorian capital.

Chapter 12

Radio drama panics

A cross-cultural phenomenon

It is something of a surprise to learn that the first radio play written for French radio in 1922 was banned by the Sea Ministry because the depiction of the story was regarded as too realistic and the state authorities anticipated the potential for panic. This meant that Maurice Vinot (writing under the pseudonym Gabriel Germinet) and his co-writer Pierre Cusy never had the pleasure of hearing the drama unfold for the radio audience. *Maremoto* dramatised the shipwreck of an ocean-going passenger liner. Ten years after the demise of the *Titanic* the French government may well have had an understandable apprehension of the psychological impact of the realistic plot and writing. It is rather remarkable that the first adventure in specific creative writing for French radio should be censored. It is equally remarkable that the prediction and fear of panic predates the *War of the Worlds* event by sixteen years. It is a shame that *Maremoto* was not broadcast to the limited French radio audience of under 100,000 people. It would have been interesting to have been able to assess the mechanism of panic if the play had the actual effect feared by government officials. Would the panic have been spread by the radio audience to the non-radio audience? Would the panic have been more potent at sea?

Panics and deceptions are achieved in different ways and they are always linked to the *War of the Worlds* broadcast as an iconic reference or source of inspiration. A television spoof in Germany in 1982 which dramatised an extra-terrestrial landing prompted thousands of viewers to telephone police stations demanding advice to help them survive potential death and destruction. The same technique of interrupting an established show with a news flash reporting the arrival of a flying saucer in a field in Duisburg generated panic and confusion. A BBC local radio station in Sheffield in the same year created consternation in an imaginative but somewhat foolhardy programme marketing stunt through the device of a spoof news bulletin in the middle of a regular sequential music programme. The news flash declared that Soviet bombers and intercontinental missiles were on their way to London. Many of the listeners in Sheffield tried to contact their relatives living in the Greater London area and police stations in and around Sheffield were deluged with telephone calls demanding advice and guidance on the subject of civil defence.

The BBC Radio 1 FM's production of *Independence Day* (1996), featuring the network's well-known presenter Nicky Campbell, was an example of imitation. The invasion of British locations by aliens had powerful parallels. The opening narration and text is very similar to the opening of Orson Welles's and Mercury Theatre's *War of the Worlds*. Using the well-known British astronomer Patrick Moore to play the equivalent of Orson Welles's Professor Pierson is another similarity. The unfolding of the story using a Radio 1 FM disc jockey on an RAF AWACs type flight investigating unidentified flying objects (UFOs) creates a bed of contemporary broadcasting texture to support the unfolding fantasy.

The promotional material says that 'Independence Day UK overtakes Radio 1's regular programming – and as London is razed to the ground, Nicky Campbell and Patrick Moore become part of the action, joining the crews of the RAF Tornadoes and Sentry aircraft in a series of desperate dogfights in the skies over the United Kingdom.'[1] The writer, director and producer had the rights to the original movie's sound effects and the credits read like those of a feature film. However, how effective was the broadcast in successfully engaging with the psychology of the listener? Fortunately, the 1 hour production has also been marketed very strongly on the Polygram Spoken Word label so the cassette version is available for study.

Audio indulgence is served with a cinematic-style surround sound mix. The *Daily Telegraph*'s radio critic, Gillian Reynolds, described the production as 'big, bold, allusive and funny'. However, I believe it can be argued that it may lack much of the charge of the Mercury Theatre broadcast because the script and performances sometimes become cartoonish and wooden. Dramatically the tension is weak and overwhelmed by the impressive technical sound design which becomes overpowering for a listener not equipped with a surround sound decoder and five speakers. Nobody is fooled and more critically I would venture to suggest that there is not an effective suspension of disbelief. But as Roland Barthes would say, that is probably one of the production's strengths. The production is one dimensional through its over-the-top pursuit of the burlesque. It has something in common with the wrestling matches appreciated as fake spectacle by working-class audiences. The opening narrative refers specifically to the 1938 panic and makes the interesting point:

Sixty years later throughout the world radio's influence has withered. It is a spent medium. It could never happen again . . . could it?[2]

Such a question creates a portent which is virtually impossible to achieve. But subjective evaluations very often depend on the context of the comparison. The lack of depth in characterisation and in the script's literary quality is also very much the hallmark of an original and potent form of radio drama. Dirk Maggs had previously created very short episodic *Audiomovie* series of early comic strip stories such as *Judge Dredd*, *Batman* and *Superman* for Radio 1 FM and this production was an extension of that genre. Judged in its broadcast and audience context, the *Audiomovie* increases in value as an innovative form of storytelling for the popular music format station. Maggs has also produced another *Audiomovie* blockbuster production of *An American Werewolf in London* for the same network – again structured in very short sequences that run to the same time as an album track and are then fused together in an omnibus at the weekend.

The programme started with a pretend BBC Radio 1 UFO special, full of the station's jingles and realistic references to the geography of RAF communications and defence infrastructure such as Government Communications Headquarters (GCHQ) and RAF Wentworth. The cast included former 'Doctor Who' Colin Baker and the versatile actor Toyah Willcox, who performed the role of a fighter pilot. Nicky Campbell and Patrick Moore give rather convincing performances of themselves. The use of BBC Radio 1 music as normal programming in the switch between the studio and outside broadcast was another concession to the 1938 production. Patrick Moore speaks to an old professor friend at a Russian observatory, as an incoming signal becomes attached to an approaching object from space. By the time it arrives over the surface of the earth, fragments the size of the Isle of Wight break off to hover over the important cities of the world. Another concession to the 1938 broadcast was the shameless mimicry of the 1996 British Prime Minister John Major and Opposition leader Tony Blair. This was reminiscent of the Mercury company actor who imitated the voice of President Roosevelt in the 1938 broadcast. The sound design of the programme included typical *Newsbeat* jingles and musical beds. Maggs cheekily included the Radio 1 announcement:

> Apparently the other radio networks and television can't opt out of their regular programming till half past seven to cover these events so Radio 1 is at present the only source of information on what is happening.[3]

What better way to account for the normal programming on other radio channels which reassured some Mercury Theatre listeners in 1938 that they were listening only to a radio play.

Another blatant parallel lies in the several seconds of silence that followed the 'live ad-libbed' description of the UFO's streaks of destructive light somewhat melodramatically presented by the *Newsbeat* reporter in a police helicopter. It was a dramatic pause that replicated the silence which followed Karl Phillips' description of the Martian spaceship at Grovers Mill, New Jersey. Both productions underpin the dramatic value of extended silence, but perhaps *Independence Day UK*, playing more of the role of imitating *War of the Worlds*, leaves a vacuum of tension that creates an almost suffocating void at the very core of the listener's imaginative experience which is intensely psychological.

The Phoenix, Arizona, radio station KTAR 620 AM produced a 1995 version, placing the *War of the Worlds* story in contemporary Arizona, engaging the entire on-air and production talent in the project. Producer Doren Fronterhouse went to St Mary's Basilica in downtown Phoenix to record the bells as they chimed on Hallowe'en night 1995. The station also warned its audience for many weeks that this programme was going to be aired as its special Hallowe'en 'trick or treat'. This production was not just a simple replication of the original Mercury adaptation. Unlike *Independence Day UK*, the Arizona station achieved the communication of new dramatic truths by creating a more convincing atmosphere. The sound design had rather more clarity than the surround sound sweeps of Steven Spielberg's *Jurassic Park* style productions. There appeared to be a greater dramatic cohesion in the nature of the storytelling. Rather than riding on the back of a hit movie, the KTAR station in Phoenix obtained modest sponsorship from 'Ottawa University – providing educational programmes for adult learners'. *War of the Worlds 1995* sets out to create 'a simulation of what an alien invasion might sound like if you were listening to KTAR'.

A low pitched announcer concludes his opening introduction with the words: 'Turn the lights down low, close your eyes and don't panic. Welcome to the end of the world.' The station's manager, Mark McCoy, then presents a charming analysis of the 1938 Mercury Theatre production using illustrative sound extracts. Here the homage is more honestly and clearly stated. McCoy observes that it was incredible that the Mercury production was all done live. Rather than lowering esteem for the sound/radio medium, McCoy offers the interesting view that:

> It will live forever as a moment in time that illustrates the power that a simple broadcast can have over the public – a power that in today's media culture just isn't utilised like it was in the beginning. There was a time when listening to the radio was an incredibly visual experience. We believe it still can be. There has never been a television show, movie or photograph that can approach the splendour, the warmth, the horror, and the majesty of the picture your imagination paints as you listen to sound.[4]

The alien invasion begins during an eccentric phone-in programme called *Strauss's Place*. The Princeton Observatory is updated to become the orbiting

Hubble telescope. Flash news reports refer to an expert professor from NASA (National Aeronautics and Space Administration). The developing narrative uses the station's regular phone-in news talk format to provide the mechanism for dramatising the increasing tension and panic of the story. The legendary presenter opens his broadcast with the delightful line: 'Boy, I have never started off a show before with explosions on Mars! I've got a rather interesting show tonight. In fact some might say it's a rather spacey show keeping with the tone that has already been set.' The charm and alarm technique of plot development is struck early with an intention to broadcast an interview with somebody advocating the healing powers of eating pasta. The accelerating interruption of urgent news bulletins frustrates the pasta Shaman's broadcasting debut. Bill Strauss declares: 'You know what? I am going to make an executive decision here. A big one. I am going to blow off the pasta guy.'

As more urgent news bulletins cascade into his programme from the newsroom and remote broadcasts, he is given the delightful line: 'Boy. What a night! I know it's not O. J., but if any of you would like to talk about what is going on – you've got to have thoughts on this – the gases from Mars, the meteorites, we're learning things about astronomy that I'd forgotten from grade school – give us a call.' 'O. J.' are, of course the initials of O. J. Simpson, the American athlete, actor and media personality accused in that year of the murder of his estranged wife and her friend in Los Angeles.

The first call to the *Strauss Hour* comes from Gloria in Scottsdale and succeeds in giving the production an uncanny ring of truth. Gloria believes they are being hoodwinked by a conspiracy on the part of NASA to generate more funding from Congress. One of the first callers taken on the overnight programme I presented when Diana, Princess of Wales was fatally injured in Paris, advanced a conspiratorial plot by the British establishment to prevent the mother of the heir to the throne marrying a 'Muslim playboy with an Egyptian background'. Life seemed to imitate art. The KTAR outside broadcast reporter Ned Foster peppers his language with 1995 cultural references such as 'It's something out of the X-Files'. Ned Foster's dramatic descriptions in outside broadcast links are terminated after screams and the streaks of alien flames incinerating fields and people. Rather than replicate the Mercury Theatre's 5 seconds of silence, Bill Strauss is left floundering with the desperate words: 'Ned? . . . Ned?'

The KTAR production avoids making the character Bruce Babbit, the US Secretary of the Interior who hails from Arizona, sound like President Bill Clinton. The identification of Ned Foster's charred body leaves Bill Strauss signing off with 'I can't handle this'. Outside connections from the newsroom to National Guard interviewees are lost as the Martian invaders disseminate destruction from the WW Ranch. Radio communications with Air Force fighter pilots who are liquidated by alien firepower are dramatic and realistic. The description of the destruction of Phoenix is given authenticity as the bells of St Mary's Basilica in the city's downtown location can be heard in the background. KTAR produced another version for the sixtieth anniversary of the *War of the Worlds* broadcast in October 1938. They were not alone. Scores of public and commercial broadcasters throughout the world imitated the CBS broadcast with new productions. Some were more imaginative and local than others. Some broadcasters such as the British national commercial station 'Talk Radio' simply repeated the classic. There were no reports of any panic. The event which seems to be the pre-eminent legend of radio drama has become something of a quaint and burlesque historical curiosity.

Chapter 13

Moving from burlesque to propaganda and news

Fictional narratives are not exclusive to the field of entertainment. Comedians and social subversives are motivated to expose the gullibility of audiences to highlight the allegation of a false trust. Fictional narrative is also the objective of propagandists. Scholars up to now have concentrated on the model and study of the *War of the Worlds* phenomenon. Palestine in 1948 was the scene of a most catastrophic panic generated by radio with social and political implications that have a tragic reach into the contemporary age. About 750,000 Palestinian Arabs fled their villages and homes in UN Palestinian Arab state designated areas following the massacre of combatants and civilians in the village of Deir Yassin just outside Jerusalem. The panic was attributed to the hysterical and false radio coverage by the Palestinian Arab radio service of what had happened when Jewish irregulars from the Stern gang and Irgun Zvei Leumi attacked the village.

It would appear that television has not been able to match up to radio for the force and terror of 'broadcast panics'. A UK ghost-hunting programme featuring celebrities such as Michael Parkinson created a murmur of alarm one Hallowe'en night in the 1990s. The programme was mentioned in the suicide note of a teenager, but it is felt that the individual succumbed to other psychological pressures and it would appear that the programme was a coincidental reference key to his distress. BBC Television's *Panorama* April Fool's Day joke about the spaghetti harvests in Switzerland had a fair number of people fooled in 1957. Television was a relatively new medium of mass communication and the authoritative introduction and endorsement by Richard Dimbleby helped emboss the item with credibility. It could be argued that television's reduced potency in generating panic can be attributed to the fact that radio was the only electronic medium available during the celebrated panics so there was less opportunity for audiences to verify; regulation in the television age has been more rigorous, and television is less of a psychologically based consumer experience.

However, television as much as radio does seem to have become the victim of increasing deception or faking to aggrandise its popular viewing appeal. The £2 million fine imposed on Carlton Television in 1999 for broadcasting a documentary on cocaine drug smuggling, which was exposed by the *Guardian* as having fabricated interviews and filmed sequences, and the beginning of a BBC inquiry into research standards following newspaper allegations that actresses had been employed to simulate documentary realism in talk show formats in February 1999, is evidence of this. German programme maker Michael Born served a prison sentence in 1996 after it emerged that he had faked more than thirty documentaries. In one example he had filmed six of his friends who had dressed up in the white cloaks and hoods of the Ku Klux Klan and staged a book-burning ritual in the Bavarian mountains. At the Sheffield Documentary Festival in October 1998 he said he was responding to the demands of a 'medium driven by ratings'. Television channels perceived a public demand for constant entertainment and stimulation and Born argued that he was feeding the insecurities and fantasies of his audience. If audiences are perceived to expect the same drama and satisfying endings served to them in established drama it can be argued that factual programme makers will be faced with increasing pressures to fabricate structures and scenarios, particularly when the real nature of life in all its tedious and awkward dimensions fails to deliver the source material.

The degree of deception employed against broadcast audiences seems to be quite complex, particularly when linked to the need to maximise ratings and succeed in a more competitive media market. Michelle Hilmes in *Radio Voices* (1997) gives a compelling account of 'false authorisation' in the case of the supposed involvement of the celebrated film director Cecil B. DeMille in the Lux Radio Theatre series of the 1930s and 1940s.[1] De Mille was credited as being the director and producer when he had no involvement in the productions. It sounded as though his prologues and epilogues were ad-libbed when in fact they were scripted. The popular BBC Television satirical series *Have I Got News for You* in the late 1990s is presented as live and spontaneous comedy. Viewers are not told with any emphasis that at least 25 per cent of the content has been scripted, sometimes rehearsed and the entire programme pre-recorded.

Michelle Hilmes reminds us that similar arguments for Cecil B. DeMille false authorship can be attributed to Orson Welles and his Mercury Theatre On The Air. Despite his influential and charistmatic acting and direction, there appears to be growing evidence that he worked on the CBS productions only on the final day of rehearsal and live broadcast with the bulk of scriptwriting being undertaken by freelance writers such as Howard Koch and production planning and development by his partner John Houseman.[2]

The presentation of an integrity of authorship and the potential for deceiving audiences achieves a sense of almost exquisite irony in the production and broadcast of a British Channel Four television programme on hoaxes, *Faking It* (February 1999). The researcher and producer for the programme used the benefits of the unpublished draft of this entire section of the book to support and guide their programme production. Furthermore the producer engaged me in two hours of consultation on the cultural and media issues of the media hoax phenomenon, particularly in relation to radio, and said that I would be used as an academic commentator on certain extracts to provide an 'informed media perspective'. It even got to the stage of bleeping me over a weekend to discuss availability for filming. Then there was complete silence and a few weeks later the programme was broadcast using a BBC Radio 4 presenter as 'the media critic' and with no credit or acknowledgement to my contribution during the programme or in its closing subtitles. The producers could argue that the substantial nature of the research for the programme had been determined by them. But this case history is an ironic context for analysing the source of authorship. It is further evidence of a strong current of insecurity about the process and mechanism of production and the nature of its presentation to audiences.

Orson Welles's 1938 portrayal of the expert astronomer, Professor Pearson, who is lost for words and has nothing to say in *War of the Worlds*, underlines how the audience's reliance on experts and information icons can be used to deceive and panic. It is also worth bearing in mind that the year 1957 belonged to an era when recreational travelling abroad was still the preserve of only the few. So faked pictures of growing spaghetti combined effectively with the voice over: 'Spaghetti cultivation in Switzerland is not on anything like the scale of the Italian spaghetti farms . . . Many of you will have seen the huge spaghetti plantations in the Po Valley.' Richard Dimbleby's sign-off cue 'And that is all from *Panorama* on this first day of April' was too subtle a remark for those who had been easily deceived. Viewers wrote in to ask where they could buy spaghetti plants and one viewer asserted that the programme had got it wrong; spaghetti grew horizontally, not vertically.

Further research yields much richer examples of panic caused by radio spoofs and mistakes. A relatively little known broadcast by the BBC from Edinburgh on 17 January 1926 convinced many listeners that a revolution in London had resulted in the destruction of the Houses of Parliament by trench mortars and the Minister of Transport being hanged from a tramway post.

The similarities between Father Ronald Knox's burlesque talk entitled 'Broadcasting the barricades' and the *War of the Worlds* fiasco are intriguing. Once again the cultural context is relevant. The Bolshevik revolution of 1917 had created a moral and political panic in the west. British, American and French troops had been actively fighting alongside the White Russians seeking to crush the Soviet state. A communist revolt in Munich had been put down by the German Weimar Republic in 1919. In the same year the police had gone on strike in Britain. In 1924, the first Labour government had been brought down by the fake Zinoviev letter published in the *Daily Mail* falsely alleging collusion between Labour and the 'expansionist international communist conspiracy'. Britain was only a few months away from the General Strike. Radio was generally the preserve of the high disposable income middle classes, although by this time it was being played in public places such as pubs and cafes.

Father Knox's burlesque was transmitted at 7.40 p.m. The spirit of the talk was punctuated by periodical announcements 'We will now switch over to the dance band' or other light music. The *War of the Worlds* was broadcast at 8 p.m. US Eastern Standard Time. The tension of the unfolding drama was heightened with frequent announcements such as 'We will now return you to Ramon Raquello and his orchestra' after frequent interruptions from flash bulletins. Father Knox's script told the story of a mob of unemployed people assembling in Trafalgar Square and being incited to sack the National Gallery. Having sacked the National Gallery, it surged down Whitehall, attacked government offices, destroyed wildfowl in St James's Park with empty bottles and then blew up the Houses of Parliament using trench mortars. As Big Ben had fallen to the ground, listeners were informed that in future the BBC time signals would be sent out from Edinburgh. The burlesque became a representation of reality because the talk was deliberately infected with human fallibility. A report that Mr Wutherspoon, the Minister of Transport, had been captured and hanged from a lamp-post was later corrected. He had in fact been hanged from a tramway post.

The *War of the Worlds* broadcast reproduced the realistic fluffs of a live outside broadcast at the farm where alien spaceships had landed. Reporter Carl Phillips stumbled and asked his interviewees to speak louder into the microphone. Another astonishing similarity is that Father Knox's talk finished with the mob marching on Savoy Hill to destroy the BBC's then headquarters. *War of the Worlds* scriptwriter Howard Koch took some delight in wiping out the CBS building a few minutes before the end of the 1938 drama. The Father Knox broadcast was accompanied by stage-managed sound effects of explosions and a yelling, screaming mob. Listeners contacted newspaper offices and the BBC asking 'What is happening in London? Is it true that Big Ben has been blown up? Has the National Gallery been sacked? Is the Government calling upon loyal citizens?'

In June 1944, the Germans had been given ample opportunity to appreciate the imminence of the Allied invasion of France. A 23-year-old teleprinter operator from Camden Town working in the London Fleet Street offices of Associated

Press accidentally ran the tape message that General Eisenhower had announced a landing in Europe three days before the actual event. The punched tape of the practice flash had been fed into the live teletype machine. It took Joan Ellis only two minutes to realise her mistake. By this time US radio networks had broadcast the news. It had also been distributed across four continents. It was timed at 4.39 p.m. on 3 June 1944, Eastern Standard Time. The competitive US radio networks were 'on the trigger' to be the first to announce the news. In fact CBS veteran sportscaster Ted Husing interrupted his account of the Belmont Stakes with the news 15 seconds after the Associated Press false report reached the New York newsroom. There has never been such a rush of apologies and corrections in the history of broadcasting. Police stations, government departments and broadcasting stations were still besieged by inquiries from millions of people who had been convinced that the invasion of Europe had begun. Joan Ellis became 'The Girl Who Was Too Keen' and 'She Told World "D-Day Is Here" – Apologises'. Fortunately the location of the landing had not been disclosed in the news flash.

Since the 1990s radio has been effective in developing a 'skit genre' which engages the listeners in ironic entertainment rather than fooling them. This is the realm of the spoof broadcaster who uses mimicry and verisimilitude to deceive ordinary people, politicians and public figures into making fools of themselves. *Candid Camera* is the television equivalent. It is copied across the world and provides huge entertainment. It also has the capacity to satirise and play a subversive role. However, the spoof call can go wrong when recognition descends on the 'voice in disguise'.

In 1976 BBC Radio London reporter Denis MacShane was sacked after being unmasked as the angry caller making hostile observations about the Conservative politician Reginald Maudling during a phone-in on his own radio station. The London *Evening Standard* critic Victor Lewis-Smith developed a reputation for being a radio phone-in prankster in 1989 by posing as a listener from Doncaster who berated the then BBC Radio 4 controller, Michael Green, with vituperative denunciations of the ill-fated radio soap opera *Citizens*. His mimicry was so convincing everyone was fooled into thinking he was a genuinely aggrieved Radio 4 *aficionado*.

Lewis-Smith has a website at www.lewis-smith.com/newindex.html which profiles his book publications and advertises a cassette containing recordings of some of his spoofs. He targets leading figures in the media and entertainment. The objective is to expose hypocrisy, conceit and dishonesty. Lewis-Smith and the younger Chris Morris have something in common in terms of beginning their careers in BBC local radio: Lewis-Smith at BBC Radio York, Morris at BBC Radios Cambridge and Bristol, and then contributing to BBC Radio 4's *Loose Ends* programme presented by Ned Sherrin. For a number of years there appeared to be rivalry between them, although we cannot be sure if it was synthesised. Lewis-Smith is reported to have observed 'imitation is the sincerest form of being an unoriginal thieving bastard'. Both have moved into the television medium. Lewis-Smith's Channel Four programme was called *TV Offal*.

Oliver Stone's film *Talk Radio* (1989) dramatises the life of an aggressive phone-in presenter who adopts an almost live 'fictional persona' humiliating callers with abusive and belittling insults. The film was based on Eric Bogosian's stage play of the same name which in turn was derived from the story of radio talk-show host Alan Berg – assassinated with a spray of machine-gun bullets in the driveway of his Denver home on 18 June 1984. Alan Berg's 'performances' had enraged a right-wing neo-fascist organisation called 'The Order'. Berg was a self-styled 'Wild Man of the Airwaves' and he built his country-wide audience on KOA-AM by enraging and provoking callers and then cutting them off during explicit discussions about oral sex. His angry ramblings on gun control, racism and Christianity carried across thirty-eight US states on KOA's powerful signal. On a previous station five years earlier Berg had provoked a Ku Klux Klan activist to storm his studio with a gun and scream 'Prepare to die'. The interesting question remains whether Alan Berg's on-air personality was a fictional exaggeration of his real character. The border between reality and creative extension for the purposes of entertainment in this field pushes the presentation of attitudes and opinions into the realms of fantasy and the edge of that performance may have generated a degree of realistic provocation which proved fatal for Alan Berg.

In Britain Chris Morris has developed the technique of live spoofing performances on Radio 1 FM and transferred these skills to his Channel Four television *Brass Eye* series. Previously he had been one of the major scriptwriters of the BBC Radio 4 series *On the Hour*, which was an effective and satirical pastiche of contemporary styles of broadcast news reporting. Actors portrayed the stale conventions of broadcasting and the idea was transferred to television as *The Day Today*. But with his own Radio 1 FM show he took on the task of improvised live skits. The irony was in a pure form. The listener always knew that Chris Morris was assuming characters but the targets of his satire were being fooled into caricaturing themselves in a funny, cruel and embarrassing way. Kim Wilde was trapped into expressing sorrow over the news that homeless people were being clamped like illegally parked vehicles and the leading British black politician Paul Boateng was recorded showing familiarity with non-existent rap artists. Morris rarely gives interviews or photographs. In the *Guardian* (25 July 1994) he was quoted as saying: 'it's just one way of substantiating an idea, of giving authority to any bollocks you invent. Another way is to act it out, as in a Radio 3 series I did with Peter Cook. Or to put on a newsy voice. The point is not being cruel, but substantiating those ideas'.

I would suggest that the BBC Radio 3 series he was referring to, *Why Bother?*, is probably the most inventive and exciting comedic improvisation he has been involved in.[3] As Peter Cook's biographer Harry Thompson has observed:

> Morris was one of the few performers able to match Peter [Cook] for speed of thought and surreal invention, giving the programmes a collaborative edge. The improvised content pushed taste boundaries. For example one of Peter Cook's characters is asked about the discovery of the fossilised remains of the infant Christ, cloning Christ and faxing him in DNA form and various dry runs for the resurrection.[4]

On BBC Radio 1 FM Chris Morris has achieved a sophisticated level of entertainment as well as exposing the cynicism of the media's relationship with politicians and pressure groups. Morris rang the Conservative politician John Selwyn Gummer, posing as a news reporter seeking advance interview material on European political issues. Morris humiliated Gummer by continually asking him to produce soundbites which matched hypothetical scenarios. Gummer was reduced to producing remarks such as 'Labour has signed up with the European Socialist manifesto' and when asked to provide a statement on the basis of Labour doing a complete U-turn he volunteered the observations 'This Labour Party will say anything to get a vote . . . We've pushed them and flushed them out . . . They're frightened and they don't want to stand up for what they've signed up for only a couple of months ago.' In the same programme Morris tricked a media celebrity into volunteering inanities about the value of dogs, particularly in war. Morris observed: 'Sometimes they've been tools'. She replied: 'They've been total tools'. Morris's final riposte, 'I suppose we all are sometimes', and the celebrity's agreement, 'Well, all of us are, yes', provide an exquisite point of irony which is also rather artistic.

In July 1994 Chris Morris made the headlines by generating a rumour that the senior Conservative politician Michael Heseltine was dead. He clearly challenged the borderline of good taste because Mr Heseltine had suffered a heart attack in Venice the previous year, with his agony being caught on television; the stress of the Conservatives' worst election performance for 150 years on 1 May 1997 contributed to another. Morris's programme *The Cutting Edge* took on the appearance of a breaking news programme by punctuating the content with announcements such as 'If there is any more news on the death of Michael Heseltine we'll let you know'. The sketch generated a flurry of rumours in the gossip-riddled corridors of the Palace of Westminster. While the real Mr Heseltine was making a speech in Manchester, many of his parliamentary colleagues were trying to come to terms with his demise. The sketch was built around the scenario of Morris pretending to be the BBC's obituaries editor and contacting the then Conservative MP for Harlow, Jerry Hayes. Hayes was asked to offer an elegy because 'the BBC always compiled obituaries on everybody over the age of 55'. Mr Hayes believed he was talking to a genuine BBC journalist and offered a tribute which credited Mr Heseltine with having been 'a great parliamentarian'. The House of Commons was not amused. Morris was suspended by the BBC. Mr Hayes said after the broadcast: 'I am absolutely appalled and horrified. It's so tacky and dishonest and I'm delighted to hear that Chris Morris has been suspended, even though I have no idea who he is'. The Broadcasting Standards Council also condemned him for exploiting an elderly woman by getting her to read on air a script containing obscenities of which she was unaware.

Chris Morris has never achieved the fame and notoriety generated by Orson Welles, but he continued his mischief months later by searching the world for a willing taxidermist to stuff the corpse of the former Radio 1 disc jockey Johnnie Walker. He posed as BBC Radio 1's then controller Matthew Bannister, who was seeking to stuff the veteran broadcaster's body so that it would stop decomposing in one of his studios and take its place on an exhibition stand at the 'Museum of Broadcasting'. A British taxidermist tersely observed that what was proposed was against the law. Using an excruciating franglais style of schoolboy French, Morris found that the taxidermists of France were more willing.

> MORRIS   Nous avons de lui stuffer pour un exhibition de radio. Vous pouvez faire le taxidermie sur le disc jockey?
> FRENCH TAXIDERMIST   Oui, Oui.
> MORRIS   Quel prix vous demandez?
> FRENCH TAXIDERMIST   Ah, a . . . c'est dur.

The deal was clinched at 30,000 French francs and the corpse would be delivered to Paris the next day. This skit had considerable poignancy because Johnnie Walker had previously been one of Radio 1's disc jockey icons. Entertainment was being created by the network ridiculing its own heritage and tradition. Chris Morris transferred the idea on to Channel Four television and created disturbing and uncomfortable programmes where well-known politicians and media celebrities were made to look fools by being tricked into recording reactions to fictitious scenarios. Morris created a new drug menace called 'Cake' and the resulting interviews parodied the hollowness of public pronouncements on 'the evils of drug taking'. He even managed to fool television personality Noel Edmonds into recording a condemnation of the drug and exhorting the public to fight its evil effects. This was an exquisite sting because Edmonds regularly humiliated unsuspecting viewers in *Candid Camera* style stunts on his prime time Saturday night entertainment programme. Morris turned the exploitation of ordinary 'viewer naivety' into the judicious embarrassment of celebrity. But some of the programmes took on a cruel edge and the then Channel Four Controller Michael Grade sought to apply censorship for sequences which he thought had reached the extreme in bad taste. Morris responded by including a subliminal message 'Michael Grade is a C***' in a subsequent programme.

Morris has now moved from the live improvised format to a much more highly produced, edited and part-scripted production series *Blue Jam* on Radio 1 FM after midnight. The programme uses the ambient style of Californian *Over the Edge* sound artists and develops more rounded reflective characters but retains the anarchic juvenile approach to cynical humour. There is evidence that it has been acquiring an element of university student cult status. Oxford students are said to be performing transcriptions of the programme and the BBC began to buy advertising in broadsheet newspapers such as the *Independent* and *Guardian* to promote the cult quality. It can be argued that Morris has been the first radio producer and performer to generate student interest in dramatic/creative radio since the *Hitchhiker's Guide to the Galaxy* in the late 1970s. He is certainly pushing the boundaries of good taste in language, as this example of an argument between two fictional doctors demonstrates:

Michael I don't think there is much point in . . .
They're fucking right there isn't you serial rapist
Right I'm going to leave now . . .
That's right play the little erupted fish arse when it suits you . . . I hope some mustardy cock explodes in your cocoa valve . . . Jesus . . . The rubber twat ball. Sorry about that.
Unbelievable clit.

America's legendary shock jock Howard Stern has used spoofing as just one of the many subversive mechanisms to lampoon the world around him. Stern has encouraged and cherished the phoney phone-call as an art form. His posse of fans and supporters have made a speciality of breaking into prime time news and current affairs programmes on US radio and television with assumed identities, making talk show hosts look utterly stupid and signing off with their trademark catch-phrase 'Baba Booey'. Sometimes the Howard Stern 'phone-in guerrillas' have exposed the naivety and failure of the programming infrastructure during dramatic live news coverage of catastrophic events such as the Oklahoma Federal Building bombing in 1995. One of Stern's devoted followers, Tom Cypriani, who calls himself 'Captain Janks', has managed to get to air on the *Larry King Live* show. He has broken into news network coverage of earthquakes and major international political crises. His intervention on CNN during the aftermath of the Oklahoma massacre exploited the news network's competitive desperation for eyewitness accounts:

CNN PRESENTER   Could you tell us where you are and what happened when the explosion occurred this morning?

CAPTAIN JANKS   Well I own a Radio shack next door to the Federal Building. We first heard the explosion. We went outside. We thought it was a sonic jet or something like that. The whole side of my building is devastated . . . There are so many people standing outside. The building just . . . just totally exploded. I don't understand how it happened. But I think it was the after effects of Robin Quivers' new book *A Life*.

CNN PRESENTER   Ok . . . ah.

CAPTAIN JANKS   Baba Booey Ya?

Montreal Radio's Pierre Brassard began to achieve international notoriety when on his *Blue Powder Drive Home Show* on station CKOI he successfully duped His Holiness the Pope, Queen Elizabeth, and Brigitte Bardot to engage in what they originally thought were going to be meaningful conversations. In October 1995, Brassard convinced the Queen that he was the Canadian Prime Minister Jean Chrétien. He was able to persuade her in a 17-minute telephone conversation that it would be a good idea if she could broadcast an appeal to the French-speaking province of Quebec not to break away from Canada in yet another nail-biting referendum. Part of the extraordinary conversation was in French with Brassard asking 'Are you wearing a costume for Hallowe'en?' She replied: 'No, no. It's for the children'. This scam was achieved through the skill of Brassard's cheek and mimicry and the Queen's misfortune that her officials could not confirm the authenticity of the call beforehand because Chrétien had been out campaigning. The broadcast had political poignancy because it exposed an element of bias in the Queen's attitude to the Canadian debate over Quebec's independence.

Brassard has his imitator in London at Capital Radio. The *Steve Penk Show* uses former *Spitting Image* comedian Jon Culshaw, who in 1998 mimicked the voice of Conservative Party leader William Hague. The Prime Minister Tony Blair recognised immediately that he was talking to a hoaxer because of the actor's familiar use of the Christian name 'Tony'. Hague always formally addressed Mr Blair as 'Prime Minister', which is a constitutional courtesy. Blair kept his sense of humour and acknowledged the quality of the spoof by announcing to a packed House of Commons at Question Time: 'I took an interesting and detailed call from a hoax caller at Capital Radio who managed to persuade the Number 10 switchboard that he was the Leader of the Opposition.'

The development of phone-in and talkback programming since the early 1970s has provided the opportunity for audience interactivity so that listeners can now turn the tables against the broadcasters themselves. The limited amount of time and resources available to check phone-in contributors provides an environment 'ripe for the picking'. US 'over the edge' sound artists have already succeeded in disrupting licensed programmes through phone-in participation as well as using illegal transmitters to 'crash' on established frequencies.

It would not be inconceivable for a group of subversive broadcasters to swamp an existing news phone-in programme with realistic reports of a catastrophic event tinged with political embarrassment. Back-up calls from apparent emergency services could easily convince the station's newsroom of the authenticity of the event. More highly staffed and experienced national newspapers have been duped by lone hoaxers such as 'Rocky Ryan', whose efforts have created front page embarrassment, and the newspapers had the advantage of hours to make a proper evaluation. In radio, presenters and producers have minutes and seconds.

In the research for this book I interviewed a group of young radio playwrights who have been regularly contributing to national and local phone-in programmes with a repertoire of spoof characters. They have been copying the material to use in future stage, television and radio plays. They played back the hours of material they had generated on condition that I continued to preserve their anonymity. The degree of creativity in the improvisation and development of character was as strong as any full-length play. The playwrights also experimented with a range of sophisticated and complex plot structures and even attempted to support established rules of dramatic structure. The plots and stories would move over many weeks, sometimes months of programming. The sagas would connect local and national radio stations. The personal and intimate histories which the radio telephone can internalise and make psychologically intense travelled across the timeline of problem and general phone-in programmes. The motivation advanced by the playwrights was that exclusion from the privilege and opportunity of formalised BBC Radio 4 production meant that live programming was the only outlet for their creativity and storytelling skills.

The late comedian Peter Cook used an assumed character to communicate on the overnight programme of the London independent station LBC. His 'live performances' began in the mid-1980s when he and his eccentric neighbour George Weiss had difficulty sleeping and became obsessive listeners to Clive Bull's early morning phone-in between 1 a.m. and 4 a.m. George Weiss wanted to promote his 'Rainbow' political movement and they would work as a double act with George Weiss appearing as a live guest in the studio and Peter Cook continually interrupting his political appearances in a variety of phone-in disguises. According to Harry Thompson's biography of Peter Cook, the comedian managed two appearances on Pete Murray's phone-in programme when the subject of abortion was being discussed. He popped up first as a defrocked priest and then returned as a German called Fritz who kept developing a nonsensical analogy with breeding budgerigars.

It was as the character 'Sven from Swiss Cottage' that Peter Cook's creative characterisation took on a more fundamental dimension. Clive Bull encouraged the participation of regular characters and Sven, who styled himself as a Norwegian fisherman, began to mount his own kind of soap opera whereby the fluctuations of his love life stimulated waves of advice from other callers. Sven's outpourings became a metaphorical expression of the agonies of Peter Cook's own life. He portrayed himself as a lonely and upset Norwegian whose wife Jutta had left him quite justifiably and he was now reduced to picking up girls in launderettes, which was not a suitable substitute for the happiness that he once had. The parallels with Peter Cook's actual alcoholism and the fact that his beloved wife Judy had left him for a less traumatic life in the country are rather close. Clive Bull recalls that 'it became a kind of agony hour and callers would ring in advising him on what he should be doing; but the predominant theme was always fish, which would somehow be wangled into every conversation.'

Sven's mood swings would sometimes reflect the personal despair being experienced by Peter Cook in the middle of the night, as the following passage illustrates:

SVEN   I just want to say, Clive, I mean, I have been so gloomy in the past, always talking about how miserable my life is and how these women are making me miserable, but it is up to me.

BULL   It is, yes.

SVEN   It is up to me to just go out and say, 'Look, I am alive, I am a man, I have a Mackintosh'.

BULL   So you're going to go out there and grab life by the –

SVEN   Grab life by the throat, wrestle it to the ground and kick it to death.

BULL   Well we're all thinking of you.

SVEN   Because I get miserable and I feel my mood switching at the moment, I could go downbeat any moment.

BULL   No, no, you hang on upbeat.

SVEN   For goodness sake try and keep up my confidence Clive.

BULL   Hang on there upbeat, we're all rooting for you.

SVEN   Thank you Clive.[5]

Eventually Clive Bull was tipped off that 'Sven' was actually Peter Cook, but he decided to continue the artifice and not allow Peter Cook to know that he knew. George Weiss has kept a vast number of off-air recordings of this extraordinary interaction between the reality of a phone-in programme and one of the world's foremost comedians performing a live fictional characterisation that developed from night to night. George Weiss's 'Rainbow' political movement continues and he remains a witty and subversive contributor to my own overnight programmes on the same radio station. Peter Cook's unrivalled improvisational talent combined with that of Chris Morris in 1995 when they worked together on a series for BBC Radio 3 which has been entirely forgotten, but provided a remarkable arena for what can only be described as spontaneous radio storytellers.

North America is very much the home of a curious counter-culture movement of 'guerrilla media' who specialise in jamming licensed frequencies with pirate interventions that infect regular programmes with foul-mouthed Mickey Mouse impersonations and other audio obscenities. The San Francisco audio college band 'Negativland' specialised in this subversive intervention. The band's *Jamcon '84* CD defined the motivation of culture jammers as wanting to add 'pimples to the face on the retouched cover photo of America'. The culture jammers include the Californian sound artist Don Joyce, who sees himself as a dissident of mainstream media. He says that if an international conglomerate establishes a prominent high-tech billboard, the media dissident 'cannot afford to put one up next to it saying the opposite'. The answer lies in the piratical transformation of the media or advertising icon.

When the media guerrillas 'catalyse doubletakes' on mainstream radio broadcasts, the listeners are being treated to a rich and satirical form of audio dramatic performance that lives for the moment in the ephemeral experience of live transmission, but then becomes a statement from the cultural underground through the distribution of cassettes and further unlicensed or licensed broadcasts of the live mixes. Culture jammer practitioners have published a manifesto which comes quite close to defining their philosophy and influences. Mark Dery's *Hacking, Slashing and Sniping in the Empire of Signs* describes jamming as

> media criticism as a vernacular art form . . . There is a continuum all the way from the medieval Carnival through the Zurich dadaists through the French Situationists in 1968 through the Yippies in America – people like Abbie Hoffman, with a wonderful sense of humour and talent for media manipulation.

The movement crosses all media. In London the anarchist pressure group 'Reclaim the Streets' attempted to distribute a spoof edition of the London *Evening Standard* to communicate their political message in a way that revenged the neglect of their representation in the mainstream media. A jamming collective in Canada, calling itself 'Guerrilla Media', raided the distribution boxes of the Van-couver *Sun* and wrapped a parodying cover sheet which satirised the newspaper's coverage of deforestation and logging in Vancouver Island. In San Francisco free-lance culture jammer Joe Matheny found airtime on public radio networks to ventilate his discovery of secret Vatican documents that proved Jesus Christ faked his own death. He also generated panic within the mainstream media by success-fully placing the hoax that media hackers had found a way of seizing control of cable television transmissions. San Francisco is very much the home of 'Bay Area Radio Junkies', who are now experimenting with skits on the Internet and World Wide Web. It can be argued that their activity is a subversive challenge to one-way monopolistic lines of media communication and an effective method of empower-ing the listener with the freedom of interactivity. Intriguingly the process involves fictional storytelling to mask the true identities of the troublemakers and create the frame for media criticism or satire.

Radio scholars have much to gain from the well-established work of Stuart Hall and Dave Morley on the television audience. Stuart Hall recognised that there is a compelling nexus between the structures of broadcasting institutions, the structure of thought and feeling within the audience and the encoded structure of the broadcast message. Again these factors are interdeterminate and interdependent and this aspect of scholarship, present in Hall's *Encoding and Decoding in the Television Message* (1973),[6] is highlighted by John Fiske in his *Introduction to Communication Studies* (1990).[7] But I also think the writing on the concept of the television bard in *Reading Television* (1978) is relevant.[8] It would be appropriate to transpose the principles of 'bardic television' to construct the concept of 'bardic radio'. Morris, Brassard, Lewis-Smith, Stern, Welles and Knox function as radio bards in a complicated interdependent social relationship. Seven important functions performed by the bard in the traditional society are served by radio as much as by television.

Radio certainly articulates the main lines of the established cultural consensus about the nature of reality. The early *March of Time* dramatisations of contemporary news events in US and Australian radio served this function. There is no evidence of any attempt to challenge the cultural consensus in these programmes. Many distinguished theorists have now clearly defined how broadcasting and radio as much as television constructs the reality as much as 'covering' or 'representing the reality'. Here I am drawing upon my personal experience of live presentation of the developing news story of the death of Diana, Princess of Wales in August 1997. Chris Morris has mischievously demonstrated that his constructs of deception in radio could not necessarily be distinguished from the reality of the 'Diana coverage'. It is intriguing that if he had attempted to construct the major deception of the death of a member of the British Royal Family in order to fulfil the bardic function of exposing practical inadequacies in the culture's sense of itself, the impact would have been socially and politically more catastrophic for himself as well as for broadcasting.

Morris and company almost qualify for the intriguing title of 'dissident or deviant bard'. This is because their mischief contradicts or undermines many of the other bardic functions. The BBC Radio 1 FM production of *Independence Day* plays no overall social mischief. It implicates the individual members of the culture into its dominant value systems, by cultivating these systems and showing them working in practice. The RAF proves the saviour of the world as well as Britain in a cultural throwback to the Battle of Britain. The only hint of challenge emerges with the depiction of a woman ace fighter pilot performed by Toyah Willcox. That aspirational model contrasts with the tension of real life women fighter pilots struggling to be recognised and appointed a combat role.

The establishment bardic function of assuring the culture of its practical adequacy in the world and affirming and confirming dominant ideologies is open to attack by the radio spoof genre. It is intriguing that Orson Welles and Father Knox affirm and confirm the value of liberal democracy and affirm the threat from alien ideological forces. In the 1926 British broadcast the unpredictable threat comes from the 'Bolshevik/Communist mob' and serves to exaggerate the potential for anarchy by dramatising the existence of a fictional anarchy. The *War of the Worlds* is more subtle in the way that the Martians are a symbol for totalitarian fascism. Knox and Welles (I use the name 'Welles' to represent the collective contribution of the Mercury Theatre) only challenged the practical inadequacy of broadcasting. It cannot be argued that they were seeking a reorientation of a new ideological stance. Perhaps Chris Morris is, but there is no evidence that the reorientation is based on political dogma. In the few published interviews available to us, it would appear that the primary ideological objective is to attack and expose hypocrisy which is a time-honoured aspect of the human condition dramatised and explored by writers.

Chapter 14

The *War of the Worlds* effect

Spoonface Steinberg?

In January 1997 BBC Radio 4 broadcast a rather low-cost audio production that consisted entirely of narrative by a fictional 7-year-old girl who was

> Jewish, autistic, very bright – and terminally ill with cancer. Her doctor introduces her to opera and she becomes fascinated with the music and the divas who have glorious stage deaths. As she tries to come to terms with the meaning of life and death the big question for Spoonface is, does nothing exist?[1]

The production was produced and directed by Kate Rowland, who within months was promoted to the position of Head of Radio Drama. She has received further promotion within the tri-media corporate edifice of television, film and radio drama production. The writer, Lee Hall, won a clutch of UK radio drama awards and went on to receive commissions from BBC films. He has been rightly styled as one of the BBC's most successful young dramatists.

The broadcast seems to have struck a chord with the Radio 4 audience and stimulated an audience reaction which had not been experienced before in the context of BBC radio drama.[2] It was unique for being a radio phenomenon. Kate Rowland certainly saw it as a watershed in the interaction of British radio drama production and audience:

> We had hundreds of letters and hundreds of calls to the Helpline. We had people writing the most incredible stories of what was happening in their own life, of what they were witnessing in somebody else's, of people wanting Lee, the writer, to visit them, to visit a dying son. The first phone-call I took after

the programme, and this had never happened to me before, a little old lady from Manchester called. She said 'I'm seventy and I've never rung the BBC before . . . oh love I just want to tell you, you've made me not afraid of dying.' She just made me weep. People I had been at college with and had never heard from for twenty years saying 'I was in a car park going to Tesco's. Never got to Tesco's. I couldn't shop. I had to go home.' I think what was remarkable was that the audience demanded something. They wanted a repeat and they got it. They wanted something concrete.[3]

Lee Hall in the preface to the published anthology of his radio plays stated that he was aware of a cultural context of loss and the feeling that people in contemporary society had been losing a sense of their certainties. He said when researching *Spoonface Steinberg* he had found accounts of terminally ill children apparently counselling their parents through the last stages of their own deaths. The children had been able to reconcile themselves to the inevitability of death. Their parents had not.[4] Lee indicated that his research was through reading.

Although it would not appear to have been deliberate, the writing and production of *Spoonface Steinberg* became a successful and profitable commodification of death and grief. The audio cassette marketed by BBC Worldwide in the 'BBC Radio Collection' became the fastest selling product and the biggest selling original play released into the audio cassette market. Kate Rowland confirmed that the packaging of the cassette was the fastest release of a BBC radio broadcast. The BBC had realised that 'Vicars wanted to use it in sermons and teachers were demanding the script. It was almost like a black market thing. I was sending out loads of cassettes because mothers were saying my son only has three months to live.'[5]

It is clear that the BBC became confused about their purpose and motivation at this point. Intriguingly Lee Hall writes in the introduction to the publication of his scripts: 'My intention is simply to provide some entertainment, and hopefully we can entertain as much with a good cry as with a good laugh.' It is also interesting that this script which had been written specifically for the radio medium was commissioned for adaptation into a film as part of a 'Children's Health' season on BBC 2.[6]

The cross-media exploitation challenged the creative qualities of the writing and the film is something of a failure in its visual communication because 40 minutes of radio narrative is illustrated by moving pictures that paint the images which were intended to be the intimate preserve of the imagination of the listener.[7] The *Radio Times* with typical commercial hyperbole promoted the television film with the following words: 'The play that moved Radio 4 listeners to tears is coming to TV – and the brave, terminally ill girl who dreams of divas is set to captivate hearts all over again'.[8]

The writer Lee Hall is quoted in a promotional feature article as saying that he insisted on Becky Simpson performing the television narration even though the film had to use a different face visually because the actress was now older than when she had produced the qualitative radio performance. It could be argued that such loyalty to the original and very small production team contributed to the film's failure as a viewing experience, but guaranteed professional reward for the young actress who performed the part for radio. If the film was a failure because of the insistence of using Becky Simpson's voice so that the central character depicted in the film could not engage in dialogue, the motive was well intentioned and aesthetic rather than polito-economical.

However, there is no evidence in the packaging of the *Spoonface Steinberg and Other Plays* book, the audio cassette and video of the film of any gesture or contribution to children's cancer and autistic charities. The BBC's purpose in this commercial exploitation of children's death, disability and their parents' grief is to make money. One-eighth of the space given to the *Radio Times* feature is devoted to the merchandising of the commodification of death and grief:

> *Spoonface Steinberg* is available on BBC video, price £12.99, audio £8.99 and in book form as *Spoonface Steinberg and Other Plays*, £5.99. (Buy all three for £22.99 and save almost £5) Send a cheque for the amount plus £1.95 P&P per order, payable to RT Offers, to: Spoonface Offer, JEM House, Little Mead, Cranleigh, GU6 8ND, or call (01483) 204488.

For Kate Rowland the words 'Spoonface Steinberg' mean that radio drama has achieved an 'attention grabbing' resonance to a larger audience. She said:

> The one thing that mattered to me when I came into radio drama was the *War of the Worlds* factor. Before I took the job I was swimming at the pool thinking do I want to work in radio drama because I'll miss out on the ABC in theatre? And then I thought *War of the Worlds* and then I thought 'Yes'. And I suppose maybe Spoonface has been my little *War of the Worlds*.

This well-meaning and well-intentioned head of BBC radio drama wanted to make plays which counted in terms of entertainment and in terms of moving the audience. She concedes that when *Spoonface Steinberg* was entered for Prix Futura in Berlin in 1997, 'they hated it in Europe. They were split. Half thought it was emotionally manipulative. They said "How dare you do that?"'[9] As explored in previous chapters, the importance of the *War of the Worlds* factor is that a significant proportion of the audience were unsure whether they were listening to a drama. The well-documented Mercury Theatre On The Air production of the *War of the Worlds* during Hallowe'en 1938 was later judged by sociological survey and study to have had its extraordinary impact because it resonated with the emotional and cultural fears and insecurities of the audience.[10]

Listeners who missed the introduction believed that the events depicted were really happening. 'The war of the worlds' potential in 1997 was limited by the fact that the audience media environment was substantially different from that in 1938. There had been no background of economic recession, international crisis, and BBC Radio 4 listeners were more media literate. Any potential deception would depend on the style of the programme content.

Spoonface Steinberg had the capacity to deceive in this way. The performance of the actress who seemed to have the natural characteristic of a slight lisp was not stylised. The director, Kate Rowland, had professionally and skilfully produced a performance which had realistic features of documentary interview. Documentary programmes dealing with emotionally wrought subjects such as children's cancer were also associated with the sound motif of musical bridges to allow the audience to cope with the emotional intensity of the interview. Rowland selected excerpts from Maria Callas's performances of opera in the EMI Classics collection *La Devina 1 & 2* to both refract and enhance the emotional intensity. The radio broadcast, therefore, had significant production values which created 'an illusion of reality'. The listener is not actually hearing a sick dying girl.

Certain myths are being employed in the construction of a narrative in order to give the impression of natural reality. The creative interplay between fiction and reality in radio has developed since the late 1970s in different ways. As indicated earlier, radio skit artists such as Chris Morris in Britain or Pierre Brassard in Quebec indulge in live deceptions with politicians and professionals in order to challenge hypocrisy and the vulnerability of the audience in terms of deception.

John Fiske makes an interesting distinction between narrowcast codes and broadcast codes in that the narrowcast audience expects to be changed or enriched by communication whereas the broadcast audience expects reassurance and confirmation.[11] The surprise and consternation created by the dissident and deviant radio bards is that they are actively engaging narrowcast objectives to a broadcast audience.

The spoof potential of radio lies in the willing desire to suspend disbelief. If this can be described as a human weakness then it is present in all of us. In radio both listener and broadcaster can now find ways of exposing the medium's vulnerability and weaken the dividing line between illusion and reality. This represents the wider proscenium arch of audio drama. The art form has a horizon that stretches beyond scripted narrative and dialogue. The capacity of *Spoonface Steinberg* to deceive and the mischief of deviant bards actively engage the views of Bertolt Brecht and Roland Barthes. Applying Brecht and Barthes to the cultural issues raised by the construction of the radio skit suggests that an implicit Marxist ideological objective may well be present.

In his essay *Mythologies* (1957) Roland Barthes was more than conscious and full of admiration for the working-class audience that goes to all-in wrestling matches because it is honest with itself and is fully cognizant that the fights are fake.[12] The art in the performance is appreciated. Curiously, televised wrestling was a staple diet of ITV viewing in the UK on Saturday afternoons during the late 1960s and 1970s. Television maintained the conceit that the contests were real fights to a substantial middle-class audience when the working-class audience present had a completely different perspective. Barthes condemns the middle-class or 'bourgeois' theatregoer as dishonest and lacking in true perception when placing so much store on the 'actor as reality'.

In the modern world the international film star is given a status with popular musical artists and sports performers which is iconic and financially powerful. But is the actor's status based on a conceit? Belief in the heroic roles performed in films, theatre and television invests the actor with a false reality that is beyond the true relative value of that individual's contribution to society.

The deviant bards in radio would please Barthes by highlighting the conceit of representing a social construct as nature or reality. Barthes was fascinated by the ability of individuals in sophisticated societies to be moved to tears and rage by the dramatic communication of stories that for most of the time do not exist, never have existed and could never exist. Barthes seeks to maintain a distinction between the reality of life and the world of mass entertainment and imaginative narrative. The deviant radio bards know that that distinction is blurred in so many significant ways and share his aim to restore the delineation.

There is no doubt that the cultural framework of popular engagement with narrative and dramatic entertainment reinforces the psychological and cultural conceit of surrendering to the willing suspension of disbelief in the search for poetic truth and faith. William Shakespeare and Samuel Taylor Coleridge, an opium addict, knew that the successful relationship between dramatist, performing company and audience required an interesting balance between that part of the theatregoer's mind which knows that as Hamlet so eloquently states, 'actors do but murder in jest', and that part of the mind which has to pretend the reality. In this way real emotions and passions are moved by nothing but an imaginary concept. It is when the balance is disrupted that problems arise. If the imbalance is in favour of knowing too much, that the actors are not really fighting or actors are simply talking into a microphone in a radio studio, the stage play ends up being a commercial failure and the radio audience finds something better to do. If the imbalance is in favour of a permanent suspension of disbelief, then the social impact on the audience and the real life experience of author, audience and players will be subject to considerable dislocation and disruption. In Sean O'Casey's case the physical riots in reaction to his plays in Dublin led to his exile.

Barthes was an enthusiast of Brecht because the German playwright and his Berliner Ensemble put on plays that the working class could afford to go and see and he believed in writers making their audience more conscious of the kind of society in which they are living. Since contemporary society is so much of a media society, it can be argued that the deviant and antisocial bards of radio fictionalise a version of reality to demonstrate the mediated politics of lack on the part of the audience. The distinction between the hoaxers and Brecht is that Brecht's signs of narrative are explicit from the beginning. The *Verfremdung* or distancing effect of acting in Brechtian theatre prevents the audience from forgetting that it is all an illusion. Roland Barthes advanced the point in his Théâtre Populaire that Brecht's audience is never so confused about the distinction between illusion and reality that it loses its freedom. The most damning failure of bourgeois art is to convince the spectator and (in our context) the listener that it is all real and the illusion is natural. Barthes believed that Brechtian drama does not expect the audience to identify and sympathise with character, that the romantic concept of sincerity in performance is invalid.

I believe Barthes and Brecht would have reacted very negatively to the bourgeois construction of myth and the effect of emotional manipulation in BBC Radio 4's *Spoonface Steinberg* narrative. There is an argument that the audience response was influenced by representations of childhood, sickness and class. The very nickname 'Spoonface' signifies a pet name, cuteness, childishness and also deformity. The name Steinberg signifies Jewishness and the victimisation of Jews during the Holocaust, which is heavily referred to within the play. This means that the writer Lee Hall has given the play Barthesian anchorage within the Jewish tragedy of the Holocaust and there is a deliberate correlation between the young girl character as a victim of cancer and the experience of Jewish children in the concentration camps.

I qualify this observation strictly on the basis that this is a cultural effect and not a proven authorial purpose. Barthes wrote cogently on the irrelevance of authors' intentions when evaluating the meaning of drama and literature. Cultural meaning is determined by the audience. For the purpose of this study no request has been made to interview Lee Hall and he should be rightly acquitted of intending cultural manipulation.

All the ingredients of narrative appear built to appeal to the ABC1 Radio 4 audience. The girl's parents are a philosophy lecturer and PhD student. There is also an extraordinary overloading of physical and psychological disability in the play which could be accused of attempting to appeal to every kind of middle-class dysfunctional experience. The mother has a problem with alcohol dependence. The parents separate as a result of the husband's infidelity. The mother of the girl's doctor was a concentration camp survivor who sang opera to make the inmates feel better.

The relevance of the girl's autism is somewhat perplexing. It could be argued that it is enough that she is dying from leukaemia. But the presentation of the Spoonface Steinberg character seems to appeal to a stereotypical idea of what a child of Radio 4 listening parents is likely to be. She is white. She is constructed very much as 'a pretty and innocent' image with a precocity, maturity and insight beyond her years. This is a wholly contradictory fusion of the adult and the child in characterisation which Valerie Walkerdine has equated with the idea of the cinematic innocent little girl as the object of male gaze.[13] It can also be argued that Spoonface has been invested with the fantasies of male adults.

Her dream of being a beautiful opera singer framed in 'a special light with her boobs and everything' has been inspired by her (male) adult doctor who has given her the opera tapes to listen to. She wants 'to sing the dying' so that the 'people would love me'. Could it be said that these tapes impose a male fantasy of women as seductresses? The opera singers are objects of the male gaze and Spoonface who listens to them then aspires to become a diva herself. The jury is still out on an answer to that hypothesis.

Spoonface is intelligent and articulate and possesses 'idiot savant' behaviour in having an incredible mathematical ability. She is not at all typical of autistic children. David Potter of the Autistic Society told a researcher that she seems to be 'on the higher functioning end of the spectrum that we know as autism'. Furthermore it is arguable whether Spoonface equates with a realistic image of the child personality dying from cancer, or simply an idea of what adults would want a child dying from cancer to be like. There is a complete absence of anger and defiance and rather than challenging and fighting her parents' self-pity, she is characterised as accepting the philosophy, advice and inspiration of the adults around her. Her response to her parents' inadequacies is wholly passive and spiritual. This is a fictional construct which serves the emotional needs of an adult audience but deceives them fundamentally in terms of the truth and reality of the subject explored. It can therefore be argued as a matter of opinion that the play is exploitative of the agony and suffering of real children in these contexts because it denies them an independent identity and genuine voice for representation.

Diana, Princess of Wales had helped to colour the signs of her media image by identifying herself as 'the Queen of People's Hearts' even though she was never going to be Queen of Britain in the famous *Panorama* interview on BBC Television.[14] Here was an attempt by the 'social actor' playing the part to assert and control characterisation over the wider media direction of her life. But it is also apparent that she was using the most potent elements of media communication to determine her own characterisation. Whether she was successful is something that will be very difficult to establish. It will always be a struggle to distinguish the extent to which her mythical media construct influenced her individual actions and her motivation to edit and control this construct of herself through her own actions and her own communication changed or modified the construct. To make things even more complicated, it should be pointed out again that Roland Barthes[15] and the critics W. K. Wimsatt and Monroe C. Beardsley, have asserted that it is the audience which decides the meaning of media narrative and not the author.[16] Again authors' intentions do not determine the meaning of the story.

This analysis does expose the agony of the practitioner/artist subjecting the aesthetic expression of creative production to the academic rigours of cultural examination. As a fellow radio dramatist and director I remain an admirer of the writing, direction and performance of *Spoonface Steinberg*. I respect enormously the aesthetic qualities and would be the first professionally to substantially credit Lee Hall, Kate Rowland and Becky Simpson. Indeed in the 'professional/practitioner' environment this respect has been confirmed with awards and accolades. So from the point of view of the professional/practitioner it is paradoxical that the play is condemned in the context of cultural dynamics, its commodification in the context of corporate global market economics, and its place in the narrative frame of dominant ideologies.

However, the process of this analysis should be regarded as a valuable opportunity for professionals/practitioners to recognise the role they play in the overall context of the global media structure.

Chapter 15

Spoonface Steinberg

Constructing the Holocaust as a means of identification

Both the radio play *Spoonface Steinberg* and the 'Diana Phenomenon' share the association of grieving for 'dying children'. As the media constructed Diana as 'a childlike' figure in her vulnerability and alleged 'feminine frailties', and this construction was further consolidated by her brother's eulogy in Westminster Abbey, the emotional parallels with the death of 'Spoonface' become more striking. Furthermore, Diana was constructed by herself and the media as the comforter of dying and suffering children. This undoubtedly was the dimension of 'motherhood' in her media profile. The 'caring and compassionate' Diana that was at the heart of so much public/audience memory was based on the official and unofficial revelations of her visits to children's wards, and the care and sympathy she demonstrated actively with children maimed by land mines in Africa and Bosnia.

There is a myth of 'caring', emotionally recollecting the idea of 'lost childhood', and 'the destruction of childhood innocence' common to the fictional Spoonface narrative and the real life though fictionally constructed Diana narrative. Motherhood is depicted in *Spoonface Steinberg* as flawed and psychologically unstable. Spoonface's mother is alcoholic and struggling to cope with the denial of her intellectual and academic destiny as a result of the sacrifice she made to enable Spoonface's father to complete his PhD. The parallel with Diana's 'confessional' on the BBC Television programme *Panorama* during which she admitted adultery and defined the agony of another addictive disorder (bulimia) is intriguing.

The ultimate and most devastating historical icon of 'lost childhood' in the twentieth century is undoubtedly the destruction of millions of children in the Holocaust. It can be argued that such is the emotional charge of *Spoonface Steinberg*'s narrative through the characterisation of an individual child dying from cancer that no extra dimension of human suffering needs to be added. But Lee Hall does add the symbolism of the Holocaust children icon. He does it through the shared religion and heritage of Spoonface's parents and the direct family experience of her doctor. Dr Bernstein gives to Spoonface and to a considerable proportion of the BBC Radio 4 audience a measure of cultural resonance by rooting his experience, their experience and Spoonface's experience with the Holocaust.

Spoonface therefore becomes a symbol of the Holocaust and the play inadvertently moves into the dimension of allegory for the Jewish experience of children during the Holocaust. As with Spoonface, the destruction of childhood and life for Jewish children in the Holocaust was inevitable. Hitler and the Nazis were a cancer that could not be cured for Jewish children. As with Spoonface's parents, the Jewish leaders during the Holocaust fought among themselves and, to take up the Zionist argument, failed to marshal the necessary resources of defiance and resistance. Millions of Jewish children went passively into the gas chambers. Spoonface walks passively towards death listening to music as an inspiration. Dr Bernstein's grandmother, an opera singer, sang to comfort children in the concentration camp as they awaited their fate, which means that even the operatic music selected in this production is coloured with the tragedy of the Holocaust. The Nazis played music through loudspeakers to soothe and calm the millions walking to their destruction at Auschwitz, Belzec, Treblinka and other death camps. Mrs Spud could even be interpreted as the indifferent gentile onlookers (naturally working class) of the western Allies. She is the class opposite to Spoonface and her parents. She is the working-class onlooker who comes to clean and has no power to intervene. The play finishes with the Jewish prayer for the dead, the Kaddish. There can be no stronger conclusion to an allegory for the suffering and destruction of Jewish children in the Holocaust.

The lexicon of the play is entirely narrative with a curious polyglot of ersatz childlike language such as 'granduate' for 'graduate', 'centigray' for 'centigrade' mixed with the adult language, thoughts and feelings provided by the adults who populate Spoonface's family, medical and social environment. Sentence structure is abandoned so that the rhythm of speech is a meandering flow of thoughts joined by 'and', 'and then' and 'but'.

The structure of the piece interweaves fantastic depths of philosophical insight with charming and amusing anecdotes of the folly of Spoonface's parents. As with the multidimensional sound montages that fabricated the life and significance of Diana, the BBC Radio 4 production punctuates the interior monologue with musical mood that enhances emotional meaning and then takes on the tragic tonality of Shoah after it is revealed that the grandmother of Spoonface's doctor had sung to her fellow inmates in the concentration camp before their journey reached an end in the gas chambers of Auschwitz.

1 Opera music sung by Maria Callas.
2 Monologue. Spoonface describing her dream of dying like an operatic diva with light illuminating 'her boobs and everything'.
3 Opera music.
4 She reveals that her doctor has given her the opera tapes, she describes her autism, she describes the tension of her parents' relationship because of her father's infidelity with 'a floozie' who had 'big boobs'. Mrs Spud, the working-class cleaner/servant is introduced.
5 Opera music. Spoonface describes her extraordinary mathematical ability, 'the sign of genius' that is known as idiot savant behaviour but occurs only in a very small minority of autistic children. Description of her mother's alcoholism linked to the fact that being pregnant with Spoonface meant that she did not finish her PhD as quickly as her husband. Description of the break up of their relationship through the husband's infidelity. Description of the diagnosis of Spoonface's leukaemia and the fact it was terminal.
6 Opera music.
7 Spoonface's father comes round to be told the news and there is the sentimental description of both parents joining together in her bedroom to consider the sadness and tragedy of their situation.
8 Opera music. Description of further tests and radiation treatment, signs of her father coming round more often after his relationship with the other woman has broken up. Tragicomedic description of her father drinking her mother's vodka, getting extremely drunk, and communicating his morose depression to Spoonface as if she were an adult, collapsing on the ground in convulsions of misery and Spoonface being rescued by her mother. This passage includes a reference to her father telling her that she was from 'his own sperm' and there is also a reference to her mother's 'bosoms'.
9 Opera music.
10 Description of Dr Bernstein telling her that his mother had been a child in a concentration camp. Can it be argued that it is inconceivable that a doctor would communicate such horror to a girl aged 7? The detail of the description is fundamentally authorial rather than effective characterisation. Here the polyglot child language smoothes out to precise and authoritative description. The expression 'In the whole history of the world there has never been anything as awful as the concentration camps' is the vocabulary of an adult.[1] Can it not be argued that the detailed testimony of the life of suffering Jewish children in the concentration camp is beyond the recall

and communication of a child and here the production's credibility crumbles? But the emotive connotation is overlaced with the first use of music as a production 'bed'. 'Casta diva' and 'Mon coeur s'ouvre à ta voix' (My heart opens to your voice) underpin the narrative. At this point we also see an example of the undeniable beauty in the writing of this play. The metaphor of Spoonface imagining the drawings of butterflies by concentration camp children turning into real butterflies and ascending to heaven is breathtaking in its elegance. Not surprisingly Dr Bernstein's description of his grandmother singing to the children becomes Spoonface's imaginative preoccupation when she now plays the opera music tapes given to her by the doctor.

11 The inclusion of the operatic piece 'O mio babbino caro' at this point is far too predictable and packs sentimentality at the expense of subtlety.

12 Description of Spoonface receiving more radiation treatment. She now equates hospitals with concentration camps. The story moves on to her description of chemotherapy and the indignity of her hair and eyebrows falling out and the discomfort of diarrhoea and vomiting at the same time. The detail of her suffering at this point is probably the most poignant part of the play. Again her models for surviving or coping with the disease and dying are referential examples given by the adults around her. Beethoven's deafness and the suffering of Job and Jesus are evoked. The failure of chemotherapy and the introduction of pain control through morphine leads to another metaphor from the Holocaust when Spoonface's mother expresses a hatred for God. Jews who survived the Holocaust and wrote about their experiences frequently expressed such spiritual exasperation.

13 More opera music. The selection of 'Vio lo sapete, O mamma' is appropriate and reflects the emotions of the mother.

14 Again Dr Bernstein invests in Spoonface a meaning for her own life through Jewish religion. By giving her a book about the Hassidim he inspires her to produce a moving passage in which she describes the sparks within a human being which shine and light up the world in life and death. 'Shining light' and the symbol of the candle flame are familiar signs of life and memory in the Judaeo-Christian religions. The 'lighted candle', 'the beacon', 'the light of people's lives' and 'the candle in the wind' were probably the most familiar symbols evoked to represent Diana during the period of unprecedented mourning.

15 Opera music.

16 Description of Mrs Spud remembering her dead husband who also had cancer. Lee Hall skilfully weaves a narrative passage with poetic metaphor that is way beyond the articulation of a 7-year-old child but is communicated in childlike rhythmic speech so that for most of the audience the

willing suspension of disbelief is maintained. Spoonface throughout has been given an angelic compassion and understanding for the failings and miseries of the adults around her that again may show insight well beyond her years. What is so curious about the entire script is that the adults around Spoonface, without exception, seem to be inspired by her dying to display gushing waves of self-pity about their own tragedies. This can be interpreted as the most abominable manifestation of emotional selfishness. For example Dr Bernstein upstages Spoonface with the horror and misery of his mother and grandmother's concentration camp experience. Spoonface's mother displays the depression and agony of not being able to complete her PhD because of the obligation of motherhood and caring for a dying child, as well as coming to terms with her husband/partner's infidelity. Mrs Spud talks about the loss of her husband through cancer. Spoonface's father is driven to paroxysms of existential despair by his daughter's terminal illness. The writer intended that the key adults Dr Bernstein and Mrs Spud should provide humanist and spiritual guidance so that the dying child can find meaning and comfort in the nonsensical and meaningless agony of terminal illness. This intention is entirely laudable, but there is an argument that these adult characters are serving themselves more than they are the child. The story of Spoonface drawing an 'I love you Mrs Spud' card as a gesture of thanks for cleaning her up after an involuntary defecation is one of the most touching pieces of writing in the play and from a creative point of view determines the uniqueness of the play.

17 Opera music.
18 Final passage. Spoonface with her polyglot ersatz child dialect expresses some existentialist thoughts on existence and death.
19 Opera music.
20 The Jewish lament for the dead – Kaddish.

The production constructs a role for the BBC as compassionate and understanding, and as 'representing' the Jewish children of the twentieth century denied their future so cruelly by the evil forces of racism. It achieves considerable cultural manipulation and has been demonstrated as an enormously successful manifestation of aesthetic expression in the field of radio drama. It has substantially resonated with the BBC Radio 4 audience, which in Greater London has been measured as having the second highest audience share of the overall radio market.[3]

Part IV

The theory and practice of writing audio drama

Chapter 16

The writing
agenda for
audio drama

The country near Dover.
GLOUCESTER   I see it feelingly.
KING LEAR   What, art mad? A man may see how the world goes with no eyes.
Look with thine ears. See how yon justice rails upon yon simple thief. Hark in
thine ear: change places, and handy-dandy, which is the justice, which is the
thief? Thou hast seen a farmer's dog bark at a beggar?
GLOUCESTER   Ay, sir.

(Shakespeare, *King Lear*, IV. vi)

I think a large amount of radio drama is very badly written, but this is only an
opinion. Writing constitutes the foundation stones of the radio play's architecture. Bad foundations mean the building will fall down. I also believe that bad
writing has been one of the factors making radio drama an endangered species.
Despite the documented examples of successful radio drama discussed in this
book, radio drama has not been able to take a hold of mainstream programming
on commercial radio in the UK. It used to be the mainstream in the USA and
Australia but lost out to television in the middle to late 1950s. It would seem that
at the ABC in Australia, which like the BBC in Britain and CBC in Canada has a
monopoly on public funding for radio drama, there has been an abandonment of
any popular gestures toward storytelling for large audiences. The CBC has been
eminently more imaginative, courageous and cost-effective with public money and
produced drama for the mainstream as well as the cultural intelligentsia. The live
soap opera *The Diamond Lane* run during peak breakfast time sequences is an
example of that.

There is one extreme political view that the BBC arrogantly expects people to be criminalised and mainly poor African Caribbean single mothers to go to prison so that they can continue to make the radio drama they want to make rather than people want to listen to. I think that this is too simplistic a notion as well as being highly polemical. It is also ascribing responsibility for the social injustice of public funding to the creative programme makers which is most unfair. They do not imprison or fine people for not paying the licence fee.

The BBC has relied on the longest running soap opera in broadcasting history, *The Archers*, to represent its main gesture towards large and popular radio audiences. It has tried to originate new series and serials. Although *Citizens* in the early 1990s was judged to be a failure, *Westway*, a BBC World Service soap set in a busy health centre in inner-city West London, has been a success. *Westway* represents the considerable efforts by the BBC to reflect more effectively the multicultural and cosmopolitan nature of British society.

Despite running three young playwrights' festivals (1988, 1991 and 1995), the BBC has not been so successful in generating interest in audio drama with a younger generation of writers and listeners. Some promise was engendered by commissioning a young playwright in the 1995 First Bite young playwrights festival to produce the beginning of an original five-minute episodic series. However, it would appear that the writer received 0.5 per cent of the total budget. He had to write a series of letters over two years to beg the BBC to allow him to listen to half the produced material and Radio 1 FM refused to broadcast any of the work anywhere on its 24-hour channel. The explanation that it had difficulty scheduling drama in a popular music format station was illogical. Radio 1 FM had been content to serve up pastiched 3–4 minute cartoon dramatisations of *Superman* and *Judge Dredd* which had about as much relevance to the younger generation of listeners as Humphrey Bogart and Lana Turner. Other public broadcasters have been more inventive. Eva Stenman-Rotstein at the publicly funded SR (Swedish Radio Broadcasting Corporation) has steered a series of evolutionary changes to young people's radio drama which has captured a new generation of listeners in music format radio. Story-telling for children and young people has reinvented itself and 'delivered' new audiences.

It could be argued that culturally the BBC has been blighted by what could be called 'the pompous paradigm'. This is an elitist attitude to radio drama which buttresses an arrogant and patronising attitude to anything produced in independent radio and anything which tends to be successful because people of all ages and background like what they hear, or because another broadcast organisation has originated the form. Evidence for the origin of 'the pompous paradigm' may reside in the history of the BBC's attitude to popular 'radio soaps'.

A key figure who restricted the UK development of the radio soaps was Val

Gielgud, head of BBC Radio Drama between 1929 and 1963. He had a personal hegemony over radio drama almost as long as Edgar Hoover's reign in the US Federal Bureau of Investigation.

The concept of the radio soap opera was invented by the Americans and developed by the Australians and Latin Americans with huge success. While women in British broadcasting were still cleaning the toilets and typing letters, in the USA talented programme makers such as Irna Phillips invented the soap opera. With three university degrees behind her, she began in Chicago Radio in 1929 and by the 1930s was writing 2 million words a year and developing six different soap series at the same time. Her main rival was another creative woman, Anne Hummert, and her husband Frank. The genre challenged the representation of women in mainstream media. Many of the leading characters in these soap operas were women prematurely widowed and displaying tremendous strength of character in the way they coped with adversity and the harsh economic conditions of the Depression. Many of the lead women characters were characterised as starting their own businesses and careers.

Britain's earliest soap, *The Robinsons*, first appeared during the Second World War. It was an import, not a home-grown and tried programming product. Canadian comedy writer Alan Melville was directed to devise a radio soap to be broadcast to the USA and Canada on the BBC's North American Service with the political objective of demonstrating British pluck, courage and resistance to Hitler, the Luftwaffe and the Blitz. Its first title was *Front Line Family* and it showed the Robinson family bravely coping with rationing, bombs, their RAF aircrew son going missing, their daughter Kay falling in and out of love. It was a hit in North America. Other overseas services started to broadcast it and service personnel on leave and dial-twiddling Brits were finding it a welcome alternative to Lord Haw-Haw.

Throughout the 1930s Val Gielgud had prevented the development of a BBC radio soap. He considered it vulgar and a bastard form of drama from the USA. While *Front Line Family* was renamed *The Robinsons* and became a huge success on the Home Service, Gielgud issued a directive to members of the BBC Repertory Company that working in a radio soap would be a breach of contract. It does seem extraordinary that the prejudice, pomposity and elitist discrimination of one man could be responsible for holding back the tide of one of the most significant radio programming forms of the twentieth century. But Gielgud's belief that soap opera was cheap and nasty was echoed by the BBC's senior management. *The Robinsons* mutated as a result of broadcasting becoming an informational propagandist weapon. The audience popularity for dramatic storytelling in the soap opera form was a benign and accidental side-effect.

Gielgud's opposition was predicated on all the wrong reasons. He believed that if actors became household names in a soap opera they would end up demanding more money until they were being paid as much as the more distinguished repertory thespians. Gielgud believed that serial actors were not in the classical thespian league. He believed that the soap opera was 'deliberately constructed to hit the very centre of the domestic hearth by playing variations on the theme of all kinds of domestic trivia'. He also believed that the British public would not like it because they would realise that soaps are capable of achieving a quite unreasonable influence. He was wrong on all counts.[1]

It is now possible to acquire a boxed set of an entire 24-hour period of broadcasting by the CBS station in Washington DC in September 1939.[2] It is an opportunity to make the astonishing discovery that most of the programming was radio drama in 15 minute episodes – mostly soaps and popular series. Putting aside arguments about high brow, midcult and low brow narratives and production values, that fact is something worth considering. At 8.45 a.m. radio listeners in the US capital could hear 'the continuing story of Dr. Bob Graham, who, during the Great War, promised to care for his dying sergeant's two daughters. One daughter, Ruth Ann, eventually marries his best friend'. It was billed as a 'realistic portrayal of American life'. The 15 minutes featured on this Thursday morning were devoted to the story of Dr Bob 'taking a case to the legislature'. On this one day on a key network American radio station twenty-four different radio drama programmes were scheduled and broadcast, including *The Columbia Workshop* at 9 p.m. Eastern Standard Time. It was billed as 'experimental theatre; a place for innovations in sound effects and production, and a showcase for young writers and actors. Orson Welles, Archibald MacLeish, William Saroyan, Dorothy Parker and Stephen Vincent Benet were among the host of talents who contributed scripts.' On this night the audience heard a play called *Now It's Summer* by humourist-playwright Arthur Kober.

The radio drama writer was therefore responsible for about 85 per cent of the output of mainstream radio programming in the biggest and most powerful economy and society in the world. Now it would appear to be less than 1 per cent. The reduction has been over sixty years. Yet I would counsel against pessimism and make a somewhat heretical point to the writers and directors who make up the bulk of craft guilds in the English-speaking world. Radio is alive and well throughout most popular musical and talk programming. They have completely missed it. Particularly in the USA radio dramatists sometimes write and constitute up to 15 minutes of any hour. Their work will not win a Prix Italia. They work in the 30 second, 1 minute and sometime 1½ minute form. These are the 'radio copy writers': nobody calls them dramatists. In the USA they are more deserving of this title than in Britain where the quality of commercial production writing is, generally, lamentable.[3]

Most UK radio adverts consist of overpaid totalitarian or cynical voice-over artists haranguing and shouting at listeners in an undignified rush to keep the advertiser happy in the 30 seconds allowed. Thus has about as much grace as an encounter between a prostitute and client in a brothel or a hysterical rant by Hitler and Mussolini. In the USA and Australia where sponsoring and selling radio time for entertainment and storytelling has been culturally entrenched over many more years, copy writers have a tradition of writing effective characterisation and witty and poignant plot lines with a product or message that is logically part of the soundscape.

Sometimes, and I regret to say that it appears to be the exception rather than the rule, a 'commercial message' can have more resonance and dramatic power than a two and a half hour dramatisation of a classical text on BBC Radio 3. Here is the script of an example:

Single modern young male voice. No music or sound effects
To the best mum in the world. Dear Mum. This letter I hoped you'd never receive because it's the verification of that terse black edged card you received some time ago. Tomorrow we go into action. No doubt lives may be lost. But if this leaves the world a slightly better place then I'm perfectly willing to make that sacrifice. Don't get me wrong though mum. I'm no flag-waving patriot. No. My little world is centred around you and Dad. You are worth fighting for. And if it strengthens your security in any way, it's worth dying for too. I want no flowers, no tears, no epitaph. Just be proud. Then I can rest in peace knowing I've done a good job. Surely there's no better way of dying. I loved you Mum. You're the best Mum in the world. Goodbye. Your son.

Older and quiet male voice. Still no music or sound effects
This letter was written by a young private the night before he died in battle. At the Imperial War Museum we don't try to glorify the war. We try to give an idea of what it was like to be part of it. We're open between ten until six every day. Nearest tube is Lambeth North. The Imperial War Museum. Part of your family's history.[4]

This piece of radio was created and produced by Mandy Wheeler, one of the most elegant radio advert makers in the world. Its success is in its faithfulness to the true values of radio drama and feature making. The 'mini-dramas' of commercial production have the potential to use the full panoply of dramatic structure and storytelling devices.

The music format that dominates most of the contemporary radio throughout the world normally consists of short segments of narrative. The majority of popular songs have a story set to music. The librettist, even in the context of rock and roll and modern popular music, has taken over the storytelling role in perhaps a minute of lyrical communication compared to the soap writer of the 1930s and

1940s who would tell the story in 15 minutes with a cliff-hanger to throw the listener's interest forward on to the next instalment. It can be argued that the emotional element present through musical instrumentation as opposed to the storytelling through song lyrics is the dominant paradigm. However, the argument that most popular music is a form of entertaining and storytelling narrative can be sustained.

If there is a threat to radio drama production in public radio services such as the BBC posed by the pressure of monetarist ideology, I also believe another threat has been generated by the complacency of authors and radio drama directors. The work is just not consistently good enough. Orson Welles was 22 when he adapted, directed and acted in the seven-part dramatisation of Victor Hugo's *Les Misérables* for the Mutual Broadcasting System in 1937. Few modern dramatisations can match the quality of his production which was produced for a highly competitive market in US radio that demanded programmes that people would enjoy, would want to listen to, and above all would want to listen to more than anything else. His trademark throughout all his radio dramas was the consistency of listenability and entertainment.

Boredom is not listed as one of the seven deadly sins, but for most people it is something to avoid. When this happens you do not exist as a dramatist. It would be a cruel judgement to make of any radio playwright who had failed that they should go back to their previous life and try something else for a living.

The BBC has closely guarded the results of specially commissioned research into radio drama listening. Having heard second-hand reports that BBC research had yielded the unfortunate conclusion that at least 50 per cent of the BBC Radio 4 audience switched off when the radio drama programmes began, I decided to attempt my own research.

I gathered together a panel of fifty listeners who had been culturally committed to listening to radio drama.[5] I did not think at this stage there would be much point asking for opinions from people who had never heard a radio play before. I once did a workshop with about thirty teenagers in an inner London school.[6] Not one of them admitted to listening to any scheduled form of radio drama. When I asked if anyone was aware of people listening to radio drama, one 16-year-old girl put up her hand and said that her mother used to listen to *The Archers*.

My panel was asked to record their views on BBC radio drama over a fortnight. I asked each participant to give the BBC a general score out of ten to reflect the number of occasions radio drama had been a successful listening experience, and 75 per cent reported four out of ten or under. While most of the panel were anxious to emphasise that the struggle to find something fulfilling to listen to justified the BBC's licence fee funding and they unanimously supported the existence of BBC radio drama with all its faults, the panel agreed on the following most common faults in the drama output:

1 Bad beginnings.
2 Very poor billings and promotion by the station.
3 Too many similar voices making it difficult to distinguish characters.
4 Stories not gripping and interesting enough.
5 Poor acting and direction (many panel members said they could 'see' the actors performing in the studio).
6 Story did not sustain length of play and the failure to repeat left panel members frustrated if their car journey had been completed or they had entered the play at a midpoint.

Radio/audio drama is theatre. All good theatre has the same ingredients for success. The principles are the same as those that apply to stage drama, television or film drama. The special characteristics and principles of radio drama writing do not dominate and override the need to communicate a good story, create substantial and engaging characters and sustain the interest of an audience. There are differences between the theatre, film, television and radio but they are not fundamental to the writing of a good script.

The most important principles are discussed below (the writer is addressed in the second person singular).

The writing rules

The beginning

The beginning is everything. If this part of the play does not work then you might as well give up as a writer. In radio when people twiddle the dial or switch off, the breaking of the broadcast/listener contract is terminal. You, the writer, have failed. If the play is a long one then so is the disaster for the radio station. It lasts as long as the play. And there is no guarantee that the listeners will come back. They might find something more interesting on other channels. They will forget about you and your radio service. You will be the playwright who provoked a yawn within the first minute of your relationship with the listener. The radio audience is not a captive one. You have not enticed a group of people into a theatre, closed the doors and turned the house lights down and effectively imprisoned people for an hour and a half. Most dissatisfied theatregoers stick it out stoically or heroically. In radio, no money has exchanged hands and the moment of departure is quick and ruthless.

So how should you start? Begin at the beginning for example? This is not an advisable course to take. If your play is 15 minutes, half an hour or even an hour, beginning at the beginning can be a long drawn out and somewhat tedious experience. What do you mean by beginning? When somebody is born? Perhaps you think you should go back generations. Explore the ancestry. That will take up all the time your play originally had to run. The key to beginning well in drama is to create a dramatic moment of arrival. The playwright should think of the beginning as a parachute jump into a battle.

Drop your listener into a high moment or significant moment of drama. Do not start with the climax. That would be starting at the end, or near the end. It would also be rather premature. But you must find the right moment to join the story. Whatever you do, avoid the slow snail's explicatory route. The background and subtext of previous histories is better explored through revelation in dramatic action. Give your listeners a rush at the beginning and whoosh them through the rapids. If you begin your play with one minute of snoring, this would be a somewhat avant-garde approach. A few people might stick with it because the unexpected is sometimes intriguing, but most of your listeners will either fall into a slumber or go elsewhere. On the other hand if you start your play with a 60-second countdown to an execution, or 60 seconds after a bomb has gone off, it tends to hold people's attention a little more.

Structure and plot: are they synonymous?

The structure of your play is the discipline of your story. We sometimes meet interesting and rather intriguing people in our lives. What they do to us and what we do to them is what really matters. The interesting people exist as a result of our experiences with them and the story of life changes their character and our attitude to them.

In some respects we can be changed too. And when the people we meet do not change, then that in itself is a dramatic storyline begging the questions why and what if? There is an interrelationship between structure and characters. But characters cannot exist on their own. The drama of our lives requires our participation in society, in a community of people, and our experience is determined by our own decisions and those taken by other people and the forces of nature. Life can be considered a series of phases. We generally hope that in the struggles that we have, there will be a resolution which is in our favour, or to our advantage. The drama of our lives tends to be determined by our character being pitched into circumstances – the set up, followed by the struggle – the conflict, battle, war or tension and then leading to the resolution, victory, defeat, disillusionment or death.

In Aristotle's *Poetics* we can find the earliest attempt to theorise about the perfect composition. The Greek philosopher emphasised the need for a beginning, middle and end. He set up a hierarchy of dramatic rules which he placed in order of importance. The first was plot, followed by character, thought, diction, rhythm and spectacle. By thought, it is supposed he meant the emotional dimension or the sentiments generated by the play's performance. By diction it is believed he meant dialogue. Rhythm related to music or melody. Spectacle concerned the scenic effects.

Aristotle was a critic at the time of Aeschylus, Euripides and Sophocles during the age of Greek theatrical tragedy. He talked about tragedy being a complete and serious action that carries magnitude and uses language which has artistic quality. The story is told through action that is steeped in fear and pity. Directors and screen writers from all around the world pay nearly £300 each to attend Robert McKee's workshops on 'Story Structure'. Mr McKee is a modern Aristotle who teaches the 'magic and mysteries of story structure'. His course defines 'The classic five part narrative structure', inciting incident, progressing complications, crisis, climax and resolution. He is a much admired figure and draws plaudits from Kirk Douglas, Denise Nicholas, Gene Reynolds and Toby Emmerlich, the president of New Line Cinema Music, who observes 'Hollywood studios don't buy great ideas, they buy great stories that can capture an audience's imagination'. Radio drama must demand that which Hollywood demands. The expectation in qualitative storytelling structure should not be any different.

I have already attempted to draw the similarities of syntactical construction between music and audio drama and there is an argument that the application of Gestalt theory, developed by German psychologists, is another relevant line of enquiry. Gestalt theory proposes that the whole is greater than the parts and that the parts of artistic structure make sense only in relation to the whole. Perception is organised by grouping parts into patterns. This means that there is a tendency on the part of media audiences to prefer structural shapes of communication which are the simplest and most stable. Audiences will prefer narrative construction which has symmetry, balance, regularity, smooth continuity and closure, or a sense of completeness. The clear relationship between interpreting musical tunes and constructing pleasing and entertaining radio plays is in the demand for balance or equilibrium, the commitment to symmetry in subplots and main plots, particularly between the beginning and the end.

The Gestalt theorists claimed that satisfaction through the smooth arch shape of artistic construction could be attributed to innate brain function. Modern psychologists believe it is more a matter of cultural convention and linked intrinsically to the experience of learning and expectation. Disrupting a cultural convention such as the smooth arch structure of communication does bring on the agenda of the avant-garde and the advantage of surprise through breaking the rules of convention in art.

I think it is important to be on our guard about 'writing by numbers'. I remain sceptical that script editors, who have never written anything significant in drama, can guarantee effective teaching of the subject. There is a risk that production infrastructures in drama will be dominated by commissioning editors and multiple layers of script editors who determine writing quality by the precision and pitching of a half-page treatment. Detailed deconstruction and analysis of the human alchemy of creativity contains the risk of establishing cultural conventions which become oppressive and mutually exclusive to the members of the production hierarchy. I do not believe you can discover and produce great radio drama through formulas. Discussions on how to write and the practice of storytelling can only debate rules and principles which are given to aspiring writers as a matter of advice.

There are five main dimensions to the structure of communication in audio drama:

1 The word through voices: dialogue and narrative.
2 Music through instruments and choral voices.
3 Sound effects: natural atmosphere and spot effects or abstract sounds synthesised or natural sounds that have been symbolised.
4 Post-modernist use of previously recorded actuality, archive or sound history, or previously recorded narrative and dialogue.
5 The imagination of the listener: this is physically a silent dimension. In terms of consciousness it is immensely powerful. This is the existence of a significant part of the play in the imagination of the audience, i.e. the listener. It is what I have defined previously as 'the imaginative spectacle'.

These dimensions represent tracks or streams of narrative direction. The structure of radio drama involves the multi-tracking or sequencing of these dimensions, their balance, their juxtaposition and combination or divergence.

I would contend that writers tend to be more interested in the creation of their characters, while audiences (in radio's case we are talking about the listener) tend to be more interested in the plot. Dramatists are called playwrights not because they write plays but because the art involved the wroughting of plays. It was and still is a skilled trade. A 'wright' was a person who constructed or repaired something, hence the relationship between playwright and shipwright. Nowadays you could call it a science. Without good construction the play will, like a badly designed building, crumble. It might even collapse. Whatever little delights you had for the top floor – moulded frescoes, glass panelled facades and an overall impact on the environment which involves dominating light and shadow – without solid foundations and sensible engineering, the building will be condemned by the failings of its structure.

The plot, the story and the structure: defining the difference

The story is the span of the narrative which contains the play as a concentration of action and drama. The pattern or system of action and drama is the plot and the design and engineering of the plot is the structure.

Playwrights need to have a full understanding of the principles and differences between narrative and drama. If we consider anthropological myths about the origin of storytelling or even consider anthropological evidence from cave paintings, we can begin to appreciate the seeds of theatrical communication in a contained space. It is assumed that the first stories may have been based around hunting, the danger involved in tracking and capturing wild animals that could fight back. When such stories were acted out underneath animal skins the first audiences were presented with drama. The story was being performed live with action and physical movement. The word 'drama' is derived from the Greek word meaning 'to do'. The performance is dramatic because it communicates conflict, tension, contrast and emotion.

The theatre we are familiar with has according to various sources been derived from the ritual of ancient and prehistoric rites, and religious practices. The christening ceremony, circumcision ceremonies, rites of passage ceremonies for boys and girls reaching puberty, marriage rites and funerals often represent the conflict of human against human in the search for food, shelter, territory and companionship or spiritual maturity and fulfilment. These ceremonies are characterised by a build up of tension through dramatic conflict between characters involving a climax and resolution and during which the central characters undergo a fundamental change.

When recollected with single voice accounts structured in mnemonic verses with rhyme and metre to aid memory and ensure the survival of an oral culture, the first audiences were presented with narrative. This is storytelling about the past. The Aborigines of Australia cherish sagas and myths which have been handed down from family to family. All cultures from Africa, Asia to Latin America have an oral tradition of singers and storytellers from the past.

These epics formed the basis of literature when human societies first began to keep a tangible 'letter form' record of their cultures. We could never be sure which was the first and which was the oldest. Archaeological discoveries in the mid-nineteenth century revealed a system of writing called cuneiform which was produced by the Sumerians 3500 years BC on the banks of the Euphrates river in the Persian Gulf. Cuneiform is made up of wedge-shaped strokes in little soft clay blocks that later hardened in the sun. Twelve of these tablets found in the library of King Assurbanipal have revealed the Gilgamesh Epic, a heroic tale about humankind's vain attempts to comprehend moral destiny. Gilgamesh learns from an all-knowing wizard type character called

Utnapishtim that nobody on the earth can escape the inevitability of death. Utnapishtim said:

> There is no permanence. Do we build a house to stand for ever, do we seal a contract to hold for all time? Do brothers divide an inheritance to keep for ever, does the flood-time of rivers endure? It is only the nymph of the dragon-fly who sheds her larva and sees the sun in his glory. From the days of old there is no permanence. The sleeping and the dead, how alike they are, they are like a painted death.[7]

It is clear that this early written form of storytelling depends on a narrative rather than dramatic structure. Dramatic speech is reported or narrated as something from the past.

Radio drama is a medium that originated in the twentieth century after a significant period of human history had been devoted to storytelling through literature which had more of a narrative focus than a dramatic one. Curiously radio drama has much in common with literary prose and poetry. The active audience in the line of communication is one person. Radio's fifth dimension of narrative communication, the listener's imagination, is central to the cognitive, metaphysical and subconscious experience of the reader of written poetry and prose. However, listening to radio plays, like watching live stage theatre performances, involves a limited time frame. The listener's imagination may not be the contained space of the theatre, but the commitment in time is contained in the same way. The reader of literature can stop and resume, can vary the pace of imaginative interaction, which in radio drama and stage drama is controlled by the performance. In this regard audio drama has a strong similarity with music. The composition depends for its expression on interpretation and performance. This is not so with literature.

This means that radio plays can apply some narrative elements with great effect in the construction of plot, but because of the exigencies of contained time and the fact that radio drama is performed rather than read silently, the emphasis in structuring radio plays must be on the dramatic rather than the narrative.

The purpose of plot in radio playwriting is to create a dramatic and narrative structure which can convey aesthetic meaning. It should be able to accommodate characterisation and subtext, establish a firm hold on the listener's attention through a 'trussing' of question marks which swell the listener's anticipation and interest in accompanying the story to the climax. Plot in radio playwriting has to achieve the objective of warding off the enemy which includes the heat and cold of distraction from outside stimuli. The temperature of human communication from within the radio play has to be pleasing and sensuous. The gravitational pull of internal emotions which can 'switch off' the listener's imagination has to be 'buttressed' through an ascending and accelerating structure of dramatic storytelling. The gravity of conscious concentration has to be harnessed through a coherence of dramatic narrative. The rising of each scene's upward momentum secures the listener's direction of understanding.

The building materials for dramatic plotting are as follows.

Central character

The main character force and focus usually provides the point of view for the play and is usually represented by the idea of hero or heroine.

Secondary characters

These are the character forces who create disruption in the original equilibrium of the central character's life, offer the conflict resistance which strikes the play's essential tension, or generate the developing crises of experience for the central character. Secondary characters can fulfil the role of representing a potential reward, deceive the central character through the role of false hero, false helper, or assist and ally the central character through genuine guidance and direct help.

Main plot

This is what Russian writers would describe as the *syuzhet*. It is the deliberately constructed architecture of storytelling which drives the central character from the opening crisis or issue to eventual climax and change/resolution.

Secondary/subsidiary plot

The separate strand of *syuzhet* weaves a balance of what Ken Dancyger has described as 'charm and alarm'.[8] It frequently serves as an opportunity for comedy and can create an anticipation of alarm by heavily hinting in the early stages of the play that the subsidiary plot has the potential for overtaking the main plot or offering an explanation of the play's central enigma.

Crisis

This is the dilemma or problem that should be immediately apparent from the beginning of the play and it is often the overall determining atmosphere or psychological and social environment that preoccupies the internal and external existence of the central character.

Sub-climax

This is a significant device which builds tension and increases the grade of suspense and excitement for the listener. It can be a climactic resolution of the secondary plot. It can be the final level or stage prior to the summit of climax for the main plot.

Main climax

An exploding and dramatic reaction of conflicting forces that have the effect of resolving and displaying the consequences of the plot's human imperatives. The climax usually discloses the play's essential enigma.

Linear and lateral time frames

A linear time frame unfolds a story chronologically. A lateral time frame unfolds the story through flashback, or begins a narrative at the end and proceeds to explain the enigma and mystery of the end as a narrative that then switches to the beginning and proceeds by intriguing the listener with a explanation of how 'B' was reached as a result of a journey from 'A'. Lateral time frames can slide or 'elide' historically, futuristically, or both. Quentin Tarantino's film *Pulp Fiction* (1994) is an excellent example of a *syuzhet* with a lateral time frame. It enables central and key characters to exist in the *syuzhet* but to have died or been killed in the overall *fabula*.

Narrative cohesion

This means telling a story with narrative passages interspersed by dramatic scenes. The narrative voice can be neutral and omnipresent, sometimes resembling the idea of authorial voice, or it can be a character providing a frame narrative that tells the story from that character's point of view – Michel Chion's 'acousmatic voice' (see p. 85). A dangerous and potentially problematical device is to invest authorial voice and character presence as narrative via interior monologue in dramatic action. The novel is usually constructed by way of narrative cohesion. Charles Dickens invested his narrative voice with all the energy and identity of the authorial voice which in some ways existed and commented on the drama of the story. His voice was so distinctive that it would inevitably undermine and confuse the voices of his dramatic characters if they were ever used to convey narrative description. The interior narrative existence of the character would become that of the author. This would contradict the nature of the character as represented by exterior dialogue and monologue. Narrative cohesion can be present or past tense. Anna Hashmi's *Farewell Little Girl* (IRDP for LBC 1993) is clearly an example of narrative cohesion although the central character's attitude to the listener is present time. She is referring to past history in a dramatic expression of present identity.

Dramatic cohesion

This is the presentation of the play's story through dramatic action where character is established and communicated by dialogue and present time interior monologue. The *mise-en-scène* and imagistic physical and social environment of the play is expressed by sound atmosphere, music and sound effects. There is no narrative voice whether neutral or character linked. Simon Beaufoy's *Saddam's Arms* (IRDP for LBC 1993) is an example of dramatic cohesion. The play consists of a series of action and dialogue scenes. Monologues are present time active and not referring to the past. The script *Broken Porcelain* (see pp. 194–7) is still dramatic cohesion even though the narrative direction of the characters' communication is single voiced. The voice is present tense, dramatic and directed in a scene of active participation with others. Another example of dramatic cohesion is *Restless Farewell* by William George Q (entered for Prix Futura 1998). Four male characters dialogue during a wake for their best friend who has died prematurely. He leaves the legacy of their friendship in his multimedia computer. The entire play is framed by drama. James Payne's *Shiver Breathing* (LBC 1995) is entirely action based with dialogue. The time transitional build-up is highly sophisticated, taking the listener on a series of steps in different time-lines so that understanding of the *syuzhet* is gradually revealed through switchback and switchforwards in the *fabula*.

Time transitional lintel

This is a sound symbolism or musical bridge which facilitates the lateral transference of the listener's understanding backwards or forwards in time, or in some instances on to a parallel time narrative line. The effectiveness of such a bridge can contain its own narrative or dramatic line. It can exist as a subplot. For example, in a dramatisation of Joseph Conrad's *The Secret Agent*, a poetic mix of echoed and recollected voices picked out oppressive and intimidating vocabulary from the scene. This constituted Adolph Verloc's flashback. The flashback was dramatic rather than narrative, but the narrative lintel or time transitional bridge was poetic and symbolic. Rather than remaining the same, it changed and developed in its symbolic content and had the potential to contain its own *syuzhet*. Such time transitional lintels can be more abstract and devoid of words. Sound effects can be used.

In Tony Duarte's *Coffee and Tea 90p* (IRDP for LBC 1991) the somewhat avant-garde sound of an old-fashioned shop bell, heavily reverberated and processed so that it was in reverse, linked the central character between the exterior existence and the interior existence. It had the aesthetic effect of whooshing the mind's eye from the National Theatre coffee bar with the punctuating sound of a modern till bell into the central character's interior consciousness and recollection of a past event.

The switchbacks and the switchforwards in time transitional lintels do not have to be surrealistic or point up to a 'dreamy' or consciousness evaluated experience. The time transitional lintel can simply transfer the listener into different historical points in the *fabula*. The most important aspect of its function is to clearly signpost to the listener that this is happening.

Interior to exterior consciousness transepts

These are well represented by the reverse shop bell sound in Tony Duarte's play. There is some merit in taking a detail of the soundscape from the exterior existence and exaggerating its properties (*rendering* from Chion's sound vocabulary) to suggest the increased imaginative intensity of the interior consciousness. The transept could be a simple cross-fade. However, more elaborate or finely crafted transepts which are mutated to indicate a forward passage in the plot tend to create more intrigue for the listener. In Anna Hashmi's *Farewell Little Girl* the transept was achieved by a long and soft lingering of reverberation from interior to external existence that varied from blowing dust from the surface of a book, flicking book pages to stirring of a tea cup.

Fifth dimensional dome narrative and drama

The dome narrative on the fifth dimension involves characterisation and plot line substantially in the imaginative spectacle of the listener. It means that the central character does not even utter a word during the production. The characterisation is usually constructed by the dialogue and monologues of other characters. Anthony Minghella's Prix Italia winning play *Cigarettes and Chocolate* on BBC Radio 4 is an example of fifth dimensional dome drama. The key character has no present time active participation in the drama around her. It would appear that she has withdrawn from the society around her. A similar dynamic is established in Andrew Smith's play *Still Stationery* (produced for LBC in London and short-listed by Prix Italia in 1996). The key character Frank has 'disappeared' and the developing anxiety and concern about his absence is dramatised through his three girlfriends, squash partner, parents and cat and the junk mail spilling through his letter box. The dome drama character in the fifth dimension lives and breathes, thinks and feels solely in the mind and heart of the listener.

Conscious and subconscious transepts

The conscious and subconscious transepts represent the elegance and style of moving from scene to scene in the unfolding play. They tend to be punctuating words, expressions, thoughts through words or sounds which blend or echo the beginning of the following scene. Anthony Minghella in the Oscar-winning film *The English Patient* (1996) established sound based transepts through sound symbolism. The tapping of a finger or pencil on paper would cross-fade into the rhythmical drum beat of North African musicians. The conscious transept is the utterance of words or phrases by characters which 'cue' or are overlapped by ironic utterance of characters in the following scene. The subconscious transept is a sound or idea in the interior consciousness of a character which elides for echoing, parallel or ironic effect with the mimetic or mirroring sound and language of a character's communication or presence in the following scene.

Long scene pacing

This is the pacing of scenes in long and involved interaction between characters. It tends to be more reminiscent of stage theatre plays' structures where the physical presence of the audience invites greater depth and development of character and story in single scenes and sets. The technology of stage theatre does not encourage short scene pacing. I heard one radio drama director condemn long scene pacing in radio drama as anachronistic and borrowing too heavily from stage drama. While he had a point, I think it would be wrong to exclude the intensity of drama psychology that can be present in plays with long scene pacing.

Short scene pacing

This has a more exhilarating drive of narrative and dramatic cohesion. The short, punchy, almost staccato rhythm of structure is reminiscent of modern film and television drama. There is a risk that an over-reliance on short scene pacing will stunt the growth and representation of characters as well as confuse listeners.

Long/short scene pacing

A varied rhythm of scene construction is advisable. There is a danger of repetitive and predictable patterns of structure and euphony having an hypnotic or mesmerising effect on radio audiences. If it sends listeners to sleep or becomes unexciting because of its predictability, then the play will be substantially flawed. David Mairovitz's Prix Italia winning BBC Radio 3 play *The Voluptuous Tango* (1997) undermined audience concentration by repeating a Tango dance based musical phrase.

Pyramid narrative

This is a plot structure beginning with at least two and sometimes several subplot origin points building as parallel story lines, occasionally crossing through the common strand of characterisation and conflicting relationships into a climactic point of resolution. The building tension with ironic resonance and a growing pressure cooking of suspense achieves an explosive dynamic of story resolution.

Inverse pyramid narrative

The inverse pyramid has a multi-strand subplot development that arises out of one incident or one original story line event and builds into a range of differing experiences and parallel consequences, intertwining irony and significant points of tension. The resolution has a lateral rather than linear line of coincidence between the subplot lines of narrative development.

Arch narrative

This is a process of providing the exposition of the story after the event. The listener begins the play with the event or crisis which is the source of the story's

167

drama. The play then begins to explain how the central and subsidiary characters reached this point.

Arcaded narrative

Arcaded narrative is a process of story exposition using traditional techniques of story revelation on a progressive time-line. Methods used include investigative and interrogative scenarios in interviews, inquiries and courtrooms which can elicit confessions and recollection. In the relationship between characters, exposition of narrative can be struck through direct and indirect questions, arguments, gossip, confessional intimacy and advice. More key information can be revealed in conflict and battle with authority demanding explanation, correction and clarification. Sound technology can also provide mechanisms of plot revelation in arcaded narrative structures. Examples include answer machines, public address systems, media publication through the Internet, radio, television and film, and tape recorders. Dictaphones, telephones, mobile phones and radio surveillance technology provide further methods of sound technological exposition.[9]

Ironic framing

This is a narrative structure embedded and woven with ironic lines of information for the listener. Sometimes the irony is refracted, with ironic knowledge being shared by characters and the audience.

Contrapuntal multi-track

This is a narrative structure with paralleled main plot and subplots which contrapuntally combine at key points and with a gathering momentum of excitement combine at the end in a climax of contrapuntal harmony.

Time frame overlap

This narrative structure shuffles time-lines like moving sheets of mica. The time dimensions can be past, present and future. The successful use of this technique rests in the coalescing of characterisation purpose, dramatic objective of plot, and the use of the time frame for ironic impact.

Spiral staircase progression

The spiral narrative progression towards climax involves a spiral oscillation with interruption and delay before the story's tension is ultimately resolved. The success of this technique requires the ability to convince the listener that safety or security is assured and then stir the engagement of listening with the disruption of renewed tension.

Direct staircase progression

This method of narrative development generates the conceit of the listener already knowing the end of the apparent story. The plot line is therefore direct, transparent and incontrovertible. However, the tension and conflict in the play lies in more subtle and ironic nuances of characterisation, internalisation and exposition. In every play there has to be a desirable and worthy goal which the central character needs to strive for and achieve. If listeners share that objective, they will normally identify with and emotionally participate in the struggle. The failure to achieve the moral or material objective will often define a play as a tragedy. Conflict is created by placing and generating opposing forces in the way of the central character's drive to achieve the desired goal. Dramatic action arises out of the clash of opposing wills.

Creating a scenario

It is advisable to create a scenario before writing the full text of your play. This should begin with an outline and analysis of characterisation followed by a detailed outline of the plot and an analysis of its dynamics. This might sound formulaic but you can guarantee that basic mistakes in plot construction can be avoided by adopting this approach. That it is not to say that great plays can never be written without thought and written preparation of characters and plot outline. However, I have never known of a sophisticated, well-constructed building being erected without an architect's plan.

The essence of a play should be communicated in a short narrative of 200–300 words and attempts should then be made to draw out more of the detail, dropping in the occasional exchanges of dialogue or linking narrative. Character plotting should include a life story leading to each character's entry into the play. This work can always be changed as a result of the creative germination that arises through completing the writing, but it will be of enormous help in the play's production when the director needs to provide background material for the actors.

You cannot divorce the relationship between character and plot. The actions of all the characters should be consistent with their natures and personalities. There has to be a harmony and logic between action and the truth of character. Art cannot always effectively imitate life without planting essential 'seeds' of anticipation. The skill of a playwright is in planting seeds that do not undermine the essential need for surprise. Seeds should sprout small plants that provide a covering of plausibility. Another vital structural discipline is the eradication of any speech, scene, line or character that does not serve the dramatic purpose of the plot. There is not much point in constructing a huge atrium in the middle of a five bedroom chalet which takes up all the space needed for the bedroom accommodation. There is not much point building a tower on the roof of a bungalow. This principle of eliminating the unnecessary is called unity of action.

Two other essential principles need to be attended to. All radio playwrights should bear in mind that they deprive their listeners of the obligatory scene at their peril. This is where the plot has built up a degree of anticipation for listeners where considerable pleasure and emotional relief will be provided through the resolution of that tension and set up. There is little to be gained by leaving listeners with an abiding sense of frustration after the play is over. However, there can be purpose in frustrating listeners through the tantalising development of plot through struggle and towards resolution.

One of the greatest *bêtes noires* of plot construction is the intervention of the *deus ex machina* device which was roundly condemned by Aristotle when he wrote *Poetics*. The mechanism means 'a god from a machine'. The entry of this technique is normally confirmation of a failure in plot construction. If 'God' has to fly in to untangle a convoluted knot of crisis and climax the human characters have lost control of their own destiny. The play has lost its logical momentum. You see its modern manifestation in special forces arriving to rescue characters in a hopeless hostage situation.

Analysing the plot

An analysis of plot will require the identification of the following building blocks.

The beginning

This has to be arresting with a dramatic moment of arrival. The character relationships need to have clarity; powerful question marks in the mind of the listener need to be struck immediately.

Conflict and attack

There has to be evidence of an emotional, financial, moral, human or physical struggle that provokes listeners into laughing, crying or experiencing fear and pathos. If you cannot arouse strong emotions within your audience then you will lose it. The play's central conflict needs to be decisive. It needs to be effectively timed and the opposing polarities or extremes need clear alignment. The art of storytelling is exploring the extreme limits of human psychological and physical existence. One polarity needs to be pitched against another.

Rising and balanced action through plot

The plotting needs twists and turns. It is advisable to have a main plot and depending on the play's duration to have one or two subsidiary plots which are linked logically to each other and help contribute to the rising tension and pitching of polarities. Most successful plays have a major and minor story line linked to one another which twist and turn and then resolve climactically at the end. There has to be an element of surprise in this development but pay attention to the need for the obligatory scene and avoid the need for a *deus ex machina*. Ensure that neither plot nor characterisation predominates over the other completely. If your main plot is character intensive, make sure that your minor plot is plot intensive.

Tension and humour

You may have heard the expression that 'life always has its ups and downs'. The structure of radio plays needs to reflect this basic truth of human existence. It is rare indeed for life's experience to be unrelenting suffering, crisis and agony. The essential rhythm of human experience contains a balance of tension and humour. Humour is the survival mechanism of the tragic experience. I would recommend that the emotional rhythm of the play dances on the listener's heart and mind: tension, humour, tension, humour, charm and alarm, charm and alarm. It is vital that the two emotional dimensions are linked. The central character uses humour to react to an absurd but painful obstacle. Only one character should use humour to deal with difficult situations. Keep the use of humour verbal: slapstick belongs to the stage, television or film. It is also important to ensure that the use of humour is consistent with the character and you do not have a play where characters take it in turns to be funny. Your play will be changing into comedy or sitcom if you go down this route.

Emotion and ambience

You must have generated an emotional response from the audience, particularly in relation to the main character. Emotion can be defined as love, hate, admiration, disgust or even a paradoxical pity. The emotional connection between the writing and the listener guarantees good radio drama. The fifth dimension of imaginative involvement with the listener requires detail and relevant detail establishing the play's atmosphere and ambience so that they become a picture palace in the mind of the listener. This can be created by sound effects, imagistic narrative detail, music, and observation through dialogue.

Dialogue and purpose

There needs to be predominance of dialogue and dramatic communication over narrative. Dialogue is how we engage dramatically with the world: characters inform, argue, amuse, outrage and argue through the ebb and flow of dialogue. When we do, we talk and that is how great radio plays are made. Your characters must talk in dramatic dialogue. Do not forget Aristotle's golden rule of unity of action. Every word, every line, every scene must serve a dramatic purpose in terms of the play's characterisation and plot development. You must drop anything which is redundant or superfluous to the play's drive, theme and issue and anything which is inconsistent with the development of the main character towards the main crisis and climax.

The main character

The listener must be able to identify and experience empathy or sympathy with the main character. Without this you do not have a play which is going to maintain interest and audience loyalty. You cannot afford to fail in this area because the audio audience is not captive and can leave you in an instant. The central character is essential to the drive of the play. The main character's aspiration has to be definite and forceful and that is the mechanism by which the characterisation would normally win the sympathy of the listener. The obstacles and opposing forces need to be strong enough and relevant so that the main character's struggle is purposeful. The conflict arising from this needs to generate a dramatic intensity which resonates and is consistent with the issue and theme of the play.

Turning point and climax

There is an element of sexual metaphor in the terminology used by dramatists and dramaturgists in analysing the dynamics of play construction. I cannot imagine that the film director Ken Russell would disagree with me when I make the observation that better sex has foreplay, development, sustained excitement, sur-prise and affection, maybe even love, followed by an explosion of ecstasy. Good radio drama is not all that different. As my shorthand teacher used to tell me: 'If you don't use it, you lose it'. Marilyn Monroe used to complain that having sex with President Jack Kennedy was all 'humping, and no foreplay'. History showed that that was a relationship which did not prosper. It has also been observed that 'one night stands' do not make for a fulfilling sex life. In relation to radio play construction, you need to make sure that the central crisis of the play emerges naturally from the play's basic conflict. The central problem needs to be realised or resolved. One force needs to dominate over the other. The climax has to represent the highest peak of emotional intensity in the play and the central character or the audience need to emerge from the experience with an element of enlightenment or change. The developing plot and rising crisis need to have changed the character and/or audience in a fundamental way. This has to arise as a result of the battle between the polarising forces inherent in the plot.

Issue and theme

There has to be a euphonic balance between the stating of the play's issue and its clarity. If the communication is too subtle it will be lost. If it is overstated then the play will founder on self-consciousness and a level of didactic propaganda which defies the listener's willingness to keep an open mind and suspend disbelief. Bear in mind that complicating the presentation of an issue can cause confusion. There is a saying in art that 'nobility is gained through simplicity'. All plays are built around a theme and the central character must be the metaphorical agent in the dramatic depiction of the theme. It is important to confirm that the motivation of the central character and the momentum of the plot is determined by the play's basic idea.

Structuring a radio play

Radio play structuring requires a fine understanding of the principle of building and developing scenes. Every scene has to have an introduction whether by word, sound effect, atmosphere or music. It should be underpinned by the conflict of two character forces each with an aim and objective. The aim represents the first character's aspiration for himself or herself. It may not be fully resolved in the individual scene if it has an arc of progress that reaches to the play's climax. The objective represents the outcome for the other character intended by the first character. The other character also has an aim and objective which may be diametrically opposed to those of the first character. But the key to maintaining a momentum of story drive in play construction is to ensure that at least one of the character forces achieves an aim or objective. Every scene has a specific purpose to serve the overall direction of the plot. Well-constructed scenes are tagged so that at the end or even sometimes during its time span there is a pointer to the next scene or the presence of one of the characters in the next scene. I use the term 'character force' because the force of character may not be a human being. Character can be a metaphysical presence, an anthropo-morphic dimension or stream of sound symbolism. Every scene leaves the listener with tantalising and resonating questions that future scenes are expected to answer.

Theory of narrative

Most creative writers are likely to be astonished that an entire legion of philo-sophers and theoretical writers mainly from the linguistic and anthropology dis-ciplines have analysed and reflected on the concept of communication and social narrative. This has advanced theoretical writing on the subject of dramatic narra-tive from the early consideration by Aristotle. More importantly the analysis has been rooted in the social context of the twentieth century and the social inter-action between the individual and the new phenomena of mass communication: radio and television and more recently the Internet and World Wide Web. Film is a very significant and rather popular medium for analysis by academia and it has also been ground into very fine particles of deconstruction by the philosopher's stone.

Colin McArthur stated in a British Film Institute publication that narration has a 'central ideological function' which confers authority and elides contradictions in ideological discourses.[10] This point underlines the fact that narration is more than a technical convenience. It is recognised as an ideological mechanism. The concept of the narrative paradigm sees people as storytellers. Storytelling is central to human discourse and interaction. The autumn 1985 edition of the *Journal of Communication* developed this field of debate and communications theory sought to distinguish the socio-philosophical role of the narrative paradigm from the dramatic paradigm. Walter Fisher stated that the narrative paradigm sees people as narrative beings because they have an inherent perception of narrative probability. This is seeing the world from the point of view of a coherent story and narrative fidelity giving people an understanding of whether stories ring true in terms of their own lives and experiences. The dramatic paradigm sees people playing parts or prescribed roles with the scripts structured by existing social and psychological situations, political and social institutions and cultural patterns.

Creative writers and radio drama directors meeting this theoretical approach would probably translate these notions as a realisation that storytelling and plot construction through narrative or drama have always had a social or ideological function. The expression art imitating life or life imitating art is a close parallel explanation of the dramatic paradigm. The engagement between practising narrators and storytellers in audio theatre, and I would venture to suggest in any other dramatic field, begins to resonate with greater relevance by considering the texts produced by Bulgarian structuralist Tzvetan Todorov, Russian critic and folklorist Vladimir Propp, French linguist Roland Barthes and French anthropologist Claude Lévi-Strauss.

The value in studying the theoretical debate is that for the creative artist there is the potential for understanding social and philosophical purpose as well as defining the technical architecture and craft of practical expression and construction. Creative communication is also dependent on its meaning. Meaning is the way it resonates within the heart and mind of the listener. In this context we can find a most valuable contribution to communications theory by Swiss linguist Ferdinand de Saussure. By studying language and its relationship with thought and emotion he came to the conclusion that there is merit in differentiating between the name, the naming and the meaning of what is being named in language.

This is a structural approach to communication and he has bestowed as his legacy on media and communication the terms signifier, signified, signs and signification. Putting it very simply the sign is the building block of human communication. The sign is composed of the signifier, which is the physical existence of the sign – the word – and the signified, which is the mental concept that denotes the word. Signification represents the charge of external reality or the connotation of meaning. What is the relevance and parallel with audio drama? Here are some simple examples.

The central character in a radio play is a matriarchal despot who ruthlessly destroys dissidence and insubordination through assassination and exile. She controls her 'council of power' meetings with a claustrophobic menacing authority. She never raises her voice. She hisses and whispers her orders and commandments. When anyone dares question her opinion or inadvertently provokes her anger, she has a reputation for saying 'Hush' and drawing out the final 'sh' sound of the word for several seconds which fades into a deafeningly intimidating silence.

So the signifier is the physical utterance of the word 'hush'. The signified or mental concept is the admonishment, generally regarded as mild rebuke, to people to quieten down. But the external reality for the other members of the council of power and the matriarch's 'subjects' is that the expression of this word is portentous and a sign of potential retribution which is likely to be tyrannical and totalitarian. The word 'hush' then takes on a social or culture-specific meaning. When parents say 'hush' to their children it takes on a more dangerous and threatening power. Political radicals and satirists use the word mockingly to expose the matriarch's abuse of power and the need to overthrow her malevolent authority. When people say 'I'll hush you' it becomes the equivalent of a threat to kill. Saussure's theory can be applied to the modern connotation of the adjective 'gay', the image of the hammer and sickle, or the sound of Big Ben which is inextricably linked with the urgency and authority of mainstream news communication.

Russian theorists from the 1920s have very helpfully distinguished between plot and story with the terms *syuzhet* and *fabula*. As indicated earlier playwrights need to be aware of the separate existence, prior and future, and sometimes the lateral direction of story as opposed to the dramatic presentation of plot within the play. *Fabula* as story is now defined by media theorists as all the events in a narrative, both explicitly presented and inferred. They include the things that must have happened during time transpositions and the history prior to the listener being plunged into the immediate crisis which sets up the dramatic charge of the play. They can also include the information and story withheld from the listener as the critical plot device leading to surprise, enlightenment and resolution in the final climax. *Syuzhet* as plot is everything audible through sound and visible through imaginative generation in the mind's eye. It is the construction of deliberately selected parts of the *fabula*. *Syuzhet* can be recognised when the dynamics of storytelling succeed in providing entertainment and 'suspension of disbelief' retains its equilibrium so that the resolution of the play does not challenge logic and sympathy.

First person singular narrative

In our practical and theoretical debate about narrative and drama, I think it is rather interesting to consider the definition of the first person singular narrative force in audio drama. Is it narrative or is it dramatic? The answer is not absolute. It can be either and it can be both. In Tony Duarte's radio play *Coffee and Tea, 90p* the central character presents his first person existence as a present consciousness recollecting internally a past experience or 'narrative'.

The time and communication relationship with the audience at this stage is a dramatic dynamic because the disturbing recollection is set in the time present of the coffee bar of the National Film School where the central character is struggling with the conflict between resolving or reliving an internal emotional pain and the external interruption and frustration of dealing with complaining customers making unreasonable demands. Leaving aside Sigmund Freud's fascinating analysis of personality and the exhaustive although never conclusive philosophical debates about the meaning of existence and our individual identity in the universe, we can begin to define the dimensions of a character's existence and storytelling role in a radio play.

Internal existence for character

The internal is represented by an internal voice which speaks to the character itself and the audience. Its intimate quality is enhanced by the audio relationship of one person to one listener. This is emotionally confidential.

The internal existence is not limited to one voice. The notion of a character's identity, motivation, feeling and origination can be represented by different voices which take on different characters and emotions. In Samuel Beckett's *Words and Music* the ostensible story of a poem's creation is an internal experience with a dynamic of conflict between Croak (the central consciousness) and Bob and Joe dramatised and articulated through the form of words and music, and those words and music have a voice that is clearly the expression of character.[11] When the dynamic of an internal interaction of voices or sound is in the present then the communication is dramatic. The internal existence can also be narrative when the character accesses his or her mental 'film school' of the past. The 'film school' of memory is in sound, vision, smell and touch and the recollection of memory can engage with any of these sensory mechanisms for 'flashback'. The experience of recall is narrative, but the experience of the presentation of recall is dramatic if it is scenic and involves the playing of parts in mise-en-scène.

Internal existence can be conscious as well as subconscious. In everyday language, conscious internal existence is sometimes defined as day-dreaming or 'what's on your mind'. The subconscious existence tends to be defined as your internal experience when unconscious or disconnected by way of external communication and reception with the outside world. I cannot exclude the sub-conscious existence of the individual while conscious and interacting with the outside world.

External existence for character

The external existence is represented by the words, the emotions and force of the character's presence in society. It operates by way of action and dialogue and of course external monologue although the soliloquy in radio is normally predicated on the idea that this is communicated internally to the character and is listened to only by the listener. It is not unknown for radio dramatists to suspend disbelief and develop stories where all characters or only some characters can connect with each other's internal existence. Conflict can be created by the invisibility of internal existence as well as ignited by its transparency.

Subtext

You cannot exclude the force of internal existence colouring and transmitting through verbal and action codes on the plane of external existence. This is the fundamental position of subtext. Subtext is the subsidiary communication of thoughts, feelings, ideological objectives and other messages through voice, words, music, action and presence. Subtext can be generated with silence. More is said by answering a question with silence than with a lie. Subtext is saying one thing and meaning the opposite or something completely different.

This can be hinted or subtly communicated by implicit performance. Resorting to internal dramatic monologue or narration would be explicit. There is a presumption that audiences prefer to participate in dramatic storytelling by decodifying and perceiving subtextual messages. The subtlety of such an engagement is exhilarating and emotionally and intellectually stimulating. It helps bond the process of sympathy and empathy between characters and audience. Subtext is also the internal reaction to the reception of external language and action in a dramatic scene. Again it is conveyed or connoted through external language. The mundane banal exchange of 'How are you doing?' with the reply 'I'm fine' has a dramatic potential which is multidimensional through the layered and subtextual dynamics of internal and external existence. The performer can play the line 'I'm fine' with aggression and this can hint although not explicitly state that the character saying 'I'm fine' wishes to express a feeling that is rooted in the *fabula* of the play. Perhaps, for example, the person who says 'I'm fine' has been diagnosed as suffering from cancer and wishes to express defiance of the disease. The defiant delivery of the line 'I'm fine' is intended to communicate to the person who said 'How are you doing?' that today there will be no compromise, no concession – the character saying 'I'm fine' will not be defeated. Similarly the presentation of the seemingly banal question 'How are you doing?' can be played with huge indifference and lack of enthusiasm. The subtextual dynamic is therefore inevitably dramatic by surprising the audience and raising the question why? It is unusual for people to say 'How are you doing?' in such a way that it sounds as if the character is not in the least bit interested in knowing the answer.

The power of subtextual communication of internal existence is exquisitely demonstrated in the opening sequence of Canadian playwright Jeff Green's production of *Somebody Talking to You* (1989). The central character Mercury enters the play from the point of view of his external existence. He arrives home in his eccentric apartment where sound files play when he opens the door and his life and character is portrayed through a series of answer-machine messages. The listener experiences the construction of the *fabula* through the introduction of the *syuzhet* plot device of communicating a medley of characters which define the identity of the central character. This is enhanced by his reactions. The narrative of his life collides dramatically with present time conflict between what people intended to say about him in time past in the form of answer-machine messages and the response he presents externally as though they are still there to hear what he has to say. He knows that they are not there.

The interesting question is whether what he says would have been different if they were there in time present. There are two calls in particular which are rich in subtext. The first call from this character results in no message being left. The second call is a young woman's voice which says 'Hello?' and then hangs up. Mercury's response is minimalist. He says 'Ah . . . Mandy.' We pick up or 'denote' from the subtextual message of this curious exchange that Mandy is probably an ex-girlfriend who has been struggling to summon up the courage to ring Mercury.

She has been frustrated by discovering that he is not there and cannot bring herself to communicate explicitly through an answer-machine message, but she has left enough sound to communicate to Mercury that she wants to talk, that it is now time to talk and there is unfinished business. Mercury responds by communicating an identification of what Mandy has done but also about what he feels because in two words 'Ah . . . Mandy' Mercury communicates regret, sadness and sympathy. We can speculate how different the communication externally and subtextually between these characters would have been had they met sonically in 'time present' for a clash or interaction of their internal and external consciousness. But Mandy's presence is by way of a past recording conveying her past internal and external consciousness, but disconnected from the internal and external reaction of Mercury's consciousness. Internal existence is psychological and philosophical. External existence is social and political.

The listener's point of view whether through first person singular narrative or third person dramatic development provides the potential for ironic entertainment and appreciation. When the listener knows something, another character, unaware of dramatic irony, is identified and the listener's coded engagement can be implicit through subtext or explicit through past and present internal monologue within a character.

For example, a multimillionaire is travelling in a ship which has struck an iceberg. In his past he has persecuted and exploited his workers. In fact one such workman who stood up to his tyranny is travelling to the USA to start a new life after being sacked and denied any further work opportunities in his town because of the stigma of his union agitation. The worker does not know that the multimillionaire is travelling to the new world to expand his business and secure lucrative markets for his business's products. Neither knows the other is on the ship, but we do – and the fact that they are both travelling on the *Titanic* to search for new horizons is ironic.

When the ship starts to sink, the worker and his family are prevented by the millionaire from leaving their accommodation area because priority is being given to first-class passengers. But fate decrees that they are confined to an area of the ship where there are more spaces in the lifeboats than there are women and children. This means that the worker and his family can survive the disaster. In the first-class area there are so few lifeboats that the millionaire's wife and children drown. He himself is struggling in the water and shouting for help. The worker cannot identify the drowning man's voice and reaches out to save him, only to discover that he has rescued the very man who did everything to destroy his livelihood and past security and nearly destroyed the lives of his wife and children. Despite the past, the worker cannot help but feel sympathy for a man who has in fact lost his wife and family. This story is a veritable onion of ironic construction, stripping away one layer of irony to reveal yet another.

In some of these examples creative writers and audio drama directors are now beginning to engage with a body of significant and modern theory in communications from the linguistics tradition. It is called semiotics or semiology. We will explore this further. In the meantime we must continue our analysis of the dramatic value and social function of first person singular narrative. In Tony Duarte's play *Coffee and Tea 90p* the listener is locked into three essential dimensions of dramatic storytelling. We are experiencing the central character's internal existence. He is tormented or traumatised by the memory of coming home to his shared flat and discovering his girlfriend naked in bed with another woman.

Emotionally and intellectually he is trying to come to terms with the implications of his girlfriend's bisexuality and also her infidelity. The central character's external existence, or time present, is the story of how he is coping within a society while obsessed and preoccupied by the unfolding flashback of the experience of this discovery in his private life. What is he going to do about it? It seems from the development of his internal existence that he feels motivated to exact a revenge of some kind, or at the very least force a confrontation.

The third dimension of storytelling is the recollection of the previous experience of discovery which is fragmented, detailed and jagged in its gradual disclosure because of the exigencies of *syuzhet*. The confrontation has an anticipation of violence because of the central character's tendency to be overly aggressive to people challenging him in time present scenarios and his vandalism towards objects such as cardboard boxes, which he rips apart violently with a knife.

This dramatic action in time present is clearly an external symbolic manifestation of the anger and hurt that he feels towards his girlfriend. The plot construction controls the amount of information in the linear disclosure through flashback of the central character's experience of finding his girlfriend *in flagrante delicto* lesbian style.

The play contrapuntally weaves the dimension of internal existence expressing present time emotion, internal existence recollecting past dramatic experience with external existence being presented through the dramatic journey towards a new confrontation with his girfriend and her lover. The adverb 'contrapuntally' reflects the appropriateness of theoretical musical vocabulary to define and describe the construction of radio plays. Contrapuntal singing or chorus is the progression of different melodic journeys within a piece of music where all the singers start and finish with the same melodic direction. In *Coffee and Tea 90p* the central character's existence is time present for the listener within the *syuzhet* framework. The time-line is virtually chronological within the span of the play's duration.

We start in the National Film Theatre coffee bar and then accompany the external existence of the character as he finishes work and journeys to confront his girlfriend and girlfriend's lover. The climax of the play is anti-climactic in the external existence of the central character whereas the presence of powerful climax is to be found at the end of the development of the unfolding and tortured memory of an event rooted in time past. The author sets up a worrying anticipation of *crime passionnel* which in reality is challenged by the sensitivity and humanity of the central character's genuine response to the news that his girlfriend's father has had a heart attack and is in hospital. The absurdity of life events has intervened to challenge the emotional logic of motivation and intention.

The play ends with a somewhat existential conclusion. The only remaining presence of the central character's internal and external existence is represented by the sound of his footsteps in the urban landscape. The footsteps are heard although not commented on by the internal consciousness, which has nothing to articulate, and the external existence is symbolically represented by 'a walking away'. The reality is the sound of footsteps, but the symbolism may be a continuing journey along the route of absurd existence. The central character remains alive although he has been consigned to a future existence which is uncomfortable and confusing. He may well have been changed. The priority of human understanding or conflict is transformed by the presence of grief which transcends and nullifies the petty jealousies and sexual pride engendered by infidelity.

The first person narrator in Billy Wilder's film *Sunset Boulevard* (1950) presents first person internal existence at the beginning as a traditional narrator. He is introducing a story from the past, and the audience then becomes dramatically engaged with the story as the central character exists externally but with subtextual expression of inner consciousness always present. The conceit in *Sunset Boulevard* is that the central character who began the film with the opening narrative finishes up riddled with bullets, floating face down in the swimming pool and closing the film with the final narrative post-mortem. This is a delightful example of existence not belonging to a mortal reality. The metaphysical tradition of religion and philosophy means that we can enthusiastically spiritualise existence so that it has a voice and dramatic validity before, during and after death.

Codes of narrative

Barthes has established an impressive framework which is now being described as 'codes of narrative'. They arose out of his intriguing attempt to 'deconstruct' or in ordinary language 'analyse' a short story by Balzac called 'Sarrasine'. It needs to be stated that the theoretical writings of authors such as Barthes and Propp are not doctrinaire 'bibles' by which the world of narrative can be defined and explained. They are simply modern philosophers struggling to mould a vocabulary of explanation. So Barthes's narrative codes are not straitjackets by which narrative construction should be pigeon-holed.

His codes are proiaretic or action codes, which loosely defined means the voice telling us what happens. The Voice of Empirics tells us about events and provides the sequence of the story.

The enigma code or hermeneutic code sets up the question marks which puzzle the listeners, hold them in suspense and are finally disclosed at the end. It is described as the Voice of Truth.

The cultural or referential code references the historical, literary, physical and scientific landmarks of knowledge that define the cultural context of the story.

The code of the seme is the Voice of the Person, or character. The semic or symbolic code is simply the Voice of Symbol. This system of analysis is an eloquent mechanism to examine texts. Barthes himself states very clearly that his network of codes represents a 'galaxy of signifiers, not a structure of signifieds'.

Tzvetan Todorov's main contribution to the theory of narrative is to underline the traditional technique of storytelling beginning with an equilibrium which is challenged by an event, setting in train another series of events which result in a new equilibrium or status quo. This is as relevant to a society or community as it is to an individual character.

Chapter 17

Creating the character and effective use of characterisation

As I indicated earlier writers prefer to concentrate on the creativity of character creation rather than the intricacies and construction of plot. There has to be a main protagonist character in any sequence of drama who represents a point of view which the listeners can believe in and identify with. The BBC Radio 4 series *Girlies* (1997) by Sudha Buchar and Shaheen Khan depicted the lives of five 'thirty something' Asian women who all met at the local comprehensive school in the 1970s. It spanned four half-hour episodes and it can be argued that the main plotting weakness was its inability to focus on any one character for each episode.

However, it created a powerful charge of storytelling despite the overlapping of plot and subplot and an ensemble of five equal forces in characterisation. The fault may have been present in the scheduling. Four episodes cannot effectively serve a quintet of relationships between a group of women who meet regularly for 'Girlies', a ritual weekly evening meeting where men and children are barred. It could be argued that strengthening the focus on main characterisation and bolstering the dominance of main plot over subplot would be a way of fine-tuning a highly entertaining and promising series. It had a second series run, but in my opinion it also had the potential for being permanently established as a regular 'soap' series. The characters and scenarios had a life and appeal which went beyond four half-hour instalments broadcast on FM at 10 a.m. on a weekday.

The quality of the writing in *Girlies*, which was directed by Kristine Landon-Smith, demonstrates the fact that characters have to be believable and recognisable. Unity of action requires characters that always have function and dramatic purpose. The main character and other characters must be active. There needs to be a dynamic relationship between the activity of the character and the urgency of the plot. When one of the women has an extramarital relationship with her 22-year-old Tamil student, Ramesh, the crisis and climactic tension created by his desire to change the terms of the relationship beyond a secret affair with the threat that he will inform her husband engenders a response and character development which is consistent with her character and feeds back into the plot. The fact that she has a relationship despite the appearance of 'a perfect' multicultural marriage with a white Englishman is surprising but, in the context of her action and emotions revealed in dialogue with Ramesh and her 'girlie' friends, it is believable. She reveals herself as a selfish person, but her flaws can be forgiven and intriguingly the majority of the audience does not wish her husband to be told about the affair, causing the likely ending of her secure and generally happy family life.

At this stage it is worth debating which should come first. Should we be creating a plot first from which the characters hang, or should we create our characters first from which the plot hangs? John Galsworthy said that the writer who does the former rather than the latter is committing a cardinal sin. He may be right. Most writers on writing seem to think he is. Plot construction tends to be mechanical and I think that the creative impetus of character creation must come first. It is better to begin with the idea, follow with the characters and then tell the story.

If we consider the plays that have survived their periods, it is those that are dominated by the power of their central characters which have endured. When people think of Shakespeare they think of *Hamlet*, *Macbeth*, *Romeo and Juliet* and *Richard III* first and plays such as *Taming of the Shrew*, *As You Like It* and *Twelfth Night* later. Plays which have titles that are not eponymous with the central character also survive when the force of their dramatic energy emerges through a central character who is unforgettable and embodies some powerful truth about human nature. Farce and melodrama which depend on situations and the course of action tend to belong to their cultural time.

It is easy to spot the play where the character has germinated in the writing of narrative and dialogue. Here the characters are not in tune with the plot. The story of the character's life and origin overwhelms the dramatic cohesion of the play's idea and development. Profiling of characters should be done before a word of the play is written. Professional production of plays where there has been insufficient profiling often exposes inconsistencies or illogical contradictions in the characterisation. Performers are compelled by the nature of their own artistic instincts and method to invest creative interpretation which challenges the purpose and behaviour of the character in the play. Background, antecedents and history should be determined by the writer and not by directors and actors. As a writer you need to know your characters' strengths and weaknesses, ambitions, aspirations and insecurities.

You need to have a full understanding of each character's anxieties, fantasies and guilt and to have worked out what it is that the character hates about himself or herself and what it is the character loves about himself or herself. It is also important to understand how your characters deceive themselves. What was the worst thing that ever happened in your character's life and how did the character come to terms with that experience? What is the best thing that ever happened in your character's life and how has that experience resonated intellectually and emotionally? What was the character's relationship with the mother and father and any siblings? What is the experience that your character has had with grief and profound emotional suffering? What experience has your character had with death and serious injury? Has your character stared death in the face? Does your character fear death? How would your character want to die and what would be the worst way of dying for your character? What are your character's religious and philosophical beliefs? What has happened in the past to change them?

What is your character's sexual orientation and history? What was your character's first sexual experience and how did he or she lose their virginity? Has your character been in love? How many times? How would your character exhibit attraction to another person? Has your character suffered from a broken heart? What would it take to break your character's heart? What does he or she want out of human relationships? What drives the force of envy and jealousy within your character? What does your character think about his or her body? How would you pitch the quality of your character's self-confidence? How does your character day-dream? How does your character respond to fear and danger? How does your character exhibit extreme anger and what would provoke your character to this point? What would reduce your main character to gales of laughter and how does your character have fun? What was the most foolish thing your character ever did? What is your character most ashamed of? Your characters have an internal and exterior existence and consciousness. The exterior is not necessarily determined by the interior although they often have direct cognisance of each other. They are often in conflict. The complex juxtaposition sets up the paradoxical nature of dramatic existence. Exterior consciousness may be dominated and preoccupied with the ecstasy of making love, but the interior consciousness may be tortured, confused and stung by the guilty realisation that this action is a betrayal of an exterior human relationship and also an attack on an interior notion of self-esteem and moral rectitude.

Your understanding of your character is probably as intense an intimacy as you will ever experience in your own personal relationships. When you give your characters private moments during a play and allow your listeners into the minds and hearts of your characters, you are sharing the privilege that you have with your listeners and it is a powerful opportunity for revelation. Enabling your characters to drop their guard for the purpose of plot development enriches the intensity and quality of characterisation as well as enhancing the listener's appreciation of the story.

I would advise a policy of giving each character a dominant physical or behavioural characteristic and for this characteristic to be purposeful. This helps to establish immediate engagement for the listener and supports rapid identification of characters who are essential to the unfolding of the plot. I heard one experienced writer suggest the imbuing of a stereotype to ensure rapid recognition which is then twisted to strip away the clichéd surface. There is merit in challenging the homily that there is nothing new under the sun by making it new under the moon.

If your characters have been fully imagined you will find that the natural course of their impulses will write the play for you. When you make your authorial decision to place your central character in a specific social, physical and emotional environment the action will be determined by this nexus of human dynamics. In tragedy the impetus of dramatic characterisation is determined by a striving for a goal that the hero can never attain. The tragedy is accentuated by the unrelenting failure to overcome the obstacles thrown in the hero's path. Tragedy tips over into melodrama when the dynamics of the social and physical environment of the play dominate the focus of characterisation. In comedy the drama depends on the dramatic portrayal of the central character's response and reactions to the social and physical environment. In farce the dramatic entertainment is derived from the dynamic force of the actions on character rather than character on actions. Comedy and tragedy are the drama of characterisation. Melodrama and farce arise out of dramatised situation.

An essential ingredient of character construction is understanding the principle of the hero or heroine. Listeners need to look up to main characters and want to admire them because, to use the line of a popular contemporary song, we are all 'searching for the heroes inside ourselves'. Our psychological existence depends on a fantasy that transcendent people and transcendent moments always conquer adversity. One of the most enjoyable plot developments in characterisation is the transference of the hero from the obvious to the humble. By investing greatness in apparent inferiority you are engaging the well of human generosity which thrives on a recognition of the potential for human dignity.

Your main characters need to be attractive from the point of view of personality. They need charisma. They need to resonate conviction and intensity. They may not be perfect but we are attracted to them because they are not unlike ourselves. Human beings are not drawn to people who appear to be 'too perfect', lack a sense of humour, take themselves too seriously and seem to be devoid of beliefs. If your main character is burdened by these characteristics you will lose your audience.

In your plot construction try not to forget that your main character has to change and be changed by the plot. Drama requires conflict which can only be generated when you have drawn characters who are extreme in relation to each other. Clarity of characterisation and plotting also requires a polarity between characters where the central personality undergoes internal and external changes as a result of the twists and turns of the plot, but the secondary characters should be more singular in their characteristics. The best way to define this is that your secondary characters should already be committed at the moment of the listener's arrival into the story, while the main character is still weighing up the options.

At this stage you should be in a position to recognise assured characterisation in a radio play. The main character should be central to the plot and possess dominant characteristics. Your listener must like and care what happens to the main character. Your listener should dislike and have the potential to hate the antagonist and your main character should be developing through the plot. Your play's structure should be engineered with a gripping and captivating plot with twists and turns and it should be launched with a crisis at the beginning which is dramatic. The play should have emotional intensity, with the plot hitting high points in action and drama as conflict escalates to an explosive and defining climax. In this journey remember to modulate charm with alarm and alternate tension with humour. Strike the colours of the world of your play with detail so there is a rich imaginative atmosphere setting mood and emotional, cultural or political ambience. The sympathy or empathy with the main character on the part of the listeners needs to be passionate, emotional and committed and struck powerfully against antipathy, dislike and apprehension for the antagonist or villain. Keep surprising the listener all the way through the plot and tantalise the listener with a cascade of fascinating and demanding questions.

Vladimir Propp's *Morphology of the Folktale* (1928) was a comprehensive attempt to deconstruct the social and creative dynamics of the Heroic Wonder-tale.[1] He believed that it was possible to identify eight character roles and thirty-one functions of narrative which propel or direct the forward movement of the story. They include a prohibition or ban on the hero, and the significant enlightenment of the hero about some aspect of the villain or vice versa. The eight character roles were defined as villain, hero (the seeker of an objective), donor (provider of an object with magic property), helper (aiding the hero), princess (reward for the hero and object of the villain's schemes), father of princess, who rewards the hero, dispatcher (figure who sends hero on the journey) and false hero. Propp's work in this area was valuable in deconstructing the narrative function of character. I believe it is possible to draw out his analysis to highlight more general functions of character in audio play construction.

Chapter 18

Writing dialogue

There are a number of essential principles which distinguish the dialogue of drama from the conversation of real life. The language used by characters must be a response to a situation, plot or action. The exchange between characters should be a response to each character in the scene. Dialogue can serve an excellent function as comic relief during intense and emotionally overladen sequences. However, humorous dialogue is not simply a matter of characters cracking jokes, but the construction of carefully crafted lines responding to the dramatic situation. The dialogue should also be written and constructed so that scenes are connected. Such lines and exchanges can serve as effective conscious and subconscious transepts.

The quality of dialogue is determined by the presence of active, direct and emotional language as opposed to reflexive, passive and neutral communication. Believability is increased by specificity. Quality is also improved when dialogue is more specifically constructed in relation to a character's background and emotional state. If dialogue is reacting to action or situation then it must be dramatic and poised on polarities. The goals of the characters in each scene should be different and the language should explicitly or implicitly dramatise this. It is also crucial that dialogue should have continuity, with the characters taking tags from one another by repeating the last word spoken. The dialogue of each character must relate to his or her dramatic function, so it is perfectly acceptable to mix direct and indirect dialogue between two characters when they have different goals.

Dialogue can be divided into two major styles. It is possible to mix them, but more often playwrights tend to commit to one style in single plays. Heightened language could be described as the language of the theatre. Ken Dancyger has described it as 'high octane' communication.[1] It is often poetic, philosophical and highly charged with authorial expression. It not only serves the development of the plot and character, but also presents the view of the writer. It could be argued that radio is the natural medium for heightened dialogue. There is now a tendency for more naturalism in UK produced radio drama. Radio producers like to go out on location and explore realism. In these situations there is a tendency to accentuate the use of naturalistic dialogue.

In naturalistic dialogue there is a tendency to find more simple language. There is less use of vocabulary in the exchange between characters, shorter words and a relationship to action and characterisation. Lines between characters are often crossed-over and crashing into each other. This tendency is normally a sign of a struggle by both characters to say something first.

In heightened dialogue there is a greater capacity for description, and the presence of the writer's conviction can sometimes give the impression of preaching. Longer words and more complex use of metaphor, simile and vocabulary are further signs of a heightened style of writing. In the ensuing passage from the dramatisation of Joseph Conrad's novel *Heart of Darkness*, the Greek chorus style interaction of the acousmatic voices of Conrad, Kurtz and Marlow is clearly heightened dramatic language. In a sense they are engaged with each other through the communication of indirect dialogue. Conrad's voice is like a wide-screen cinecamera. Marlow's voice is the restricted vision of Marlow's stereoscopic eyeline and his thinking and feeling. The Voice of Kurtz is more naturalistic and is disconnected from the present narrative direction. It is a resonant echo seeping into Marlow's present time consciousness as a memory of the last words Marlow heard him speak. Kurtz is also an acousmatic and immortal spirit who has been present throughout the dramatisation and joins the chorus at the end.

The structure of the writing emphasises the dramatic irony of the Intended Woman seeking a recollection of Kurtz's last words that will bring comfort to her. The dramatic question is how will Marlow respond? Will it be with the truth? Marlow lies because the communication of the words 'the horror, the horror' would be too emotionally traumatic. But the added irony is that by lying he has corrupted himself, and by joining the voices of Conrad, Marlow and Kurtz as one the drama implies that they have lost their ability to distinguish one from the other.

Examples of tagging occur in lines 23 and 24 in the use of the word 'example' and in lines 37 and 38 in the use of the expression 'his last word'. The dialogue language of Intended Woman tends to be more indirect because her focus is on her grief. Her goal is to extract from Marlow her lover's last words. Marlow's goal is to deliver the bundle of papers, leave as quickly as possible and avoid conveying to her the truth of his understanding of Kurtz and his end. Marlow's dialogue language is therefore more direct and minimalist.

Dramatisation as a writing function is very much a cultural representation of the time of the adaptation. While European authors have celebrated the text of *Heart of Darkness* as one of the most influential books in the twentieth century, Nigerian author Chinua Achebe has condemned it as negative stereotyping of Africans. In a highly influential essay he has accused Conrad of being a thorough-going racist. Achebe discourses a western psychology which 'set Africa up as a foil to Europe, a place of negations at once remote and vaguely familiar, in comparison with which Europe's own state of spiritual grace will be manifest.' Achebe renders the novella as a controversial issue in the growing debate about 'Orientalism' – the denigrating and political representation of non-European and English-speaking history and culture.

The adaptation has been written with these cultural concerns. The acousmatic voice of Conrad has been delineated as a voice and joined with that of Marlow and Kurtz. African representation has been established through ironic, authentic musical and choral chants by Paa 'C' Quaye and Clairvalle Aboh. Additional writing, particularly in dialogue, has reversed the Orientalist paradigm.

[*Rhythmic tramping and clanking sound. Bush actuality. Cocking of rifle.*]

1 GUARD   Stop! [*Clanking stops*] You! You! Stop! Who are you?

2 MARLOW   D'accord! It's all right . . . D'accord! . . . I'm from the station . . . Arrived today!

3 GUARD   Ha! From far all white men look the same . . . Haha!

4 VOICE OF CONRAD   Uniform jacket with one button off, rifle clutched laconically at the middle. Large white teeth in rascally grin . . .

5 MARLOW   What are you doing with these men?

6 GUARD   These are criminals . . . Mistah Manager say savages . . . I don't know this word . . . Savage? Perhaps you tell me?

7 MARLOW   Where are you taking them?

8 GUARD   [*Laughing somewhat maniacally*] Hahaha!

9 MARLOW   Why are you laughing?

10 GUARD   Masta you know where! We are together no? Together we conquer . . . we rule . . . We make lots of money . . .

[*Loud crack of whip and guttural 'Ha' sound.*]

11 GUARD   Move . . . Savages . . . Hahahah [*laughter into the distance with clanking chains.*]

12 VOICE OF CONRAD   Past some vast artificial hole, dug out on the slope. No quarry, no sandpit, just one vast hole. Piles of smashed drainage pipes. Into the shade and rushing noise of rapids, that fills the mournful stillness.

[*F/X Groaning from tired dying men.*]

End of *Heart of Darkness* by Joseph Conrad [2]

Dramatisation script by Tim Crook (1989).

1 VOICE OF CONRAD   The vision of Kurtz, stretcher, phantom-bearers, crowd of wild, obedient worshippers, gloom of forest, the glittering reach between the murky bends, the beating of a drum, regular and muffled like the beating of a heart, the heart of a conquering darkness. The wilderness of triumphs.

2 VOICE OF MARLOW   The vision of Kurtz, his abject pleading, his abject threats, the colossal scale of his vile desires, the meanness, the torment, the tempestuous anguish of his soul. Immense and wide stare, embracing, condemning, loathing all the universe.

3 VOICE OF KURTZ   The horror . . . the horror.

4 VOICE OF CONRAD   The dusk is falling. Tall marble fireplace, cold and monumental in its whiteness. The grand piano gleams darkly, like a sombre, polished sarcophagus.

5 VOICE OF CONRAD   His intended all in black. Her pale head floating in the dusk. For her he had died only yesterday. Such desolation, such sorrow.

Domestic interior. Large grandfather style clock ticking.

6 INTENDED WOMAN   I had heard you were coming. Well, it has been a year . . . I have survived.

7 MARLOW   Here . . . He asked me to give you this.

8 INTENDED WOMAN   You knew him well?

9 MARLOW   Intimacy grows quickly out there. I knew him as well as it is possible for one man to know another.

10 INTENDED WOMAN   And you admired him. It was impossible to know him and not to admire him. Wasn't it?

11 MARLOW   He was a remarkable man. It was impossible not to . . .

12 INTENDED WOMAN   . . . love him . . . How true! How true! . . . But when you think that no one knew him as well as I! I had all his noble confidence. I knew him best.

13 MARLOW   You knew him best.

14 INTENDED WOMAN   You were his friend. His friend. You must have been, if he had given you this, and sent you to me. I feel I can speak to you – and oh! I must speak. I want you – you who have heard his last words – to know I have been worthy of him . . . It is not pride . . . Yes! I am proud to know I understood him better than anyone on earth – he told me so himself. And since his mother died I have had no one . . . no one to . . . to . . .

15 MARLOW IN NARRATION   I listened. The darkness deepened. I was not even sure whether he had given me the right bundle. [*Start next line of* INTENDED WOMAN *here and fade and keep low under* MARLOW, *increasing the level at the end of his narration.*] I rather suspect he wanted me to take care of another batch of his papers which, after his death, I saw the manager examining under the lamp.

16 INTENDED WOMAN   You see, I loved that man. My family disapproved of our engagement. He was not rich enough. He did not have the means, so he was continually struggling, and it will be my eternal tragedy that he went out there to make such fortune that would drive the poverty from his life and impress my family . . . Who was not his friend who had heard him speak once? He drew men towards him by what was best in them. It is the gift of the great . . . But you have heard him! You know!

17 VOICE OF KURTZ   The horror, the horror!

18 MARLOW   Yes, I know.

19 INTENDED WOMAN   What a loss to me – to us! To the world . . . I have been very happy – very fortunate – very proud. Too fortunate. Too happy for a little while. And now I am unhappy for . . . for life . . . And of all this . . . of all his promise . . . and of all his greatness, of his generous mind, of his noble heart, nothing remains – nothing but a memory . . . You and I . . .

20 MARLOW   We shall always remember him.

21 INTENDED WOMAN   No. It is impossible that all this should be lost – that such a life should be sacrificed to leave nothing – but sorrow. You know what vast plans he had. I knew of them, too – I could not perhaps under-stand – but others knew of them. Something must remain. His words, at least, have not died.

22 MARLOW   His words will remain.

23 INTENDED WOMAN   And his example. Men looked up to him. His example shone in every act. His example.

24 MARLOW   True . . . his example too. Yes, his example. I forgot that.

25 INTENDED WOMAN   But I do not. I cannot. I cannot believe – not yet. I cannot believe that I shall never see him again, that nobody will see him again, never, never, never . . .

26 VOICE OF MARLOW   Never see him! I see him clearly enough now. I shall see his eloquent phantom as long as I live. I shall see her too, tragic and familiar. Shade, stretching out her black arms, with clasped pale hands across the fading light. She resembles that other tragic woman, bedecked with powerless charms, stretching bare brown arms over the glitter of the infernal stream, the stream of darkness.

27 INTENDED WOMAN   He died as he lived.

28 MARLOW   His end was in every way worthy of his life.

29 INTENDED WOMAN   And I was not with him.

30 MARLOW   Everything that could be done . . .

31 INTENDED WOMAN   Ah, but I believed in him more than anyone on earth
   – more than his own mother, more than – himself. He needed me! Me! I
   would have treasured every sigh, every word, every sign, every glance.

32 MARLOW   Don't, please . . .

33 INTENDED WOMAN   Forgive me . . . I – I have mourned so long in silence
   – in silence . . . You were with him – to the last? I think of his loneliness.
   Nobody near to understand him as I would have understood. Perhaps no
   one to hear . . .

34 MARLOW   To the very end . . . I heard his very last words . . .

35 INTENDED WOMAN   Repeat them . . . I want . . . I want . . . something
   . . . something to . . . to live with . . .

36 VOICE OF KURTZ   [*Heavily echoed*] The horror, the horror, the horror, the
   horror . . .

37 INTENDED WOMAN   His last word . . . to live with . . . Don't you
   understand, I love him – I loved him . . . I loved him . . .

38 MARLOW   The last word he pronounced was . . . your name.

39 INTENDED WOMAN   I knew it. I was sure! [*She begins to weep with grief.*]

40 VOICE OF KURTZ   I wanted justice . . . only justice . . .

41 VOICE OF MARLOW   I couldn't, I could not tell her.

42 VOICE OF KURTZ   The horror, the horror!

43 VOICE OF MARLOW   It would have been too dark, too dark altogether . . .
   [*Thames river actuality*].

44 VOICE OF CONRAD   Marlow ceases talking, sitting apart, indistinct and
   silent, in the pose of a meditating Buddha. The offing is barred by a black
   bank of clouds. Tranquil waters of the Thames flow sombre . . . flowing
   under overcast skies to the uttermost ends of the earth . . .

45 VOICES OF CONRAD, MARLOW AND KURTZ   . . . leading to the heart of an
   immense darkness.

[*The end*]

In the ensuing short story drama script the language is both dialogue and
naturalistic, but it is unique in leaving the conflicting subtextual line and opposite
direct lines in the imaginative spectacle of the listener. This is fifth-dimensional
dome narrative. The young boy exists only in the minds of the audience: his
interior existence and exterior language are exclusive to each individual listener.
Each speech appears in rhythm to be in the style of a monologue because each
speech addresses the selfish concerns of each character. Although orientated to the
young boy, it is as though the young boy is not there and the final speech from his

sister strikes up the irony of this truth which the listening audience has been appreciating as the play unfolds with its emotionally cruel implications.

Broken Porcelain by Tim Crook (1988)

1 FATHER   I know you think I'm a bastard . . . I probably am . . . I didn't give you the bike as some sort of . . . you know sop . . . the sweet before the left hook . . . Huh! . . . We . . . we . . . both of us . . . went together to buy it for you . . . because we still love you . . . whatever happens we still love you . . . Do you understand that? . . . It's not going to make any difference . . . We're still a family . . . Even when we're apart . . . You can still see me . . . anytime . . . Well you'll have to phone during the week . . . not during the day of course . . . I'll be working . . . but later . . . On second thoughts why don't you write . . . it'll be cheaper . . . People don't write enough nowadays . . . Well I don't think so . . . You write . . . and I'll ring . . . that's a promise?

[*Sound of domestic destruction. Faster bicycle on gravel.*]

2 MOTHER   Subtle wasn't he? . . . A twelve speed racer and a Piss off . . . I hate your mother . . . I'm shacking up with some slut . . . I'll introduce you later sort of thing . . . Don't look at me like that . . . It's not my fault . . . I'm not the one who's been screwing around . . . I'm not running out on you . . . I'll still be here . . . Washing, and cleaning and cooking and working now . . . I'll be working now . . . To keep you in the style to which you're accustomed . . . Yeah! . . . I'm bitter . . . I'm sorry . . . but how can you know what I'm talking about? . . . at your age . . . What do you know about bitterness . . . twelve years . . . That's how old you are isn't it? . . . Twelve years . . . You . . . Yes . . . You . . . One of life's accidents really . . .

[*Sound of domestic destruction. F/X bicycle. Continuous run on road. Traffic passing.*]

3 SISTER   Wasn't much of a surprise was it? . . . I'm glad really . . . They've been kicking lumps out of each other for years . . . I can't remember when there was ever a day they didn't scream at each other . . . I can't remember a day when there was peace . . . Why do people marry? . . . Why do they have kids? . . . Well I'm leaving soon . . . Thank God! University! Freedom! I won't have to hear mum going on and on about what a sod he is . . . It's so boring . . . So you'll be on your own . . . with Mum of course . . . At least there won't be the arguing . . . Silence and space . . . Air to breathe . . . lots of it . . . You're lucky really . . . Tell you what . . . You can come up and see me at college . . . Oh but you'll be at school won't you . . . And I've only got a small room in a hall of residence . . . So you can't stay for more than a

day . . . but then it's a long way isn't it . . . it's a long way by train . . . Perhaps Dad could run you up when he's not working . . . When is he ever not working? . . . I'll write . . . Yeah . . . I'll write . . . Remember . . . we're in this together . . . brother and sister . . . Nice bike . . . Bet it cost him!

[*F/X approaching and skidding to a stop.*]
[*Sound of domestic destruction.*]
[*Telephone actuality.*]

4 FATHER   Yeah . . . I'm sorry your Mum isn't in . . . I had something to tell her . . . I needed to talk . . . Well . . . Look you'll do . . . You had to find out in the end . . . I'm sorry . . . God! I'm always apologising . . . Well I am sorry . . . It's . . . It's . . . When you're older you'll understand . . . course you will . . . you'll understand . . . I promise . . . You've got to believe me . . . I'll come to the point then . . . This holiday we'd planned . . . well we'd only talked about it . . . It didn't really get beyond the discussion stage . . . Something's come up . . . I really argued . . . but no can do son . . . I've sent you something . . . in the post . . . Nancy helped me choose it . . . I hope you like it . . . and there's always next time eh? . . . I promise . . . So you'll tell your mum . . . I reckon she'll be pleased . . . Reckon she likes having you around . . . I'm sorry . . .

[*Telephone hung up.*]
[*Sound of domestic destruction.*]
[*Telephone.*]

5 MOTHER   The bastard . . . the bastard . . . I've always told you . . . Now you know . . . Proof! . . . You know why he's done this don't you? . . . To get at me . . . He's screwed me up for 18 years . . . and he's not giving up now . . . Did you tell him I was going on this course? If you did I'll bloody well teach you . . . You tell that bastard nothing do you hear me . . . Not a bloody word . . . What I do . . . who I see . . . It's my life now . . . I owe that pig nothing! . . . Nothing! . . . . What excuse was it this time? Something to do with work . . . God the times I've heard that . . . Why doesn't he just tell you the truth . . . Bonking Nancy in Tenerife is more important than spending a few days with you. He's probably bonking somebody else . . . Nancy won't last long . . . Some father you've got there mate . . . Well you listen to me . . . I'm going on this course . . . You can fend for yourself . . . Be a big boy and all that crap eh? It's about time men learned to cook for themselves . . . Anyway I'll sort it out when I get in . . . I'm going to be late . . . Put one of those packets in the microwave . . . don't forget to do your homework . . . and . . . I'm sorry . . .

[*Telephone hung up.*]

[*Sound of domestic destruction.*]

[*Telephone.*]

[*Sounds like she's at some sort of party, she's tipsy and a man is tickling her to leave the phone.*]

6 SISTER   Hi! It's me . . . How you doing! I'm great thank you . . . I shan't ask about mum . . . Not in the mood . . . [*To boyfriend*] Ow! Get off . . . I'm on the phone . . . [*To brother*] Bet you can't wait to leave home eh? God, University's really great . . . You wait and see . . . only six more years . . . What I want to say is this . . . Um . . . I know I said I was coming and that . . . but we've ah . . . we've got this field trip on and I can't really say no . . . I'm sure you understand . . . and anyway me and mum will just start shouting so you'll have a bit of peace and quiet . . . Oh but Mum's away isn't she . . . I forgot . . . Well then more peace and quiet . . . [*Giggling in reaction to her boyfriend's tickling*] . . . Yeah . . . this is not funny I suppose . . . but I'm sorry . . . I've got to go . . . What's that you said? . . . OK . . . I'm sorry . . .

[*Telephone hung up.*]

[*Sound of domestic destruction.*]

[*As though writing a postcard: town traffic.*]

7 MOTHER   Thought I'd send you a postcard of Cambridge. Course going well. Lots of interesting things going on. Will be ringing tonight of course, but hope this card will give some idea of where I am . . . Oh . . . I've run out of room . . . Much . . . there's nowhere for the love . . . I'll just scribble Mum near the address . . . I'm sure he'll understand . . .

[*Sound of domestic destruction.*]

[*Tapping on word processor.*]

8 FATHER   This is the latest model and I am tapping this message on it . . . Hope you like it . . . Computers are the way ahead and Nancy and me thought you deserved something special for . . . well . . . you know . . . [*To himself*] I'll delete 'for' . . . just leave it as something special . . . Ah . . . Oh yes . . . Much love Dad . . . [*To himself*] Now just tap it and save it . . . Shit . . . I've lost the last line . . . Christ the time . . . It'll have to do . . . [*Shouting*] I'm coming Nancy . . . Won't be a moment . . . Just packing the bloody apology! Kids! Who wants them?

9 SISTER   My brother . . . Well . . . I don't know him really . . . He doesn't know me . . . There's six years between us . . . I reckon Mum and Dad didn't exactly plan him . . . one of those accidents . . . We've never really got on . . . You see I think the reason it was so bad . . . specially in the last six years . . . was because of him . . . They felt they had to keep things going . . . And didn't they just . . . Like he was some sort of foam . . .

smothering all the heat and warmth . . . Our family . . . like an empty quarry . . . An ugly great scar and he's somewhere there playing about on the broken stones and kicking an old rusty can . . . That's how I see him . . . When I say love . . . I don't feel I mean it . . . He did go out didn't he? Course he did . . . Wouldn't want him to hear what I'm saying . . . I'm sorry I'm going on like this . . . Did you hear a noise . . . I thought I heard something . . . OK . . . I'm sorry . . .

[*End.*]

Part V

Constructing the radio drama/ documentary feature

Chapter 19

The phantom
distinction

Reality is not, reality always has to be discovered and conquered.

(Paul Celan)[1]

A superficial truth is one of which the contrary is not true. A profound truth, on the other hand, is one of which the contrary is also true.

(Niel Bohr, founder of modern quantum physics)[2]

Indeed documentary is drama, we think.

(Kees Vlaanderen, NOS radio documentary editor)[3]

Lance Sieveking asserted that the feature programme is 'an arrangement of sounds which has a theme but no plot'.[4] The head of the legendary BBC Radio Features Department, Lawrence Gilliam, offered this description of the 'radio feature':

> a combination of the authenticity of the talk with the dramatic force of a play, but unlike the play, whose business is to create dramatic illusion for its own sake, the business of the feature is to convince the listener of the truth of what it is saying, even though it is saying it in dramatic form.[5]

Shaun MacLoughlin in his book on *Writing for Radio* (1998) says the feature is:

> anything from a five minute report on the chicken industry, recorded on location, to an open ended Dominican Debate on the Existence of God on Radio Three . . . a creative piece of writing and production, where the elements do not consist solely of scripted drama as we traditionally understand them. Very often, as in the form called 'drama documentary' or 'faction', they will be constructed out of fact, rather than out of fiction.[6]

Paddy Scannell presented a short paper to the Prix Italia symposium on the radio documentary in June 1996 in Naples. These are some of the points he made which might be helpful. First, a special research unit was set up at BBC headquarters in 1928 (Savoy Hill, London) with the purpose of researching, creating and experimenting. The BBC regarded the radio feature as a source of original expression unique to the radio medium. Second, the emphasis was on the aesthetic qualities of 'radiogenic' expression. The Victorian notion of 'art for art's sake' encouraged an exploration of the avant-garde through voice, music and sound.[7]

According to Lawrence Gilliam, the features unit 'first formed part of the BBC Drama Department under Val Gielgud, to whose support and critical faculty it owed much from its beginnings'.[8] An examination of the output of BBC Radio in 1998 and 1999 yields the interesting observation that a considerable range of programming defined as 'drama' is in fact a complex creative mixture of documentary, drama documentary, and faction. This is certainly true of a production called *From Salford to Jericho* by Kate Rowland on homelessness in Manchester, which was broadcast on the 9 to 10 p.m. 'new radio drama slot' on BBC Radio 4 in 1998. The montage of documentary monologues acquired through actuality interview with poetry by Simon Armitage and the multilayered use of music did not distinguish the fictional from the factual. Its total effect was poetic.[9] Its intrinsic component included the real.

A similar creative dynamic was established in the BBC production of Len Deighton's novel *Bomber* in 1995. The story of the final mission of RAF Lancaster bomber WF 183 (call sign O – Orange) which took place one night in 1943 became the documentary story of all the many men and women – British and German – whose lives were irrevocably changed by that night's bombing raid. The result was intriguing and culturally resonating. The acting performances of Tom Baker (narrator), Frank Windsor, Samuel West, Emma Chambers and Jack Shepherd in dramatic dialogue were juxtaposed with moving and authentic interviews with veterans.

The broadcast in eight half-hours was scheduled to equate with the real life chronology of a 24-hour sequence in the life of a bomber crew and the lives of people in a market garden town in Germany which experiences the horrors of 'carpet bombing'. Transmission on a Sunday on BBC Radio 4 with the resulting interruption of an existing and normally fixed broadcast schedule was also ground breaking. By escaping from the straitjacket of habitual listening Radio 4 had disrupted expectation and excited anticipation.

This was a production which combined outstanding creative talent and achievement. From the script by Joe Dunlop to the direction and production by Adrian Bean and Jonathan Ruffle, a powerful range of dramatic values was engaged to elicit a significant response from the audience. Other people deserving credit for this highly significant radio drama event are the then editor of series and serials, Marilyn Imrie, the then Head of BBC Radio Drama, Caroline Raphael, and the then controller of BBC Radio 4, Michael Green. It is remarkable that it did not win any of the entertainment industry's awards in Britain and was not entered by the BBC in any international awards. A close analysis of its content results in the incontrovertible conclusion that this was not 'pure drama' but drama 'feature' because of the presentation of 'recollected reality' through documentary interview.

The definition of the radio feature by practitioners varies according to whether there is political-economic agenda or an aesthetic one. At a radio documentary festival in Amsterdam in 1995, BBC features maker John Theocharis said: 'The importance of the radio documentary as a form of the art of radio is increasingly obvious when our ears are constantly attacked by trash and meaningless noise.'

Another political observation was made by Piers Plowright, whose international reputation in features production is very high: 'We have to say to the bosses: in the end, if you allow us to be imaginative you'll get more listeners because listeners are getting fed up with children's food. They want something stronger.'[10]

In his Prix Italia talk Paddy Scannell went on to explain that the crash of 1929 and the economic and political insecurity of the 1930s spawned the actuality based features where constituent parts involved taking the microphone out of the studio into 'real life'. He said: 'a purely aesthetic concern with radio for its own sake was increasingly difficult to sustain as the clamour of the times grew louder'. He cited the transformation of eyewitness first-hand accounts of social conditions by commissioned commentators or by staff commentators to 'a new style of social reportage' of bringing twelve people to the microphone to provide authentic accounts of their experience of the dole.

Some selected feature-making landmarks and key British radio feature makers[11]

Lance Sieveking

Sieveking worked during the 1920s and 1930s; despite considerable research it would appear that original feature broadcasts prior to 1933–4 have not been preserved for archiving. This means that Sieveking's radiogenic experiments are available only in scripts. Some of his drama scripts were published in *The Stuff of Radio*.[12] He also included script representations of what he described as 'Plays too purely radio for reading'.[13] They are derived from the productions *Kaleidoscope I*, *Kaleidoscope II*, *The End of Savoy Hill*, *The Pursuit of Pleasure* and *Love*. In 1931 Sieveking produced *Crisis in Spain*, a creative mixture of telephone and radio ambiences to dramatise the abdication of the Spanish king. It was described at the time of broadcast as the 'first English example of the reporting in radio form of contemporary events'. A recording of this piece seems to have been reproduced in the late 1930s as a training exercise and was played to me by former BBC features producer Bennett Maxwell.

Tyrone Guthrie

The Squirrel's Cage (broadcast 3 June 1929) and *The Flowers Are Not for You to Pick* (1930). Scannell says that *The Squirrel's Cage* 'is usually hailed as one of the first real radio plays'.[14] Drakakis observes: 'Rather than simply reproduce with the aid of verbal imagery a kind of quasi-photographic verisimilitude, Guthrie was drawn towards an exploration of "the purely symphonic possibilities of the medium".'[15]

Louis MacNeice

Christopher Colombus (1942) and *The Dark Tower* (1946) with music by Benjamin Britten. MacNeice highlighted the dramatic function of the radio feature and believed it could go beyond mere documentary journalism: 'The radio feature is a dramatised presentation of actuality but its author should be much more than a rapporteur or a cameraman; he must select his actuality material with great discrimination and then keep control of it so that it subserves a single dramatic effect.'[16]

Dylan Thomas and Douglas Cleverdon

Under Milk Wood (1954). It is not very well known that Cleverdon reproduced the *Play for Voices* for London's commercial radio station Capital Radio in 1982 with the participation of the original narrative voice, Richard Burton. Cleverdon said that the feature 'has no rules determining what can or cannot be done. And though it may be in dramatic form, it has no need of a dramatic plot'.[17]

Lawrence Gilliam

'Opping 'Oliday (15 September 1934). Scannell says that this was the first documentary feature which allowed 'people to speak for themselves', although he qualifies his enthusiasm by concluding that the programme was essentially about the casual Cockney hop-pickers of Kent rather than for them.[18] The representation in this programme can be usefully compared with the creative literary treatment by George Orwell in *A Clergyman's Daughter*.[19] I would argue that Orwell's phonetic dialogue representation arises out of the modernist inspiration of radiophonic expression.

D. G. Bridson

March of the 45 (February 1936), *Aaron's Field* (1939), described by Drakakis as a 'highly politicised verse Morality play',[20] and *The Christmas Child* (1948). Bridson is responsible for the first example of what I have been able to establish as a positive representation of black culture on British radio in a collaboration with the Harlem poet Langston Hughes. *The Man Who Went to War* was produced in the USA for broadcast to Britain in 1943. Bridson said: 'it was quite one of the most popular broadcasts I ever had on air, being heard in Britain by nearly ten million listeners on its first transmission alone'.[21]

Archie Harding, Joan Littlewood and Olive Shapley

These worked during the 1930s and 1940s with D. G. Bridson in the Manchester North Region. Harding was effectively exiled to the north by Director General John Reith because of the political storm generated by his feature *New Year Over Europe* (1932), which had included the statement that one-third of Polish income was diverted to funding its Ministry of War. Harding had made a feature called *Western Land* (1930), which dramatised the lives of Cornish fishermen, tin-miners, farmers and flower-growers. He developed the idea of a fictional character travelling through Britain in search of work in a series called *Harry Hopeful* (1935). Bridson worked with Littlewood and Shapley on industrial features *Steel* (1937), *Coal* (17 November 1938), followed by *Cotton* and *Wool* in 1939. The series began to incorporate actuality inserts recorded on location. Olive Shapley made greater use of the Mobile Recording Unit and with Joan Littlewood specialised in covering 'all levels of working-class experience'.[22] The key programmes were *They Speak for Themselves* and *The Classic Soil* (both produced and broadcast in 1939).

From 1950 to 1965

In 1950 the BBC with the London publishers Evans Brothers published *BBC Features*, edited by Lawrence Gilliam. It remains a significant document on BBC Radio feature-making culture. Gilliam paid tribute to the creative contributions of Felix Felton, Herbert Reed (who co-translated Rudolf Arnheim's book, *Radio*, in 1936), Laurie Lee, J. B. Priestley, Elizabeth Bowen and Edward Sackville-West. The book also contained the scripts of features by Hugh Trevor-Roper, *The Last Days of Hitler*; Jennifer Wayne, *British Justice*; Nesta Pain, *The Brain At Work*; and Leonard Cottrell, *The Man from Belsen* (1946 – the first radio documentary on Nazi concentration camp life as seen and experienced by a prisoner). This generation of feature makers bridged the period until the early 1960s, which was marked by the work of Bennett Maxwell and Dennis Mitchell, who developed a genre of cityscape features. The features unit was shut down in 1965.[23]

Charles Parker

Parker worked throughout the 1950s and 1960s, pioneering a genre known as the radio ballad, for example *Singing the Fishing* (BBC Third Programme 1960, winning the Prix Italia in that year). Parker was based in Birmingham and worked closely with the folk composer and singer Ewan McColl and musical director Peggy Segar. *Singing the Fishing* was described as a radio ballad of three generations of the herring fishermen, told by Sam Larner of Winterton, Ronnie Balls of Yarmouth, George Draper of Lowestoft and Frank West of Gardenstown. Charles Parker's radio ballads set up a special tradition in the investigation of working-class life through the radio feature and folk music. Other landmark programmes include *The Ballad of John Axon, Song of a Road, The Big Hewer, The Body Blow, On the Edge, The Flight Game* and *The Travelling People*. A Charles Parker archive is held in the Archives Department, Central Reference Library, Chamberlain Square, Birmingham. The archive is owned by the Charles Parker Trust and holds some 5,000 tapes, his files, papers and a library of books on folk culture, music and politics. A BBC Radio 4 *Radio Lives* documentary on Charles Parker (produced and broadcast in 1993) revealed that the main inspiration for Parker's use of folk music came from listening to a tape of Norman Corwin's CBS drama-documentary on the death and funeral of Franklin D. Roosevelt in 1944.

Piers Plowright

Still making radio features and programmes in his retirement, Plowright has maintained a powerful and compelling track record in the traditional radio feature tradition. There is a need to document and analyse his work in greater depth. In 1992 Goldsmiths MA Drama student Susan Dietrich wrote a thesis on his collaboration with Ronald Hayman on Tennessee Williams and New Orleans. The much acclaimed feature *A Bus Named Desire* was broadcast on BBC Radio 3 in 1992. Other Plowright features worthy of further study include *One Big Kitchen Table* (BBC Radio 3, May 1988) and *Setting Sail* (BBC Radio 3, 1988). In the late 1990s Plowright worked closely with Alan Hall on a range of features, the most notable being an item on the blues pianist Jimmy Yancey in the BBC Radio 3 series *Between the Ears* (27 February 1999).

Peter Everett

Everett, who has generously contributed his views on features making to this section, devised a pioneering series called *Soundtrack* for BBC Radio 4 in 1983, which continued under his editorship for five years. It was the first Radio 4 strand dedicated to montage-style features. The programmes had to be radiogenic.

Other notable contemporary BBC features makers include John Theocharis, Mark Burman, Alan Hall, Bella Bannerman, Matt Thompson, Richard Bannerman, Brian King, Sarah Rowlands and Alby James. Alan Hall won a Prix Italia for the BBC feature *Knoxville: Summer of 1995*.

Some European landmarks

Walter Luigi Ruttmann's *Weekend* (broadcast by Berlin radio 14 June 1930) is regarded as one of the key moments in the development of the creative 'radio feature'. Ruttmann actually called it 'radio drama on sound film'. It was in fact a sound montage of about 11 minutes using 228 different segments of sound, some created in the studio, but most recorded on location. In 11 minutes he had recorded and mixed in a musical rhythm a representation of life over two days. The sound editing that recording sound on optical film had given him allowed maximum artificiality while preserving a series of realistic impressions. German feature production was revolutionised in the post-war period by Peter Leonhard Braun through the use of portable stereo recording machines. German documentary makers describe this development as 'the emancipation of original sound'. Key features by Braun included *Chickens* (1967), *Operating Theatre Number 3* (1970), *Hyenas* (1972) and *Bells in Europe* (1973).

Italian documentary feature production was developed as a result of acoustic editing experiments by Aldo Salvo. *La luna nel pozzo* (1947) presented an audio picture of life in an asylum for the 'insane'.

Making radio features

Scannell debated why features are made:[24]

1 Programme makers make programmes for themselves, resonant of the nineteenth-century Romantic Movement.
2 Features are made for those who are the subjects of the programme: the democratic impulse and transferring authorship from programme maker to programme participant.
3 Features are made for radio audiences: Scannell defines this as the social role of the professional broadcaster in relation to society. He is somewhat idealistic about this third notion being essential to making programmes which 'care for listeners'.

Some light can be shed on the art of radio feature/documentary production by considering the theoretical and critical analysis of the film and television documentary. Bill Nichols in his seminal text *Representing Reality: Issues and*

Concepts in Documentary (1991) established helpful definitions of documentary representation.[25]

1 Expository text: voices which address the audience directly. Arguing, questioning and analysing in a process of commentary where illustrative imagery is presented in linear and chronological flow. There is a logical cause and effect perspective between the sequences used and events presented. The climax or dramatic resolution is constructed around a solution to the essential problem or question raised by the programme.

2 Observational text: a process of production which is characterised by the non-intervention of the programme maker or author. There is an absence of commentary and a reluctance to use images as illustrative generalisations. The process of editing is designed to present an impression of real life. Juxtaposition and recurring images and situations are designed to communicate an impression of unfettered access and unmediated construction of an individual or community. It must be realised that this genre is observational in style and not necessarily observational in purpose and construction.

3 Interactive text: the programme maker or author interacts with the observation or enregistrement of the programme's theme or subject. There is clear evidence of partiality. Interviews are conducted to provide evidence for the author's argument. The genre concedes that programme makers are as much social actors as the people they make programmes about. The text addresses the ethical and political debate about the power relationship in media between programme maker and subject.

4 Reflexive text: this programme centres on the process of representation by analysing how the programme makers address and represent the world rather than reporting about the world. It employs stylistic devices to highlight the pleasures of form and signification, limitations of time and space, the constructed image and the way interviewees or 'social actors' are signifiers, and the sociological functions of text.

Nichols observes: 'The sense of vicarious transport into the historical world doubles back on the trail of representation itself.'[26]

An interesting and modern definition of the radio feature has been offered by one of its most elegant contemporary craftsmen. Peter Everett, former BBC Network Radio Editor in Bristol, responded to Sieveking and Gilliam's definitions:

These are neat descriptions of the radio feature as it existed up until the fifties, i.e. a research-based 'factual' or 'illustrative' script interpreted (usually) by actors. Things then became more complicated. I've certainly heard (and made) features that had a 'plot', and I've made features where my intention was to convince the listener that what they heard being 'said' was a load of cobblers.

We could try a broader definition, something like 'The radio feature is a creative arrangement of sound taken from real life.' But even that has exceptions, now I come to think of it. My own working definition is: 'On the spectrum of radio programmes that extends from drama to news, the feature occupies the bit in the middle.'[27]

There is an advantage in looking more deeply at Lawrence Gilliam's reflections on the nature and function of the radio feature when the form had its own BBC department and seemed to be in its heyday in the 1950s. Gilliam's personal deconstruction of the feature was in the overall context that 'feature' equated with entertainment or storytelling feature in cinema. The bill in cinema was defined by long and short features. Gilliam's definition depended for its framework on six principles:

1 A feature is the expression of one mind whatever the nature of the technique of production.
2 A feature is an authorial statement through radio with the greatest force, coherence, emotional and dramatic impact available to the medium. Gilliam claimed that it was 'pure radio, a new instrument for the creative writer and producer'.
3 A radio feature is under a compulsion to make listeners feel as well as think.
4 It entertains listeners as well as informs them, therefore there is a tendency to use the dramatised statement instead of a spoken statement.
5 It combines the authority of the talk with the dramatic force of a play.
6 Unlike a play, its business is to convince the listener of the truth of what it is saying even though the form is dramatic.

As Scannell has observed, a defining moment in the development of the radio feature was the transformation from mimetic representations of sound to 'photographing' sound by recording actuality on location. This gives rise to Gilliam's seventh law of radio features:

7 It gives shape to the stuff of reality by imposing the discipline and pattern of a form under the control of one creative mind.[28]

In the final section of the 1950 volume *BBC Features* Gilliam sets out some of the key *modus operandi* of radio feature production.

1 Feature elements: script, sound, music and voices are common to all.
2 Scripting comes in two forms:
    (a) outside commissioned writer.
    (b) written by producer.
3 The writer-producers are more common and effective.
4 Research is the starting point through libraries and interviews. Gilliam

observed: 'The search for material, the living contact with what he is writing about, is the heart of the matter.'

5 Composer is briefed immediately and set to work on any musical collaboration. Gilliam stated, as a creative objective, 'mirror the true inwardness of its subject, to explore the boundaries of sound'.

6 Planning and evaluation through lists, tests and recordings of likely and unlikely voices and sounds. Gilliam asserted: 'take the enquiring mind, the alert ear . . . and the recording microphone into every corner of the contemporary world, or into the deepest recesses of experience.'

7 Auditioning of actors for appropriate casting.

8 Prioritising of authentic first-hand information. Primary sources, not secondary sources. Gilliam said: 'Good documentary brushes aside secondary sources, dismisses the hearsay witness.'

9 Scriptwriting and then into studio production.

The feature production formula was summarised in this way:

Idea——Research——Script
Actors——Sound effects——Music
Research——Writing——Production

Final objectives? Gilliam mentioned perfecting 'techniques for the use of creative artists in broadcasting', establishing a 'true experience of deep significance communicated by radio art' and ensuring that 'the true character and flavour of the material shall permeate all that comes after in the writing and production'.

The 1950s was a golden age for British radio features and those elsewhere in Europe. In France General Charles de Gaulle was directing public radio policy on the basis of raising 'standards of taste, entertaining without vulgarity, and educating without boring the listeners'. In a country with 10 million households paying a licence fee, state radio channels were broadcasting ambitious plays, challenging documentaries and academic lectures. Even Radio Luxembourg was broadcasting *Vous avez vécu cela*, which was a popular historical drama documentary covering such themes as the Warsaw Uprising, the assassination of Leon Trotsky in Mexico and the Turkish revolution of Mustafa Kemal Atatürk.

A trend in Britain in the 1990s and into the new century has been the concept of the audio-vérité and the audio-diary. The first genre, which has been applied with considerable resources by Pebble Mill (Birmingham) producers Brian King and Sarah Rowlands, has sought to construct powerful narrative through 'fly on the wall' audio recordings in specific institutions and professional fields. The development of the small, portable, tough recorder which offers dependable digital quality has in some respects shifted and transformed the relationship between broadcasters and listeners.

The audio-vérité genre developed by King and Rowlands is an example where the programme makers have held on to their power. They have negotiated access to a secondary modern school, hospital, airport, university or general practitioner's surgery to record as much as they can over a specific period to provide a narrative picture of the life and experiences of people involved. The method of recording allocation varied from surveillance in reception areas, tapping of telephones used by key characters such as receptionists and secretaries and roving producer microphones on booms. One early discovery was that the telephone occupied a dimension of dramatic and crucial communication in everyday lives which had not been fully appreciated before. The acute level of drama was explored in a documentary that I produced for LBC in 1984 about a gangland kidnapping in London where threats, ransom demands and life and death negotiations were recorded on the telephone. That particular programme was not experimental in form although in the telephone sequences, the captivating and voyeuristic engagement of the listener in hearing something normally closed off and secret was compelling.

It was quite clear that the dramatic element in the BBC audio-vérité series was clearly engaged by the producers during a seminar at the 1991 Radio Academy Festival in Birmingham. Both King (who had begun his radio documentary career at the commercial Birmingham station BRMB) and Rowlands described how a sequence in which a GP expressed her feelings into her microphone after confirming that a husband had died from a heart attack in front of his wife in their living room was actually recorded two or three days after the incident. It transpired that the emergency call by the wife to the surgery was recorded as a matter of course and the sound of the exchange with the doctor was dramatic. But the GP's entry into the home was not 'actuality recorded' on ethical grounds. Her moving account of the events in the house was simulated, even though the programme makers assured the seminar that they had been reproduced as a performance to reflect her feelings at the time. Here was an interesting situation where the experienced GP was being asked to dramatically 'perform' her life.

BBC Radio pioneered and supported the audio-diary form throughout the 1990s, which it can be argued had the result of empowering the subjects even further because their use of the portable technology was unsupervised although directed and suggested. A wide social range of people who never thought of themselves as reporters or journalists have been encouraged to record their activities for the mass audience. The effect is vivid and refreshing. The audio documentary or feature form enters aspects of people's lives never recorded and amplified before.

The earliest exponent of the non-professional broadcaster/reporter was the mountaineer Chris Bonington, who took a small Nagra recorder with him during his climb of Mount Everest. Ordinary people undertaking the adventures of a lifetime were equipped with professional recording technology and the producers waited at Broadcasting House for their 'prodigal sons and daughters' of radio feature making to return with the source material. The extent to which shaping and control had to be relinquished after that point is a matter for further debate and discussion.

211

BBC features editor Richard Bannerman and producer Bella Bannerman deserve credit for extending the self-empowerment of reporting to more humble areas of the human experience where people are not setting out to conquer the world. The BBC rightly extended the opportunity for self-expression to marginalised and underrepresented individuals, the apparently uneducated, low disposable income citizens who do not populate the elites of society. A series entitled *Take the Plunge* dramatised through personal actuality recordings a Suffolk couple who decided to move to a primitive cottage in rural Ireland to escape creeping urbanisation, a disabled young girl wishing to obtain a place at university and the supervisor on a car assembly line who wished to become a priest.

Chapter 20

Making the documentary feature

Idea and subject matter

When things go wrong it normally has something to do with a lack of focus and in journalistic terms 'not having the story'. You cannot be a good radio producer, radio/sound artist or drama producer/director without being a good journalist. Good journalists recognise a good story and an interesting idea which is going to excite an audience.

Features provide the background and human spirit or colour to what has gone on and what is going on in the world. They explore social issues, the environment, lifestyle, leisure, ideas in the arts and philosophy. Whatever you do, the subject has to be interesting. If it is not, then your listeners switch off and you have failed in your purpose of being a programme maker.

Australian radio documentary maker Jane Ulmann said: 'To make a good radio documentary you need: passion, commitment, skill from the programme maker and the desire to communicate.' American creative feature maker Gregory Whitehead said: 'The most important thing is an idea, the passion, the willingness to follow the idea to its conclusions and perhaps a razor blade to cut your throat when you find out how much you're going to get paid.'[1]

German radio documentary maker Helmut Kopetzky believes that the competition between strong opinions is a vital and driving force in feature programmes. The presence of opinion may be the central backbone of the programme maker's presence. He observed: 'the virtue of being subjective, decisive, and radical in an intellectual sense. It means making your point in a distinctive, unmistakable personal manner, in your special "tone," including a certain amount of good humour.' In his presentation to the 1996 Naples symposium on radio documentary he said that 'provoking discussions should be a self-evident goal of media professionals . . . Radio is and always will be the narrative medium par excellence, the story teller of the media family'.[2]

Radio features have to be about people

Human characters are the essence of successful communication. If your people are not interesting and not saying something interesting whatever the subject, your feature or programme will fail.

Sounds

The feature or programme insert has to justify itself by taking the listener's imagination out of the studio into interesting and intriguing sound environments. You should be thinking about the sounds that you are going to use to deliver pictures aurally. You want to determine atmosphere, mood, sense of location and excite the listener's imagination. Think of your microphone as a television camera for blind people. Capture sound pictures of scenes which you can use to illustrate your piece. Think how sounds are iconic and symbolic. Collect them in relation to your subject. Always consider recording bits of linking script on location. Keep these short and open-ended or flexible so they can be used in different parts of your feature. Remember to record 1–2 minute sequences of useful wildtrack which is relevant to the subject. If you record interviews on location use the location ambience meaningfully. An interview with background traffic sounds similar to any location.

Represent action by recording a 'running commentary'. This involves describing an event taking place before your eyes. It is difficult but the general trick is to keep talking and continue describing everything that you see. Editing later can make the material meaningful. Another option is to invite your interviewee to have a go at describing the event or object.

Preparation and research

This has to be thorough and effective. You should not embark on any feature project without first writing it out clearly as a story. If this is not interesting, logical and effective, your feature will fail.

- Who are you going to interview and how much of each interviewee do you plan to use?
- What sounds are you going to use and why are you going to use them?
- Never interview anyone without knowing what they can say to be included in your package or feature.

The ideal structure of a short feature will have three or four speakers plus actuality and/or vox pops. At least one of your speakers should be worth at least two inserts.

Interviewing tips

1 Tell your interviewee the purpose of the feature and that the interview will be edited and used in a programme piece with other material.
2 Stop interviewees reading pre-prepared scripts.
3 Keep quiet and avoid interruptions if you want clear and well-constructed answers.
4 If your interviewee does not provide what you want, ask and cajole with courtesy and guidance until you get it.
5 Keep a clear idea of the length of interviewee inserts that you will need so that the sound bites you acquire have the right rhythm and length.

Structure is everything

You have to be ruthless. You have to have a great beginning and a great end. Then in the middle you have to have a momentum of interest and excitement through unfolding human character, storytelling and conflict. Each link and insert should raise key questions/cliff hangers that listeners want answered.

If you are using the continuous stream of consciousness technique, your interviewing should be designed to do what a narrative link would do. Insert clips should not be longer than 30 seconds and certainly no longer than 45 seconds. Links should deftly dovetail with actuality/interview clips. They should identify sounds, voices and speakers. The link must not repeat the content of a clip or actuality and vice versa.

You can mix the style occasionally, but not fundamentally. So it is acceptable to start with a link which identifies the following speaker and then continue with a speaker who identifies himself/herself, particularly if you are setting up a binary relationship.

Basic rules of structure

1 Do not mix styles.
2 Do not fail with either your beginning or end.
3 Do not tell two or three stories when you should be telling one.
4 Starting with wildtrack and actuality is time honoured but effective. It takes the listener out of the studio and can cross-fade with your opening link.
5 Montage establishing mood, voices of participants, crisis of issue and conflict is also time honoured, but useful. The danger is that your opening montage may be so good that nothing after it will be as effective and the listener will be left disappointed and dissatisfied.

6 Symmetry between beginning and end is important.

7 Repetition of something in different ways is a mnemonic oral tradition and musical device: it does have its uses.

8 If you are using an opening link, it should tell the listener where you are and what the story is. You are also establishing yourself as the reporter/producer. You have to win the listeners here and make them want to listen to the rest of the programme. You are selling yourself and your programme.

9 The structure must flow logically and match the points you have set out to make or answer the questions you have posed at the beginning.

10 Tension and drama need to be maintained and driven on in your programme.

Two participants: create conflict/binary/ping pong arrangement of voices.

Pros and cons: set up arguments for and against; with supporters and detractors.

Three participants: set up/struggle/resolution.

11 Use logical pick-up from the back of each insert to go on to the next point and clip.

12 Vary the length of links and inserts from anything as short as a few seconds to anything as long as 40–45 seconds.

Script

The script must be polite and spoken English and must tell the listener the story. Do not leave this to your clips if you are mixing the styles of communication. Journalistic etiquette and professionalism require that you do not present yourself as the expert on the subject matter of your report. Allow the listener to 'learn' with you. The listener will respect you as you unfold your experts, authorities and victims.

What to leave out

There is always a problem of leaving out rather than not having enough to put in. Time limitation is the discipline you must come to terms with. Everything has to be simple and brief. There is no room for including anything which is not essential to make sense of the story.

Linear and lateral structures

Linear structures work when there is a logical pick-up and the programme develops on the basis of questions asked, issues raised, questions answered and issues resolved. Lateral structures work when listeners are not allowed to forget the subplots in time and dimension and they all link up together at the end so that there is clear reason and purpose for the lateral narratives.

Divergence

Avoid similar voices or clustering. In radio widely divergent and rich, powerful or resonant voices help distinguish character and build vocal/personality texture.

Music

Only use music which is purposeful and which the listener will understand as being a relevant component or aspect of the feature. Avoid vocals or chorus music as beds or background to voice actuality and interview. Keep volume/decibel ratio vastly in favour of voice: five to one or four to one only in exceptional circumstances. As there is a closer relationship between hearing and emotional impact than between seeing and emotional impact, music is fundamental to an experience of feeling in any programme. It has also been observed that sudden deafness has a greater tendency to bring on confusion, disorientation and paranoia than sudden blindness. If the emotional fluidity of sound can be so powerful in these contexts then the most emotional expression of sound, music, needs to be moulded and layered as if it has the devastating psychological force of plastic explosive. Music can be used as counterpoint or to strike up a sobering contrast. It can be the backdrop of an emotional canvas. It can push the emotional experience of the listener to the very extremes of pathos. Music has the ability to expand a theme into a more universal dimension.[3]

If in doubt leave it out

First instinct should be trusted. Do not allow your ego and post-anxiety rational justification to blind your judgement.

Production process

Record sound components and material which have been ruthlessly researched and planned. Minimise the amount of material recorded. Listen and select ruthlessly only what you will use, then dub on to reel-to-reel tape or mini-disc/ CDs into files. The reel-to-reel source must be banded, i.e. yellow bands cut between inserts. Establish two feed machines for analogue mixing:

- Reel/mini-disc for interview/actuality inserts.
- Reel/mini-disc for links, which can also be done live. This is advantageous since the mental attitude and emotion of the presenter will pick up on the content more effectively.
- Music or sound effects CD/reel-to-reel/cassette source machine for atmosphere/spot effects. It is better to use a remote operation if you can.

Multi-track on a digital programme requires the same discipline of banding and a completed script and production plan before you should go anywhere near a computer system.

Breaking the rules

Break the rules only after you have followed them and know why they normally work. Experimentation and challenging orthodoxy stir the listener and are normally refreshing only for a short period. Bear in mind that experimentation with style should not be at the expense of content.

Common mistakes made by people making their first features

While everyone can be impressed with ambition and the extent of mental creativity, students are often let down by a lack of common sense in planning and in matching existing skills with resources.

Think before you run with a 5 kg load of ordnance on your back and no background of fitness training.

If you are going to do something that requires scripting, sort out the script first before you begin to organise Soho/Hollywood multi-track consoles and digital stations and unlimited use of sound effects, music and a cast the size of *Les Misérables*.

Common sense, common sense and common sense: demonstrate noble creativity in simplicity. It is the most difficult thing to achieve in human communication and art. And there is another thing . . . listeners respect and appreciate humanity and truth, not sophistication and multifarious interweaving of narrative directions.

Deliver humanity and some nobility in your features. If your feature/ programme is supposed to be a *maximum* length of 6 minutes, then 6 minutes it must be. Avoid artifice and self-indulgence even though well intentioned.

Think realistically

1 What can I do in three weeks with a portable Marantz and microphone, a chrome dioxide tape 15 minutes on each side and access on the days available within the existing studio resources and staffing levels?
2 What can I achieve with the existing skills that I have?
3 What can I achieve with the range of actors or voices I could bring to the project considering the people I know on the course and elsewhere, and the budget I might have for freelance actors?
4 How much time do I need to record the components if they have to be recorded in the studio?
5 How long would I need a portable recording kit for?
6 Since my mixing will be analogue using the existing consoles available with two or three pre-recorded sources i.e. two reel-to-reel tape machines and a CD, to what extent do I need to plan what I know I am capable of doing?
7 In a range of 4–6 minutes if I interview three people and I use three 30-second excerpts from each interview, that already makes up 4 minutes 30 seconds of sound and is without music, link narrative and any other illustrative sounds. Perhaps I can make more calculations in relation to other lengths.
8 In relation to digital operations, can I maximise the efficiency of my time at the multi-track editing station by pre-producing my banded source material and organising my sound design?

Peter Everett's guidelines

Retired BBC Radio features editor Peter Everett has contributed some recommendations and advice on feature making.[4] They could be described as the radio feature's 'Confucian Analects'. I have added observations and clarification.

Idea

• An idea is a story plus a treatment. Quite apart from telling an interesting story you must have a production plan to turn the narrative into radio listening. Everett says that the difference between an idea and a treatment can be shown by the fact that the feature *You'll Never be 16 Again* would be presented as: 'Story – the history of the British teenager since the war. Treatment – interviews over pop music and some archive.'

- What's the billing? Who are the stars of the feature?
- Be ruthless about irrelevance. You must edit out anything that does not add to or enhance the central story.
- Structure – thematic or chronological? Is the unfolding of your story on a time-line or linked directly to the subject? Everett says that a chronological structure can create problems when the actual story starts further back than the programme material collected.
- Duration? The same point can be applied to drama as well. As an experiment in improving this technique you should continually look at minimalist methods of telling your story. How much can you remove to leave the barest skeleton of the story? Everett suggests that a 30-minute feature needs a plot and a 40-minute programme needs a subplot.

Why montage?

Many producers elect montage because it is considered 'more creative' and less traditional and conservative. However, it should be realised that montage is a form more appropriate to an expression of feeling, emotion and culture rather than an analysis of news and current affairs issues.

- Montage is closer to drama than to news.
- Respect the Aristotelian unities. In his *Poetics* Aristotle set out a hierarchy of importance: (1) Plot known as action, story or fable. (2) Character. (3) Thought – generally known as sentiments. (4) Diction – often translated as dialogue. (5) Rhythm – generally regarded as the melody or music of the story. (6) Spectacle – the concept I have coined of 'imaginative spectacle' therefore takes on a different production resonance in the electronic age. During the time of Ancient Greece it was regarded as 'scenic effects'.[5] Everett says that the 'feature programme maker should respect unity of time by constructing a chronological sequence with a start and finish and no major gaps, unity of place by allowing the listener to build up the imagined landscape, and unity of action whereby everything included in the feature should dovetail with the central story or theme'.
- Montage makes the listener think because there are no clues about how to respond.
- Montage can use irony – the complicity of producer and listener.

Everett says: 'It's good to have a subtext, but it is also important not to allow that to interfere with the central story. There has to be a simple, linear "surface level" for the casual listener. It is also relevant to employ the "Brechtian moment", which is deliberately reminding listeners that they are listening to a manipulated radio programme and not unmediated reality.'

Why not montage?

- Factual narrative works better with a script.
- Montage describes how it felt, not why it happened.
- Montage focuses consensus, but does not sharpen controversy.
- Montage aims at vividness, not objectivity.
- Montage draws no conclusions.

Montage

Peter Everett's notes on properly evaluating the need for montage and the essential relationship between form and content in radio feature are enormously helpful. It is also important to take into account theoretical notions of rhetoric in the consideration of the montage form in radio programming. When we consider the verbal material in creative radio programming it is possible to establish three categories:

1 Narrative language: this communicates semantic information with words that serve a symbolic function, anchored in time. The content is referential.
2 Scientific language: this communicates purely factual information. It is the ascetic assertion of definition and does not serve any storytelling, narrative function.
3 Poetic language: this is metaphorical and structured with euphony, rhythm and melody. It is more lateral or spatial rather than linear and chronological.

In feature and drama production the components of sound and language have the potential for metonymic or metaphorical meaning. In a realistic sound recording of a character saying 'There is no glory in war', the language is metonymic. It can be scientific in itself. It can be narrative language if it represents the conclusion of a subject after telling the story of his experiences in a military campaign. It becomes poetic and metaphorical when sampled through a looping and repetitive function on a computer and echoed through reverberation. In the context of Michel Chion's vocabulary of sound design the sound has been 'rendered' with 'added value'.

Research by Goldsmiths MA Radio student Rikke Houd,[6] now producing features for Danish and Swedish Radio, has introduced the translation of 'montage' concepts debated by Danish radio programme makers and theoreticians Kiersten Frandsen and Hanne Bruun.[7]

'Montage' is a specific programming form in Danish radio. In many respects it equates with the British concept of 'feature'. It has the following characteristics:

- Montage is a subjective documentary produced by the radio producer personally.
- It has suggestive and aesthetic styles of expression.
- It records actuality on location which montages the sounds into a pattern or mosaic of recorded experiences.
- It manipulates psychological perception and cognition for symbolic effect. The multidimensional presentation of consciousness and subconsciousness is an example of 'montage' programming.
- The omnipresent or acousmatic voice is avoided to concentrate and focus on self-reflection and inner voice.
- The source material for programming montage is real documentary recordings and symbolic soundscapes and empathetic and anempathetic music to stimulate surrealistic images and feelings within the imaginative spectacle. A short definition could be 'realism in imagination'.

Frandsen and Bruun divide the montage form into two essential categories: temporal and scenographic montage.

Temporal montage

This involves the expression of time transition. The display is not only chronology but also a sense of time feeling. Frandsen and Bruun subdivide temporal montage into the following:

- Elliptic montage: sections of narrated time are omitted thereby leaving the listener to fill the vacuum in the imaginative spectacle and effectively speculate on causal connections.
- Parallel montage: the plaiting together of two sound sequences in real time so that the directions of narrative are parallel and effectively contrapuntal in rhythm and relationship. Small fragments are montaged.
- Polarising montage: the montaging of two conflicting, contradictory directions of communication sometimes striking up a fictional dialogue which creates a resonance of conflict.
- Collage form: the mixing of sound fragments from different thematic sequences and a structuring which is not chronological.

Scenographic montage

This explores in greater depth and creativity the spatialisation of psychological consciousness or 'imaginative spectacle'. It is apposite to the concept of anchoring montage in time sequence. The utilisation of simultaneous and parallel directions of sound narrative is achieved with greater refinement and the sound sources are more 'rendered' creatively. There are three subdivisions:

- Paraphrasing montage: sounds and music are multi-track paralleled with word and function as an interpretation of the verbalisation. Exploration of the stereophonic and surround sound fields in the musical and sound effect directions of narrative contribute to the impact of the 'superfield'.
- Psychological montage: several sounds montaged onto each other to give the impression of inner consciousness. This is a process of establishing inner voice and feelings through sound. The space is purely internal and psychological.
- Polarising montage: this is an echo from the temporal polarising category but in scenographic polarising montage the conflicting sounds are not paralleled, but mixed within each stream of narrative direction. The effect is to make the mixed or montaged sound polysemic.

Peter Everett's guidelines continued

Planning

- Set deadlines and work backwards. Doing now what you intended to leave until tomorrow is a useful motto to follow in complex programme projects. Starting with the last thing you proposed to do means that if you are faithful to your schedule you will always be ahead of yourself.
- Allow time for thinking. The most common mistake I have found with student feature producers is that they take on too much and lack planning or organisational discipline; the helterskelter panic towards the deadline destroys the valuable space needed to reflect and intellectually and creatively enhance a programme's form and content.
- Allow for flexibility ('negative capability').
- Shoot for the moon (but have a Plan B). While walking on the wild side has its creative benefits, there are occasions when people drink too much, slip into the Atlantic currents and are in danger of drowning. This is when a lifebelt and raft come to the rescue. It is 'Plan B'. Every programme maker should have one.
- Separate 'essential' from 'nice-to-have'. The closeness that programme makers have to their material diminishes the strength of objective judgement

in structuring. Something said by an interviewee becomes much loved rather than essential. There has to be a guard-rail against such understandable sentimentality.

Everett says: 'Somebody once told me that when a programme has been a failure you can always see why by looking at the planning stage. I think the best ideas emerge from discussion with colleagues.'

Research

- Become an instant expert. A basic requirement of journalism. Intellectual and scholarly absorption of complex subjects requires concentration and education.
- Cast a wide net. It is vital that the mind is kept open and the range of sources is comprehensive.
- Think laterally about sources. Consider the 'alternative voices' as well as the mainstream axis of authority. Bear in mind that cultural and political discrimination can distort the presentation of reality and history.
- Follow up contacts-via-contacts. This is the essence of original journalistic inquiry and bypasses routes and networks fixed by previous secondary sources.
- Revise and re-shape the idea as you go along. You have to be aware that your original research and persistence could potentially change the focus of your programme.

Everett says: 'I think you need to know enough to know what it is that you need to know. Then you need to know enough to know what you need to get and also what's irrelevant. Having said that the feature programme maker should be cautious of becoming "a know-all" because this has the risk of turning the interviews into footnotes. I think it is important to cast a wide net. I remember when we made a programme about the history of football. We threw our net further back than the middle nineteenth century and beginnings of Association Football and we were therefore able to start vividly in the Middle Ages with the Ashbourne Shrove Tuesday game.'

Ingredients

- Consider the options – archive, music, actuality, readings, film clips, TV clips etc.
- Don't over-egg the pudding. It has been said before in this book that simplicity represents artistic nobility.
- Consider consistency of style and tone. Listeners do not appreciate a phonic mixture of Andy Warhol and Cézanne.

- Avoid the obvious. More creative programming is determined by persistent curiosity about the unusual.
- Make each ingredient work hard. Every programme component needs to have a muscular storytelling and dramatic purpose.

Everett says: 'I think it is vital to avoid fashionable clichés in programme production. I will never forget hearing the *Star Trek* opening theme used three times in one week on BBC Radio 4 and then twice in the same week on television. The producer needs to ask of each programme ingredient: "What is it doing in the programme?" If the answer is merely "making me look clever" then it needs to be junked.'

Contributors

- What is a 'good talker'? A good storyteller. A bright and interesting voice. A character who expresses humanity.
- How expert is your expert? Avoid vacuous pundits and establish the credentials of your informational authority.
- Know what you need before you start. Many programme makers interview people without any sense of purpose.
- Talk first, ask for the interview later. You have an opportunity of identifying strong emotional areas of communication and talking first establishes the ground work for the interviewer–interviewee relationship.
- Don't concede a veto. This can be disastrous and sometimes happens when the friendliness of the ambience and the willingness to please become overwhelming.

Everett says: 'The former controller of BBC Radio 4 once told me: "We don't make programmes about ordinary people. We make programmes about extraordinary people who don't happen to be famous." In my opinion the definition of a good contributor is someone who is a good talker, who talks in pictures and stories, who lacks self-awareness and image-consciousness, who is enthusiastic and engaged, who uses their own words and not someone else's, who talks from the heart and not the ego, who communicates in a uniquely personal way and who is relaxed. Issues and concerns about grammar, accent, vocabulary, pace and hesitation are irrelevant.'

Interviews

- Interviews are not about information. Informational interviews belong to news reporting.
- Consider alternatives to the talking head. Actuality recordings in which

there is dynamic of movement of the subject as well as the environment around the subject generate more interesting radio.

- Record early, keep recording late. Use the time with your subject for gathering material rather than gossiping about irrelevant subjects.
- Work close. Direct to indirect sound produces greater intimacy of human communication.
- Produce the interview – remember you will be cutting the questions. Construct questions in your mind which build the spaces for the interviewee to provide the storytelling blocks or components.
- Provoke emotion. Human passion and feeling is the psychological reason most people stay listening to their radio.
- Record wildtrack. Gives you vital repair material and ambient sound for multi-tracking.

Everett says: 'My general advice is to ask open questions so that your style is not going to be like that of a *Today* presenter. You should listen hard, not think about the next question, and pick up on the cues. I've always found that the best question is "Why?" A useful strategy is to allow the interviewees to say what they're determined to say and then go for what you're determined to get. I would ask the same question for as long as you keep getting different answers. I would never ask explicitly for "funny stories" because this tends to switch people into "raconteur" mode and makes them sound unnatural. It's also a good idea to feed back on how people are coming across, for example, gentle expressions such as "You're making it all sound a bit grim" or "It seems to upset you to talk about it". If you need your interviewees to provide better responses, you can get them to do it again at the end. All you have to do is say "Thanks very much" and keep rolling.'

Editing

- Log the material.
- Set a target duration for each contributor.
- Yes, no and maybe.
- Look for links, signposts and one-liners.
- Look for irony.

Everett says: 'In my experience the best programme ingredients are those that you remember. They are the "bits which say it all". When your contributors are always saying "we used to" then this is a bad sign. Nostalgia has to connect with the listener.'

Rough assembly

- Find your beginning and end.
- Divide the programme into sections.
- Break it up and keep it moving.
- Consider texture – light and shade.
- Eliminate repetition – make every word count.
- Be ruthless with the boring bits.

Everett says: 'When I was at Radio 4 our controller Michael Green set up something known as the "drowning effect". He was responding to a montage programme about a holiday camp and said "It needed drowning twenty minutes in".'

Fine cut

- Don't over-tighten – better to junk a chunk.
- Forget the chronology of the interview itself.
- If you're going to mix in music, sound effects, etc., leave yourself options.
- Use a second pair of ears.
- It should be hell to cut to length – if it is easy you should worry.

Mix-down

- A chance to think about the sound of the programme.
- Pace it for the first-time listener.
- Listen hard and trust your ears – not the meter.
- Be meticulous.

Students' learning experiences

Here are some of the insightful and useful learning experiences submitted by students in relation to their first feature. One student submitted this updated report:

1 I have already finished the final draft of my script.
2 Recorded seven clips of actuality.
3 Collected all background, intro, and outro music.

The only thing which I believe I have wasted a lot of time in was that I have been trying to play the role of the presenter. I have carried out several experiments to try and record myself as the presenter of the programme, but unfortunately they all failed. I discovered that presenting a movie review programme is a lot different than news presenting. I guess it needs much less formality, a little humour, and using more of a casual language (slang), I will therefore ask any of my colleagues if they can play this role for me.

This student shows organisation and is nearly ready to go into the studio. He is so objective that he is prepared to find somebody else who might make a better presenter.

The following student confirms the problem of recording too much for the target feature form. She also realises the advantage and importance of character quality for the feature:

What I've learned – I guess I had too much material, but you know that already. Getting it from twenty minutes down to seven was fine, as I already knew which bits I wanted. It seems to be getting it from seven down to four that is proving tricky. I've always been a 'better to have too much than too little' type person, which does me no favours.

I also made my decision for my feature subject very late. Once I'd decided, I had the interview and all the material within two days, so that wasn't a problem. I just found it hard to choose the definitive topic for a single six minute feature, when I had a list of about ten ideas. I wanted it to be the best idea, but couldn't decide which one that was. In the end, I think the one I chose was probably going to be the easiest in terms of getting the material, as it was only one interview, and he had all the archive material at his finger-tips. Once he'd agreed to be interviewed, it was fine from then on. And plus he was a very nice bloke!

The next comment is full of wisdom and insight and confirms everything that tutors go on and on and on about:

My drama turned out to be a seven minutes and twenty-five seconds project instead of a six minutes project. If I had concentrated more on the timing during the writing of my script, this would probably not have been a problem . . . I have tried to edit out some sentences, but it is still too long. I would have to cut a whole scene to make the drama shorter. I feel that all of the scenes are too important to be left out.

I have learned that when you are going to mix your feature, you have to plan and organise the structure in advance. Not only in your head, but on paper . . . It's called the running order . . . If you turn up in studio with everything well organised – your scenes on one reel-to-reel and your sound effects on another, a written running order and your script – things will go rather smoothly.

The next student is clearly well organised and assured in his approach to the feature's construction. Furthermore he does not use the advantage of a multi-track digital programme to abandon basic discipline.

Here's what I did:

1 Assembled the plot and narratives in a linear fashion.
2 Recorded each segment and then dumped all of my completed segments to mini-disc.
3 I researched and eventually found workable sound effects and composed a music bed which were then also dumped to the same mini-disc.
4 My original aim was to dump from mini-disc to reel and then edit that way. ***** was nice enough to allow me to use SADiE. Since I am a Pro Tools fanatic, I found the transition to SADiE quite simple. I then dumped all monologues onto one track, put the music bed on another, and then the sound effects at the end, layered in a group of four.
5 Once everything was compiled, I did a basic mix using slight automation and then went right to reel-to-reel.

I would say I learned about the importance, when scripting a radio drama, of thinking imaginatively about the sound design for the atmosphere right from the start. In theory I had known this was important. In practice I realised that a well thought-out sound backdrop is vital if the play is not going to sound totally dead. So I would spend more time concentrating on this. I am reasonably happy with my sound back-drop but I would have used it more dramatically, tweaking the levels slightly differently if I had done it again. It was an interesting creative assignment, doing a six minute piece. I think I found it hard to think out how to write a sequence of several actions in that short time, but in future I think I would really try and do that. My piece was a little static and if I could have worked it in effectively, getting a few different noises would have been interesting. On the whole I'm happy with it, though, for a first attempt.

Another student said:

What have I learned? To watch the quality of the tape you dump onto as most of my time has been wasted by glitches in tape quality which destroyed my clips, three of which had to be re-recorded. Umn . . . as you said, more focus . . . and very importantly to label clips if you have four or five lying around to be spliced together as ***** very kindly tried to tidy up and threw one clip on a pile of 200 others. Also to cut the verbal diarrhoea during interviews. My own voice all over the place has given me the biggest editing problems.

A practical and theoretical question for the feature maker and scheduler is how long should such programmes occupy on the time-line? Is there a length at which the 'feature' is delegitimised? As I have advanced elsewhere it has been a misnomer to talk about the death of the radio or audio play in those broadcast environments which have deconstructed the brick wall barriers of fixed half-hour, one hour, one and a half hour and two hour programming. The mini-drama exists in commercial advertisements and public information campaigns, and the fluid, improvised serial or 'soap' exists in the subversive manipulations of dissident or deviant bard playwrights who develop complex and sophisticated skits and story lines with interleaving plots and interactive characters.

These remarkable narratives hang on the live phone-in direction of commercial and BBC talk programming. Most of the people listening are completely unaware that they are listening to fiction, or as the late Italian academic Mauro Woolf said, so-called 'friction' – a mixture of fact and fiction with a tendency to fake the documentary portrayal.[8] In the case of the dissident bards the objective is to express creative storytelling imperatives because the alternative structures of paid and celebrated dramatic production are shut to them. The hybridisation of factual and fictional programmes was motivated by panic-stricken mainstream broadcasters supplying the public's supposed need for more entertainment, particularly if it is served up as 'truth' and 'fly on the wall actuality'.

The cultural legitimacy of length is perhaps more mythological than rational. The protest in 1997 and 1998 about BBC Radio 4 reducing the maximum form for most of its drama output was erroneously based on the argument that less length meant less intelligence and cultural validity. The debate was also amnesiac in the light of a point made in Asa Briggs's first volume *The Birth of Broadcasting 1896–1927*, that the first BBC radio drama editor believed plays could not sustain regular listening for more than 40 minutes, 'should be concerned with "some situation, emotion or experience which will be appreciated, or rather, applicable to the average mind"'.[9]

The creative or dramatised feature certainly occupies the ground where the news and current affairs feature has a tendency to trivialise and provide less clarity and narrative depth. The narration in creative feature making is more faithful to its subject and the involvement of the listener potentially more emotional.

However, German radio producer and director Helmut Kopetzky (ARD/SFB) has made the pertinent point that length is not the main problem for the relevance of the radio feature in an increasingly fragmented and private radio dominated world.[10] Rather than occupying the bit in between news and drama, the radio feature or drama-documentary should be expressing both news and drama. Controversy is the future of radio features.

Guiseppe Ortoleva at the University of Turin has observed that the radio feature/documentary is also a paradoxical genre. The paradox is in four parts:

1 A live and simultaneously experienced broadcast medium depends on the process of recording and subsequent editing to achieve its most artistic expression.
2 The permanent record of documentary investigation is broadcast on an ephemeral medium with no permanent system of archiving or preserving

the text. The radio transmission flow does not carry with it random organised memory.

3 A potential information genre of programming has been categorised as an avant-garde and experimental form rather than a feature of everyday programming. It could be argued that the avant-garde radio station in Paris, Radio Nova, challenged that notion by turning the avant-garde and experimental into a daily genre of expression through its unique sound design.

4 As a programming form in radio which is supposedly dependent on pure derivation from its sonic roots it has been conditioned by the study and influence of different media such as cinema.[11]

As a conclusion I would like to advance the view that the documentary feature in radio is much less like news and current affairs than drama. It shares with the dramatic storytelling force some powerful and compelling truths that many dramatic forms miss and fail to realise. We are dealing with an individual and personal quest to express the truth. The intellectual and emotional commitment of the feature maker measures its authentic quality. Documentary features are the radiophonic landmarks of our existence and human heritage. They record and inform the world of how we live and think. Their strength as a storytelling form is in being rooted in the reality of life and human existence and exploring with great depth the beauty of human feeling.

The feature documentary as radio drama strives to reconstruct reality or a view of reality. It seeks to offer a better understanding of something or somebody and it searches for the inside view. Its beauty is in its preoccupation with ordinary people and everyday life and making them more special. The feature documentary is not the province of celebrity, intellectual scholarship or the power movers and shakers or our confusing and complicated global existence. I heard the finest metaphorical definition of the drama in feature documentary at the Naples symposium in 1996. Edwin Brys described the radio documentary maker as somebody who

> shows us people moving on the chessboard of life. Or rather people being propelled, moved and pushed by forces beyond their control. If there is one constant in the many international documentaries I have listened to, it is that it is not usually kings, queens and castles who speak, but rather the pawns. Not those who want and can get, rather those who want but can't get, or those who can get but don't want. Often it is this human shortcoming, this divide between dream and deed, which is the basis of the best documentaries I have ever heard. They speak of something unfulfilled, incomplete, unfinished . . .
>
> The best documentaries let us hear the deep, albeit subdued, basso continuo of nostalgia. Not just the nostalgia for what could have been and never was, but also the perception that something could be, but never will be.[12]

Part VI

The practice and theory of directing and performance

Chapter 21

Directorial responsibility

Who amongst us isn't aching at the chance to get up on that stage, tread those boards, hit those marks, roar of the grease-paint, smell of the crowd, look at where the spotlight shines Ma? . . . On me.

(Chris in the morning on *Northern Exposure*)

The theatre is like a virus. It changes people. It alters them.

(Maurice in the same episode of *Northern Exposure*)[1]

Directing radio plays is a professional craft in a complex and challenging artform. Despite the existence of the Directors Guild of Great Britain, and a few postgraduate diplomas in directing, there are few opportunities for professional training in this field. The BBC runs limited courses on directing for staff employees. Most people learn by experience. The demise of repertory theatre in the UK means that outside degree and drama school courses, a considerable number of directors learn their trade in poorly funded, unregulated fringe theatre. The results for both actors and spectators are dismal and disillusioning. It is bad enough that many actors have to endure profit share arrangements which are more akin to paying for the privilege of acting. It seems that on occasion they are then faced with the horror and dismay of talentless, undisciplined and appalling standards of direction by egotistic and ignorant untrained directors.

While directing a play for BBC Radio 4 I was informed about the case of a freelance director whose incompetence generated twenty-seven large spools of tape (thirteen and a half hours of recording) for a one and a half hour production, that overran to ten recording days at the expensive Maida Vale studios. The director hired live musicians for most of this period without having any real idea how to use them. By the last recording day performers were being asked to continue working until 9 p.m. The production remained unedited and the loss of one of the reels meant that the play was never completed for broadcast.

This section begins with actions and decisions on how not to be a director in radio. They are, of course, relevant to other directing media.

The priorities before director and actors get anywhere near the studio are

- organisation
- script dramaturgy and preparation
- casting.

Organisation

Directors need to be committed to ensuring that the script is prepared and ready for performance. This responsibility involves providing the necessary dramaturgical support and advice to the writer. A script accepted for production does not mean that it is a script ready for performance. Directors need to ensure the following elements:

1 Every element of the script serves a valid and effective dramatic purpose.
2 Key characters serve their dramatic purpose and the main character undergoes a journey determined by plot and involving change that is resonated by the play's climax.
3 *Deus ex machina* in plot is avoided.
4 Clarity of imaginative narration in the mind of the listener is achieved at every moment in the script.
5 The beginning is sufficiently gripping and crisis laden to hook the listener.
6 Dialogue is dramatic and representative of spoken English in dramatic communication.
7 Scene development raises ongoing questions which maintain the momentum of the listener's attention.
8 The detail of atmosphere and imaginative world is effectively described in a sound design which is realisable.
9 The use and selection of music is purposeful, relevant and realisable.

Script dramaturgy and preparation

After the selection of the script for production the director should put in place research and acquisition of the following elements:

1 Sound effects and atmospheres: pre-recorded CD and DAT effects from published collections where the rights are available for use in the production. An assessment of the need to generate original atmosphere or sound effects.

2 Music: are the tracks available on pre-recorded CD, cassette and vinyl formats? Does the production need to negotiate rights or does the carrier station have licence agreements with copyright collection agencies that require only a second-by-second usage report? Does the music require original composition and production? If this is the case a budget will need to be available and allocated and the process of commissioning the musical composition should be put in place as soon as the script has been accepted.

3 Character descriptions and profiles: *syuzhet* arches of background on characters are prepared so that performers have a history that precedes the play and may even follow it. Cultural background, accents and ages are essential information which have to be obtained from the writer.

4 The director needs to read and study every word, silence and sound in the play so that he or she can articulate an explanation of why the play has been written and develops in the way that it does. If there is any element of doubt, the director has a specific duty to seek an explanation and clarification so that he or she is absolutely sure.

5 The director needs to construct a timetabled schedule of deadlines and requirements leading up to the recording day with the actors. Then the director needs to draw up a schedule of the recording day indicating with clarity and common sense the call times for rehearsal, what is expected during the rehearsal time, sufficient breaks for rest and relaxation and the schedule of recording with a well-balanced organisation of time allocated in the studio for each scene. This planning is essential for the success of the production.

6 Research information on the period, subject or theme of the play. If it is historical and relates to real people past or living, material can be acquired from library resources. News cuttings libraries are available on the World Wide Web through newspapers for a variety of charges. CD-ROMs provide excellent resources for a variety of social history and cultural references. For example the *Daily Mail* has published a CD-ROM containing selected articles from a century of newspaper editions which can be accessed quickly through search engines. *Encarta* and *Encyclopaedia Britannica* are alternative resources. National newspapers have stored a considerable number of years on CD-ROMs and most reputable libraries have *The Times* on microfiche. Using the search engines on the World Wide Web often yields very useful background information. A good example of how qualitative research for a radio play assisted a production was *Sons of Catholic Gentlemen* by

Francis Beckett (broadcast LBC 1152 AM in 1998 and the first UK Internet Play of the Month). Set at the time of the Suez crisis in an English Catholic public school in 1956, the young actors enormously appreciated a range of cuttings setting out the social mores of the time and providing a cultural and attitudinal context for the characters populating the play.

Casting

Casting intelligence comes from the following activities:

1 Going to mainstream and fringe theatre and noting the names of actors who impress you.

2 Holding regular person to person auditions for specific plays. These sessions are not auditions exclusively for the plays being produced but general interviews looking for fresh talent; this fact should be communicated to the actors and their agents.

3 Contacting professional agents and seeking their advice on people who might be suitable on their lists of artists. Good and constructive relationships with agents mean that in time they are in a position to make recommendations and help you, particularly when some members of your cast drop out through illness or unforeseen circumstances.

4 Building up a sound casting library from cassettes and CVs sent in by actors and their agents. Arrange this alphabetically and keep it well organised. You should acknowledge by letter any actor who has taken the trouble of sending a cassette and CV to you.

5 Building up intelligence from close television and film watching as well as radio listening. In the visual medium you can often gather useful information about actors during voice overs and sound-only narrative passages.

6 It is worth keying in actors' names and exploring the Internet for casting information. Actors' agents have been somewhat slow to use the new technology but when they respond the process of gathering information will become much more efficient. Agency websites can store full CVs, photos, sound casting clips and latest information about availability.

The audition session

1 It is important to preserve professional standards and values when there is the temptation to give way to egotism, self-interest and the obligations of friendship. When so many drama productions are funded by sponsorship and personal resources the capacity for independent judgement has a

tendency to evaporate. Casting determined by bribery or friendship is disastrous.

2 In casting you must look for commitment and hunger for the part. This is not only obvious in the passion and degree of expression in the audition but also clear from the questions that an actor will ask you before offering a version of the audition performance. When an actor shows intellectual and emotional interest in a part this is often a good sign.

3 You must avoid those actors who during the audition show laziness by reverting to a stereotypical voice taken from a long-established repertoire of radio performances from the past. You are right to be suspicious about an actor who instead of engaging an understanding of the part and play that you are auditioning for, seems determined to provide every type of accent, age and voice genre in the short time that the audition runs.

4 Show your auditioning actors every courtesy possible during this session. It is an interview and actors always remember respect and courtesy at auditions because many auditions are brutal and badly organised affairs. Professional actors develop thick skins and part of their training is to become desensitised to rejection. However, making an actor feel special, appreciated and important even in the context of a competitive rejection is a skill and culture which will be appreciated. You need to remember that those people you see at the bottom one day may be at the top and way beyond your level on another day. If they have a good memory of the meeting and experience they had with you, they will remember this when the power relationship is reversed.

5 The key factor in an audition is to evaluate and judge how actors will adjust their performance according to your notes and direction. It is a positive and developmental response that you want. Therefore it is vital that you give notes during the audition and an actor has one or two more chances to offer an idea of performance. You should react well and recognise a consistent journey of improvement.

6 The professional protocol in auditioning is that the agent is informed of whether there is success or not. It is better to be up front right from the beginning on how you organise and run your auditions. Let agents and actors know for example that if you are under time constraints they should assume that the audition is unsuccessful if they have not heard from you.

7 Always watch out for same voice casting. Alan Beck in his excellent book on *Radio Acting* (1997) has described this problem as 'clustering'.[2] It is not unusual to cast correctly for each part from the point of view of acting ability and commitment to the part and end up with clustering.

Chapter 22

Managing the production

Who needs a fifth column on a film, reporting, criticising, analysing? It's like finding that the commis chef works for the Ministry of Health.

(Simon Callow)[1]

Professional responsibilities

The responsibilities during production with the actors require various professional standards. First, you have to inspire your actors to establish and express life, understanding and belief in the world of every script. This requires qualities of leadership and enthusiasm and charisma. Your understanding and knowledge of the subject as well as your enthusiasm for your cast will be instrumental in this process.

Second, you have to have a consistent grasp of the time schedule and rehearsal time. This will be aided by a clear and well-set-out plan of call times and estimated times allocated to each scene and part. This will involve an economic and efficient use of the budget which sometimes means bringing in actors for short engagements. Subsequently the play may well be recorded out of sequence instead of with consecutive scenes. In these circumstances you have to produce a plan which is realisable and takes into account things that can go wrong. When scenes are recorded out of sequence you have to remember the style and charge left by the performance in the scene previous to the one you are recording in terms of the script narrative. You then have to communicate the lead-in and continuity to your actors and you have to be ready to fill in background and context at any point.

Third, you have to have a confident and experienced understanding of the technical nature of the studio and be able to liaise with the sound design structure of recording set up by your studio manager. You need to know about 'blocking', the dynamics of the different microphones, and the nature, space and qualities of the stereo sound stage. It is always better to explain to your actors in clear language as though they are experts in their field so that they feel involved, appreciated, respected and intellectually as well as creatively engaged with the radio drama medium.

Fourth, you must provide a clarity and specificity of notes at every stage of the production. Pretentious, vague, abstract and esoteric communication is going to be a barrier to the success of the production. Actors will be confused and lose confidence; in the end professional actors will revert to their own resources of experience, which will be problematic. Actors need clear guidance on your requirements for style, pace, mood and meaning both explicit and subtextual. At any time you need to be able to tell your actors

- what the character is thinking
- how the character is expressing the words in the script
- where the character is going and what the character wants
- what the character is feeling
- where the character is coming from.

Finally, you have to have a schedule which provides time for experimentation and the creative contribution of your actors, ideas and thoughts offered by your living writer if he or she is in the studio, and similarly the creative suggestions and experience of your studio manager. This experimentation should be under control. It is enormous fun giving your company or team the chance to play. It is during these moments that creative inspiration blooms and the outstanding director will also be in a position to accept and recognise originality that should be utilised in the overall production even if the director had not anticipated or conceived the idea and special contribution. The controlled space that a director gives to the creativity of his or her company is another factor which makes the difference between the mundane, mediocre production and the outstanding and unique production.

Guiding the actors through feedback

It is in the giving of notes, encouraging and accepting the good and discouraging and rejecting the bad that a director achieves his or her role in the production process. There are no fixed formulas which will work for every actor. In order to achieve adjustments there are some recommendations. For example, every actor is different and should be treated as such. This means every effort should be made to realise and apply specific styles of communication to each individual actor. The professional relationship begins from the audition and can develop over a number of years as director and performer work together. With every actor there are often inspirational communication keys which work for them and it is useful for professional directors to keep a notebook containing this information so that it is an *aide-mémoire* for future projects and there can be a consistency and building of the professional director–performer relationship. Being able to interpret and communicate instinct and experience in this context is the challenge for every director.

Things to avoid

Do not act or perform for the actors. You are the director and if you begin to offer your representations of performance, your cast will lose respect for you. Either they will know that you will never be as good an actor as them, or they will think that you think they are so bad that you can do better. You do not want to have your actors silently questioning themselves on why they think you hired them.

Do not allow panic and pressure to transmit to the rest of your company by getting bad tempered, being rude and shouting.

Do not saturate your notes with too much negativity. Actors want to be loved and love does not involve constant carping, acerbic criticism, sarcastic put-downs and an unrelenting litany of complaints and accusations.

Avoid coming on to your actors or seeking personal relationships with them during production. This is disastrous emotionally and professionally and will guarantee embarrassment, trouble and creative disaster.

Do not promise what you cannot deliver in terms of fees, perks, success and impossible ambition. Actors like to dream but they do not appreciate false dreams. Although 'white' lying is an important mechanism of maintaining morale and achieving motivation, when you are found out the result makes this attitude utterly self-defeating.

Recognising poor acting standards

You must look out for various indications of poor acting standards on the production day:

1   Actors who turn up drunk or under the influence of drugs: sack them discreetly and seek a replacement.

2   Actors who turn up late: show your displeasure privately, but also show understanding for extraordinary circumstances that were beyond their control. All professional actors know that failing to show is professional suicide.

3   Actors who subdirect: this is sometimes done with the best of intentions and is quite common from experienced actors who wish to support rookies, child actors or actors new to the medium. You have to judge what is helpful and what becomes a hindrance.

4   Actors who consult the writer instead of you: you must stop this discreetly. Actors need one line of communication and it has to be you. Otherwise the result will be a confused production.

5   Actors who have not bothered to do any preparation: bad signs include actors who arrive without the script and notes you sent them. As they move from page to page it is clear they have not marked their script or even read it.

Recognising good acting standards

1   Actors who respond quickly and with flexibility to the director's notes and any significant changes in the direction of interpretation.

2   Actors who do not wander from the production area. They always make themselves available and they are ready on time for each scene.

3   Actors who make notes from your notes. During rehearsal and production you should notice them marking up their scenes and lines.

4   Actors who concentrate and are attentive during the communication of notes. Concentration and consistency of performance are essential when there are technical defects requiring retakes.

5   Actors who begin to demonstrate an instinct and special quality of performance appropriate to the radio medium. You can see this developing and should make a note of it when it is of a high quality.

6   Actors who are always positive about the script, writer, director, fellow performers and maintain a lively and supportive spirit and sense of humour.

Useful guidelines for actors having difficulty with the script

With a well-organised production, successful takes can be achieved at the third or fourth attempt. In order to capture the spontaneity of performers who tend to present their best work during the first take, I would recommend recording all rehearsals. You do not have to inform your actors that the recording machines are turning over. Orson Welles had grave insecurities about his acting ability and believed that his first performances were always his best.

It is sometimes difficult to make an early diagnosis of what is wrong. Here are some concerns and suggestions which can sometimes help actors having difficulty.

First, suggest that the performer recaptures the psychological experience of being surprised by the character's thoughts and reactions to the events and words of characters in the scene.

Second, you may need to deal with plosives when heavy breaths, *p* and *b* sounds blow the microphones. You can help the performer by introducing a 'popping shield': coat-hanger and stocking often does the trick. You can ask the actor to perform across the microphone rather than directly into it. You can ask the actor to consciously soften any *p*s and *b*s and draw back slightly from the microphone. You can change the microphone to one that is less sensitive.

Third, actors sometimes misunderstand directors because of the lack of precision in directorial language. Directions normally need to relate to the following characteristics of performance:

- dynamics
- tempo
- psychology and interpretation.

Suggestions for direction

The dynamics of performance relate to volume and how much effort is being given to the voice. All that needs to be said is louder, quieter, very, very quiet, very quiet, quiet, quite quiet, quite loud, loud, very loud, very, very loud, and suddenly very loud. As for tempo or pace all that normally needs to be said is slow, slow and dignified, quick and bright, fast and lively, very quick, faster, holding back, and slower. These directions are only relative adjectives for sound dynamics or the equivalent of ostension in stage theatre.

Psychology and interpretation require greater discretion and skill in human communication. It is normally enough to recollect the interior state of the character in any scene because performance can emerge only from the character's thinking. The skill and professionalism of the vast majority of experienced radio actors means they can respond to discussion about a character's internal state. A recollection or discussion about the character's attitude to the other characters in the scene is also helpful. The quality of discussion is often determined by the enthusiasm and excitement that the director has in the world of the play. This degree of commitment is always communicated to the actors and the return of this enthusiasm will further enhance the atmosphere.

The director needs to concentrate on the performance in each take so that the actors are reliably informed early on about any fluff or persistent error in reading the script. Directors should also pay attention to the blocking of the performance so that early on actors are placed in the right positions in relation to microphones.

The rhythm of direction and performance is often helped by establishing the objective of full 'takes' which run across the entire duration of scenes rather than falling into staccato retakes of speeches and short sequences. Successful drama, even in a pre-recorded medium, needs a cohesion of dynamics, tempo and interpretation. Performers tend to appreciate experiencing the momentum of a scene's 'virtual reality'. This is why direction and performance benefits often accrue from location recording. Actors respond to the imaginative engagement with a near virtual reality of performance environment instead of the bare interior of the radio studio.

A more generous budget and larger production resources can also open up the option of more experimental rehearsal time. Independent Radio Drama Productions in Britain has undertaken considerable exploration of the relative benefits of dramaturgically developing new writers' scripts in both radio and theatre. In 1994 a quartet of directors, Richard Shannon, Jeff Teare, Gerard Murphy and myself, each produced half-hour radio plays for both media. The dynamics of transcodification changed in relation to each project. Jeff Teare and Richard Shannon produced the radio version after the stage development and performance. Gerard Murphy and I produced the radio play within a day's rehearsal and performance time, which is standard for radio drama production. The theatre version was performed after a week of rehearsal. We were all intrigued by the issue of whether better results were produced in theatre before radio or radio before theatre. When I later had an opportunity for producing the radio version of an hour-long play after several weeks of rehearsal and performance in a stage theatre (*Restless Farewell*, BAC and LBC in 1996) I came to the conclusion that the space and depth that more rehearsal time provides in the stage theatre context is beneficial for qualitative characterisation and performance in radio.

Chapter 23

Experimental direction and performance

Improvisation is a little explored area of audio drama. It has the potential of yielding qualitative performance results as well as being a powerful method of research development in radio dramaturgy. Improvised performance can be both live and pre-recorded. Directors leading these experiments have been seeking to liberate the existence of radio drama communication from predetermined text on the page. There is a desire to capture the spontaneous realism and truth of human surprise that can be stimulated by improvisation. When the context has been well researched, this developing method of radio drama expression can achieve a refreshing style of production and generate an immediacy of emotional experience on the part of the actor and the listener. American radio drama director Joe Frank experimented with this genre extensively in the early 1980s in Washington, DC.

Radio Suisse Romande La Première established success with *Bergamote*, an improvised radio drama series transmitted on Sunday mornings from the beginning of 1996. The producer/director Claude Blanc set up a framework and plot for each programme so that the actors were aware of their backgrounds, and their objectives in each scene. The dialogues were not written out fully as text. The central characters Monique and Roger shared the improvised and apparently spontaneous experience of their lives with the listeners in the fitness gym, in the bedroom, unemployment office or hospital.

The production team underlined the search for realism by recording on location. Increasing and sustained listening figures appeared to demonstrate that the concept worked. It represented a modern form of radio fiction. The episode transmitted on 23 February 1997 served to stimulate public debate over organ donation. It was recorded in the intensive care unit of the Vaudio Hospital Centre in Lausanne. Actors Claude-Inga Barbey and Patrick Lapp began with a traditional 'couple's row'. The character Monique accused her husband Roger of having an affair. She wanted him to leave, which he did in a fury. Scene 2 cut to the intensive care unit of the hospital. Monique had discovered that after a road traffic accident, Roger was in a deep coma and he could not respond to sight, sound or touch. In Scene 3, a doctor, played by Daniel Rausis, broke the news that Roger was brain dead. He wanted Monique's agreement to use some of her husband's organs for transplant. The drama unfolded over 20 minutes. The performances were convincing. The dramatic values of the play were achieved through the cadences and rhythm of improvised dialogue rather than performance derived from heightened text. The success of this work has been corroborated by the fact that the recording was effectively used in the training of medical students.

Yves Ferry's audio drama *Getting It Over With* for Radio France represented a story told with greater depth and on a larger canvas using improvised performance. It was recorded like a film, entirely on location. The production, directed by Claude Guerre, was a very brave attempt to breathe new life into radio fiction. But unlike a film production there was no screenplay. Yves Ferry had defined the characters, the action and the situation. The plot was centred around an actress, Albertine, who is separated from the father of her child, Marcel. Marcel is directing her in a classical theatre production while in her private life she travels through ironic and destructive relationships.

Claude Guerre defined the direction, but the cast created the dialogue using their own intellectual and emotional resources. The language of the characters has an idiomatic and realistic attitude which is generally lacking in text-based drama. Filmic and location style recording techniques in sound drama are now becoming rather fashionable. There is no doubt that the realistic physical environment helps to psychologically root the actors in a truthful mental ambience. However, Guerre's production (broadcast on 9 November 1996) seemed to be burdened by a lack of narrative focus.

The lack of clarity, in my opinion, could not be rescued by the courage and creativity of the conceptual author, sound designer, director and actors. The sophistication of this production points to an intensity of artistic commitment and experimentation by a distinguished public broadcaster. Some might classify this attempt as an heroic failure. But it is more than likely that further experimentation will produce a narrative that works for listeners, and the drama department at Radio France headed by Christine Bernard-Sugy should be recognised for their skill and boldness in supporting this style of production.

Keith Richards in his book *Writing Radio Drama* (1991) comes to similar conclusions about the efficacy of improvisation in radio drama.[1] He refers to two examples of Australian productions when the technique appeared to work. David

McRobbie's *The Beethoven Tapes* involved giving professional actors detailed backgrounds and scenarios for their characters who at were at the centre of a fictional investigation into a fire. The actors were playing the parts of people interviewed by an investigative journalist. Richards reports: 'the response from the listeners was one of total acceptance of what they believed to be a genuine radio documentary.' Richards then goes on to describe how he collaborated with fellow playwright Ken Methold at an Australian playwrights' conference with actors and an equally rigid investigative structure around the narrative of a flying saucer hoax. Richards concludes: 'I believe this form of writing to be just as valid, and in some ways, more exciting than a traditionally scripted drama.' He successfully identifies the limitations to improvised radio drama and refers to an unsuccessful attempt by the award-winning film director Mike Leigh to produce an improvised drama in sound. The apparent lack of an imposed structure allowed actors to produce 'endless rambling conversations'.

In February 1999, the BBC commissioned and broadcast a thought-provoking experimentation with scripted material, improvised performance and an emotional resonance between 'real people' and professional performers. The hour-long *One Young Man* was in the genre of 'faction'. It sought to tell the true story of HIV positive and drug addict William McLeod, who died while on remand in Edinburgh's Saughton Prison in 1993. The play covered the 48-hour aftermath when his family sought an explanation from the police and prison authorities. A unique feature of the production was that William's mother, Phyllis, and his sister, Dawn McCormack, played themselves. The rest of the cast were made up of professional actors but also included William's cousin Lynne Killin. The *Guardian*'s thoughtful radio critic Anne Karpf raised the following questions:

> Were we moved because the cast were the actual participants? Does authenticity make good drama and having been through something necessarily make you good at recreating it? Dare one judge them as performers? And what did re-enacting their own torment do to their heads – and to ours, experiencing prurience along with drama?[2]

My own view is that Jeremy Weller's production pushed the boundaries in an intensely thought-provoking way. The signposting on authenticity, fiction and reality and the emotional investment of experience in documentary subjects agreeing to perform alongside vicarious presentation was problematical. Too many political and technical questions were engaged. However, if the 'play' is judged by its own merits, I personally found it a successful listening experience and a significant contribution to raising social issues through dramatic production.

There has also been an attempt in the 1990s to recapture the charge and resonance of live radio drama. James Roy at CBC in Canada helped develop the peak listening, breakfast-time series *The Diamond Lane*, which was performed live after rehearsal. The project had two advantages. It engaged the most listened to audience in radio and repositioned drama as a mainstream sequence. The dynamics of live performance increased the adrenalin element in acting spontaneity.

The Pacifica radio station in New York, WBAI, has been the arena for an innovative development in the art of the live community radio play. Anthony J. Sloan, WBAI's Arts Director Emeritus, is a name that does not resonate in the corridors of international radio drama conferences or festivals.[3] The critical neglect which he appears to take in his stride may have a lot to do with the residual racism that African Americans have had to contend with in their own history and the continued marginalisation of Asian and African literature, oral tradition and storytelling culture in western societies.

Anthony Sloan initiated and developed WBAI's tradition of live radio drama from 1986. He explained:

> Most people did taped drama because it's safer. BBC does radio drama every day, but it's canned. I like live radio drama because the adrenalin flows for the actors. They know that not only is this live, but guess what, it's only one-time. You get some incredible performances.

Anthony Sloan has covered powerful themes by bringing together actors, writers, and musicians to create a series of media pageants that have played the streets of New York, the studios of WBAI, the satellite frequency of Pacifica Network programming and the World Wide Web with orchestras of musical, dramatic, and acoustic artistic expression fused by bold narratives. The productions are not short half-hour or one-hour sequences. They have spanned five and a half hours of airtime. Sloan has sought to combine philosophically challenging, politically controversial, intellectually stimulating, and emotionally enervating dimensions of communication with complex sound production techniques and live, physically moving performances on the sidewalks of the Lower East Side, and other landmarks in the urban geography of New York City.

I have found it difficult to trace any other audio drama practitioner in the world who has been able to match this degree of risk in experimenting with the medium. There is evidence of artistic courage, creative originality and dramatic accomplishment. I attended a weekly workshop in the Lower East Side in June 1994 where Anthony Sloan encouraged an open access of writers, poets and performers to present and exchange their work. A live, weekly soap opera was workshopped and rehearsed. Participants were encouraged to introduce and perform new parts. It can be argued that this grassroots dimension of his work is a significant indicator of how radio drama can strengthen its identity and cultural value with its audience through an exchange of energy and ideas. This cannot be achieved by remaining in the studio, editing and producing commissioned manuscripts.

The WBAI radio drama repertoire has not been restricted to promoting African American writing, although *The Leaving(s) Project* (transmitted on the night of 26 January 1996) effectively served this purpose. The five and a half hour project comprised two storytelling events. Both were live. The first consisted of Larry Neal's seminal play *The Glorious Monster in the Bell of the Horn* presented before a live audience at the New Knitting Factory in the Tribeca section of Manhattan. The play was structured in the style of Prokofiev's musical version of the Brothers Grimm's *Peter and the Wolf* where characters were identified by musical instruments. Then the multimedia event blossomed into 'a journey piece' from different locations of the New York metropolitan area. There were six different groups of characters leaving New York for various reasons who were forced to deal with personal crises on their way to an Amtrak train at New York's Penn Station. Their interweaving story lines highlighted current social, political, spiritual and artistic issues. All the disparate journeys were acted out live to moving microphones on location and culminated in a dramatic finale at Penn Station. The realistic acoustic and geographical context of the event is indicated by the fact that the fictional characters intended to board the 3.45 a.m. 'Amtrak red-eye' service leaving New York, which was actually waiting to leave one of the platforms at the end of the broadcast. The event, which began at 10 p.m. on the Friday night, continued until 3.45 the following morning. It could be heard in stereo on WBAI 99.5 FM, was distributed by satellite to 360 community radio stations and could be heard nationally and internationally on the World Wide Web.

It would be helpful if scholars and researchers in radio could attempt to challenge the 'invisibility' of black directors and writers in radio drama. There is a tendency for the subject to be dominated by the white European cultural paradigm. If Anthony Sloan has been the Orson Welles of the 1990s, I think it could also be argued that Welles had a rival for energy and creativity as a radio drama auteur during the 1940s and 1950s. Richard Durham is a name whom very few readers would recognise. Over two years he wrote a series of ninety radio plays for the Chicago station WMAQ, an NBC affiliate. His programme dramatically illustrated the lives and achievements of successful black men and women in history. It was called *Destination Freedom*. Richard Durham had been editor of the famous African-American newspaper *The Chicago Defender*. His radio plays were not networked. Such was the apartheid nature of theatre, film and television in the USA his reputation did not carry into contemporary cultural resonance. Fortunately a volume of the scripts from the *Destination Freedom* series has been published by Praeger.[4]

Notes

1 A new media history perspective through audio drama

1 This ratio of distribution has been confirmed by mathematical analysis of texts held in the library on 2 February 1998 and 10 July 1998. The college holds its library stock on a computer database called Libertas.

2 A preliminary conference funded by the Economic and Social Research Council (ESRC) at Lincoln University on 16 and 17 February 1998 confirmed the focus of interest in 'Radio Studies'. The originator and inspiration for a Radio Institute or Radio Research Project is Peter M. Lewis at Middlesex University. Eryl Price-Davis at Thames Valley University has also successfully established a Radio Studies Group on the Internet, which is continually expanding in membership and developing an international profile.

3 The first Goldsmiths College/Kent University Radio Drama conference was held 15/16 January 1999 sponsored by the Radio Advertising Bureau; a full range of papers were provided from theorists and practitioners. Organised by Alan Beck and me, it is expected to become an annual event.

4 P. Eckersley (1992) *The Power behind the Microphone*, London: Scientific Book Club, ch. 1 'Broadcasting before the BBC', p. 42.

5 This information was available at http://www.aa.net/~ifs/kqw.htm. There have been two video programmes made about KQW and 'Doc' Herrold. The first was for educational use and produced by San José University; it was supplied to me on Betacam by Dr Fred Hunter. A more recent production (23 July 1998) was broadcast on public television with the script available on the Internet at: www.kteh.org/productions/docs/docadams.html. The

programme broadcast on KTEM in San José was researched and produced by Mike Adams. This website contains a transcript of the television documentary.

6 R. L. Hilliard and M. C. Keith (1997) *The Broadcast Century: A Biography of American Broadcasting*, 2nd edn, Boston, MA: Focal Press, p. 32.

7 G. H. Douglas (1987 [1934]) *The Early Days of Radio Broadcasting*, Jefferson, NC: McFarland, p. 24.

8 Ibid., p. 30.

9 Ibid., p. 29.

10 L. Maltin (1997) *The Great American Broadcast*, New York: Dutton, p. 13. The precise appreciation of radio drama's unique nature and purpose in targeting the imagination is reflected in the BBC's advice to listeners to *The Comedy of Danger* in 1924 to turn the lights out and listen in darkness.

11 *The Listener* magazine 24 May 1956, pp. 673–4. Again this citation is entirely due to the excellent research of Alan Beck, who provided this reference for delegates at the Goldsmiths/Kent University Radio Drama conference 15/16 January 1999.

12 Alan Beck explores and analyses the history of this period more extensively in *The Invisible Play: Origins to 1932*, volume 1 of a CD-ROM series on the history of British Radio Drama. In a Radio Studies Internet message for 11 May 1998 he explained that 'the 75th anniversary of the official birth of radio drama went by completely unremarked by the BBC. I lobbied them, including the Drama Dept., Kaleidoscope, and World Service Meridian for over 2 years beforehand. Imagine if the British had invented film, and this was the 75th birthday of film?' Alan Beck did provide the research for the BBC's commemoration of the first full broadcast of a Shakespeare production. This was a new play by David Pownall broadcast on BBC Radio 4 on Friday 15 May 1998, *An Epiphanous Use of the Microphone*. Ken Garner (lecturer at Strathclyde Caledonian University) posted the BBC's press information about this broadcast on the Radio Studies list on 28 April 1998:

David Pownall's new play celebrates 75 years of radio drama. On 28th May 1923, the fledgling British Broadcasting Company transmitted its first live radio drama – a production of Shakespeare's *Twelfth Night* . . . By undercutting between the first performance of *Twelfth Night* in 1602 and the build-up to the first ever radio production in 1923, the play shows how both the Shakespeare and the BBC ensemble of actors were forced to contend with the political and editorial vagaries of the time. Anna Massey recreates the role of Elizabeth I which she recently played with such distinction at the Royal National Theatre. Over the years Anna has starred in scores of radio dramas and has also been one of the most sought-after readers for stories and *Book At Bedtime*. Michael Maloney plays Shakespeare in this production and John Reith is played by Crawford Logan. Jane Whittenshaw plays the redoubtable actress Cathleen Nesbitt who had to deal with Reith and guide her terrified actors into the unknown as they faced a microphone for the first time. David Pownall has written extensively for radio and has won many Sony Radio Awards, scoring a major success with his *Elgar's Third*.

13 R. Pybus (1981) 'Radio drama: the Australian experience', in P. Lewis (ed.) *Radio Drama*, London: Longman, p. 246.
14 R. Lane (1994) *The Golden Age of Australian Radio Drama, 1923–1960*, Melbourne: Melbourne University Press, p. 3.
15 P. Brook (1990) *The Empty Space*, Harmondsworth: Penguin, p. 154.
16 Available as Chapter 8 of E. McLuhan and F. Zingrone (eds) (1997) *Essential McLuhan*, London: Routledge.
17 M. McLuhan (1967) *The Medium is the Message: An Inventory of Effects*, with Q. Fiore, produced by J. Agel, New York: Bantam.
18 McLuhan and Zingrone, *Essential McLuhan*, pp. 292–3.
19 Ibid., p. 285.
20 L. Sieveking (1934) *The Stuff of Radio*, London: Cassell, p. 29.
21 R. Arnheim (1936) *Radio*, London: Faber and Faber, pp. 13–14.
22 B. Brecht, 'The radio as an apparatus of communication', in J. Hanhardt (ed.) (1986) *Video Culture: A Critical Investigation*, Layton, Utah: Visual Studies Workshop, p. 53. Quoted in D. Lander (1994) *Radio Rethink – Radiocasting: Musings on Radio and Art*, Banff, Alta: Walter Phillips Gallery, pp. 18–19. Also available in N. Strauss and D. Mandl (eds) (1993) *RadioText(e)*, New York: Columbia University Press. Earlier sources: *Brecht on Theatre* (1964), ed. and trans. J. Willett, New York: Hill and Wang. Originally published as 'Der Rundfunk als Kommunikationsapparat', in *Blattaer der Hessischen Landestheaters*, Darmstadt, 16, July 1932.
23 McLuhan and Zingrone, *Essential McLuhan*, p. 292.
24 This poem appears on a special page on Weimar Republic Radio programming on the Stanford University Program in Berlin website. The address (23 July 1998) was http://www-usp.stanford.edu/drama258/sebweb/radioconcept.html. It is authored by Sebastian Turullols. It also appears in M. McLuhan (1995) *Understanding Media*, London: MIT Press, p. 298.
25 Strauss and Mandle, *RadioText(e)*, pp. 21–5. Originally published as Chapter 7 'In Praise of Blindness: Emancipation from the Body', in R. Arnheim (1936) *Radio*, trans. M. Ludwig and H. Read, London: Faber and Faber, pp. 135–204.

2 Radio drama as modernity

1 H. Matheson (1933) *Broadcasting*, London: Thornton Butterworth.
2 Professor Asa Briggs does cite Hilda Matheson in his series on British broadcasting: A. Briggs (1995) *The History of Broadcasting in the United Kingdom*, 5 vols, London: Oxford University Press. He gives her one index reference in *The Birth of Broadcasting 1896–1927*, twelve index references in *The Golden Age of Wireless 1927–1939*, one index reference in *The War of Words 1939–1945*, and no references in the subsequent volumes *Sound and Vision 1945–55* and *Competition, 1955–1974*. He acknowledges her book in the bibliographical notes to volume II.
3 Fred Hunter has been trying to properly evaluate Hilda Matheson's importance in UK broadcasting history. A significant essay by him can be found in S. Oldfield (ed.) (1994) *This Working-Day World, Women's Lives and Cultures in Britain 1914–1945*, London: Francis and Taylor. Chapter is entitled 'Hilda Matheson and the BBC 1926–1940'.
4 Matheson, *Broadcasting*, pp. 13–14.
5 Ibid., p. 109.
6 P. Tissien (1993) 'From literary modernism to the Tantramar Marshes: anticipating McLuhan in British and Canadian media theory and practice', *Canadian Journal of Communication*, 18(4). Posted on the Internet at http://hoshi.cic.sfu.ca/caljkjc/BackIssue/18.4/tiessen.html.
7 P. Scannell (1996) *Radio, Television and Modern Life*, Oxford: Blackwell.
8 M. Heidegger (1962 [1917]) *Being and Time*, Oxford: Blackwell, p. 140. Also quoted by Scannell *Radio, Television and Modern Life*, p. 167.
9 T. S. Eliot (1955 [1917]) *The Use of Poetry and the Use of Criticism*, New York: Barnes and Noble, pp. 118–19. Quoted in E. McLuhan and F. Zingrone (eds) (1997) *Essential McLuhan*, London: Routledge, p. 382.

3 The electrophone or théâtrophone: broadcasting audio drama before the radio

1 T. Askew (1981) 'The amazing Clement Ader', *Studio Sound*, September, p. 44.
2 R. Hawes (1991) *Radio Art*, London: Welds Green Wood Publishing, p. 24.
3 Quoted in C. Marvin (1988) *When Old Technologies Were New: Thinking about Electric Communication in the Late Nineteenth Century*, Oxford: Oxford University Press, p. 212.
4 Ibid., p. 215.
5 Ibid., pp. 209–10.

6 *Daily Mail Centenary CD-ROM* (1996) Associated Newspapers Holdings, designed and produced by New Media.

7 Pavilion Records at Sparrows Green, Wadhurst, East Sussex, has an extensive catalogue of archive speech, radio and sound recordings.

8 Microfiche of *The Times* kept by Information Services, Goldsmiths College Library, University of London.

9 *The Beatification of Area Boy* by Wole Soyinka. Recorded in the presence of an audience, director Jude Kelly at the West Yorkshire Playhouse, directed for radio by Alby James. BBC Radio 3, Sunday 19 November 1995 from 7.30 p.m.

10 *The Times* microfiche, Goldsmiths College Library.

11 Ibid.

12 Ibid.

13 Ibid.

14 G. Robertson et al. (eds) (1996) *Future Natural: Nature, Science, Culture*, London: Routledge, p. 190.

4 The six ages of audio drama and the Internet epoch

1 T. Crook (1998) *International Radio Journalism: History, Theory and Practice*, London: Routledge, chs 7 and 9.

2 E. McLuhan and F. Zingrone (eds) (1997) *Essential McLuhan*, London: Routledge, p. 284.

3 Ibid., pp. 284–5.

4 This theory (reproduced later in this chapter) is available on the Internet (as of 24 July 1998) at www.orst.edu/instruct/phl302/texts/bacon/atlantis.html, line 2,659. It has been scanned from Francis Bacon *The New Atlantis*, first published 1626, republished in (1901) *Ideal Commonwealths*, New York: Colonial Press. Text is now public domain.

5 Edison later recorded his remembrance of this experience in a later phonograph recording which is reproduced on Comptons New Media CD-ROM encyclopedia, Version 2 1994.

6 Reproduced on the cassette collection *Great Speeches of the Twentieth Century* (1991) Rhino Records Inc, Santa Monica, CA.

7 G. Mulgan and K. Worple (1989) *Radio City*, London: Greater London Arts, pp. 9–10.

8 The programme idea was submitted to Prix Europa in Berlin, October 1997 and details were available at www.prix-europa.de. Programme contacts listed were: Marika Kecseméti, YLE Radio2/Radiomafia BOX 17 FIN 00024 Yleisradio tel. ++358–9–1480–4341 fax ++358–9–1482–2650. Contact person for matters relating to copies and copyrights: Pirjo Rintakoski.

9 Ibid.

10 W. Murch, foreword to M. Chion (1994) *Audio-Vision: Sound on Screen*, New York: Columbia University Press, p. viii.

11 Ibid., preface, p. xxvi.

12 Quoted from the entry to Prix Europa (October 1997) at www.prix-europa.de. Contacts given: Niko Ingman, YLE Radio, Swedish-language Radio, BOX 62, FIN-00024 Yleisradio, tel. ++358–9–1480–3610, fax ++358–9–1480–3390. Contact person for matters relating to copies and copyrights: Pirjo Rintakoski, Yleisradio Oy, PO Box 99, FIN-00024 Yleisradio, tel. ++358–9–1480–3457, fax ++358–9–1480–3390.

13 Aare Toikka, Eesti Raadio Radio Drama Department,Gonsiori 21 0100 Tallin Estonia tel. ++372–2–450 959, fax ++372–2–450 959 raido@opera.tele-port.ee. Details also entered as www.prix-europa.de.

14 Funding figure based on analysing radio drama and spoken reading budgets released in the BBC Radio 4 Commissioning Brief for 1998.

5 From sound houses to the phonograph sound play

1 A published book reference has been kindly provided by Peter M. Lewis: J. Weinberger (ed.) (1989) *New Atlantis and the Great Instauration*, London: Harlan Davidson, pp. 78–9.

2 M. Drabble (ed.) (1987) *The Oxford Companion to English Literature*, London: Guild.

3 H. G. Wells (1899) *When The Sleeper Wakes*. Extracts from Project Gutenberg on the Internet at www.fortunecity.se/kista/chips/28/HGWells-WhenTheSleeperWakes.txt.

4 'Introduction' to J. Drakakis (ed.) (1981) *British Radio Drama*, Cambridge: Cambridge University Press.

5 *Great Shakespeareans* CD (1990) Pearl Label for Pavilion Records, Sparrows Green, Wadhurst, East Sussex (GEMM CD 9465).

6 Interview with the author, broadcast LBC 24 May 1994.

7 *The Great War: An Evocation in Music and Drama through Recordings Made at the Time* CD (1989) Pearl Label for Pavilion Records, Sparrows Green, Wadhurst, East Sussex (GEMM CD 9355).

8 D. Kahn (1994) 'Histories of sound once removed', in D. Kahn and G. White-head (eds) *Wireless Imagination: Sound, Radio, and the Avant-Garde*, Cambridge, MA: MIT Press, pp. 1–31.

9 K. Schöning (1991) 'The contours of acoustic art', trans. M. E. Cory, *Theatre Journal* 43: 307–24.

10 B. Stoker, *Dracula* ed. and intr. A. N. Wilson (1983) London: Oxford University Press, p. 60.
11 Quoted in Kahn and Whitehead, *Wireless Imagination*, p. 9.
12 Schöning, 'Contours of acoustic art', p. 316.
13 D. Kahn (1994) 'Radio space', in D. Augaitis and D. Lander (eds) *Radio Rethink: Art, Sound and Transmission* Banff, Alta: Walter Phillips Gallery.

6 A technological time-line

1 A. Holyer (1997) *Internet UK*, Warwickshire: Computer Step, p. 8.
2 T. Stauffer (1996) *Using HTML 3.2*, 2nd edn, Indianapolis, IN: Que Corporation, p. 11.

7 A culturalist approach to Internet audio drama

1 M. Poster (1995) *The Second Media Age*, Oxford: Blackwell.
2 G. Robertson et al. (eds) (1996) *Future Natural: Nature, Science, Culture*, London: Routledge, p. 191.
3 See J. Curran (1996) *Cultural Studies and Communications*, London: Arnold, p. 139.
4 S. Peak and P. Fish (eds) (1997) *The 1998 Guardian Media Guide*, London: Fourth Estate, p. 70.
5 Section 2, 'Radio 4 Audience Research', *BBC Radio 4 Commissioning Guidelines 1998/9*.
6 M. McLuhan (1995) *Understanding Media: The Extensions of Man*, London: MIT Press, p. 68.
7 J. Baudrillard (1981) *The Evil Demon of Images*, trans. P. Patton and P. Foss, Sydney: Power Institute, pp. 14–15.
8 M. McLuhan, 'Laws of media', in E. McLuhan and F. Zingrone (eds) (1997) *Essential McLuhan*, London: Routledge, p. 382.
9 P. Scannell (1996) *Radio, Television, and Modern Life*, Oxford: Blackwell.
10 Ibid., p. 10.
11 Reported in *The Times* 26 March 1999. Available at www.sunday-times.co.uk ('media' section) and analysed on Mediatel's website at www.mediatel.co.uk. Information provided by Richard Rudin, lecturer at Liverpool John Moores University, Radio Studies Mailbase list 26 March 1999.

8 Radio drama is *not* a blind medium

1 W. Murch, foreword to M. Chion (1994) *Audio-Vision: Sound on Screen*, New York: Columbia University Press, p. vii. He repeated this point in an interview with Mark Burman for the episode on film sound in the BBC Radio series *Lumière's Children* which was aired in 1995 and 1996, first on BBC Radio 3 and repeated on BBC Radio 4.

2 David Burrows is described as 'a lecturer in music at the New York University' in the paper 'The mechanics of emotions' presented by Edwin Brys at the International Forum on 'The Quest for Radio Quality: The Documentary' held during the 48th session of the Prix Italia on 26 June 1996 at the Maschio Angioino Castle in Naples. Attended by the author. All the papers were published by Radio Televisione Italiana, Rome, in October 1996. This quotation is from pp. 113–14.

3 At the time of writing Alan Beck had embarked on an impressive project to seek a definition and intellectual debate on 'Radio Theory'. This work was being developed on the SoundJournal website:
http://speke.ukc.ac.uk/sais/sound-journal/Beck99/index.html

4 T. H. Pear (1931) *Voice and Personality*, London: Chapman and Hall.

5 A. Crisell (1994) *Understanding Radio*, 2nd edn, London: Routledge, p. 10.

6 E. Brys, 26 June 1996, Prix Italia Documentary symposium transcript, pp. 115–16.

7 I have concealed her identity in the context of this publication to respect her privacy.

8 The sound can be obtained on the double audio cassette *LBC News 1973 to 1993*, produced by Charlie Rose and Tim Crook, IRDP (1993) *The Drama Collection* (DC521 ISBN 1–85781–166–6).

9 Pear, *Voice and Personality*, p. 99, reprinted in J. Drakakis (ed.) (1981) *British Radio Drama*, Cambridge: Cambridge University Press, p. 23.

10 A. Ingram (1994) *Wireless Wisdom*, London: Radio Advertising Bureau, p. 57.

11 Interview recorded by Peter Bogdanovich (between 1969 and 1972) with Orson Welles in Rome, reprinted in *Orson Welles and Peter Bogdanovich* (1993) London: HarperCollins.

12 Broadcast by CBS on 24 April 1939. Quoted by R. L. Bannerman (1986) *Norman Corwin and Radio: The Golden Years*, Alabama: University of Alabama Press, p. 45.

13 L. Sieveking (1934) *The Stuff of Radio*, London: Cassell, pp. 65–6.

14 I. Rodger (1982) *Radio Drama*, London: Macmillan, p. 15.

15 R. Horstmann (1991) *Writing for Radio*, 2nd edn, London: A. and C. Black, p. 2.

16 J. Raban (1980) 'Icon or symbol: the writer and the medium', in P. Lewis (ed.) *Radio Drama*, London: Longman, p. 79.

17 E. S. Guralnik (1996) *Sight Unseen: Beckett, Pinter, Stoppard and Other Contemporary Dramatists on Radio*, Athens, Ohio: Ohio University Press, p. 99.
18 Ibid., p. 100.
19 J. M. Hull (1990) *Touching the Rock: An Experience of Blindness*, New York: Pantheon, p. 202.
20 R. Barthes (1977) *Image, Music, Text*, New York: Hill and Wang, p. 62.
21 E. McLuhan and F. Zingrone (eds) (1997) *Essential McLuhan*, London: Routledge, p. 303.
22 D. Mamet (1986) *Writing in Restaurants*, London: Faber and Faber, p. 12.
23 Guthrie quoted in D. McWhinnie (1959) *The Art of Radio*, London: Faber and Faber, p. 25.
24 Chion, *Audio-Vision: Sound on Screen*, p. 224.
25 Crisell, *Understanding Radio*, p. 15.
26 M. Merleau-Ponty (1962) *The Phenomenology of Perception*, London: Routledge, p. 283.
27 McWhinnie, *The Art of Radio*, p. 27.
28 Ibid., p. 37.
29 M. E. Cory (1974) *The Emergence of an Acoustical Art Form: An Analysis of the German Experimental Hörspiel of the 1960s*, Lincoln, NB: University of Nebraska.
30 Crisell, *Understanding Radio*, p. 14.
31 'Dance of the Sugarplum Fairy' is a movement in *The Nutcracker Suite* by Tchaikovsky.

9 Sound design vocabulary

1 Sieveking's original observations are set out in L. Sieveking (1934) *The Stuff of Radio*, London: Cassell, pp. 64–8.
2 R. Barthes (1977) *Image – Music – Text*, trans. S. Heath, London: Fontana, p. 39. Quoted by A. Crisell (1994) *Understanding Radio*, 2nd edn, London: Routledge, p. 48.
3 M. Chion (1994) *Audio-Vision Sound on Screen*, New York: Columbia University Press, p. 221.
4 Sound effect no. 22 on *Human Crowds, Children and Footsteps* (1988) vol. 7, BBC Sound FXCD, London: BBC Enterprises.
5 Sound effect no. 10 on *British Birds* (1988) vol. 12, BBC Sound FX CD, London: BBC Enterprises.
6 Pear quoted in Sieveking, *The Stuff of Radio*, p. 67.
7 This point is powerfully made in a transcribed interview between Ronald Harwood and Martin Esslin in *The Listener* (6 January 1977, p. 22). Esslin's book on Bertolt Brecht in 1959 was the first major English critical study of the

German playwright and established the significance of his contribution to world theatre. 'The BBC radio drama department had introduced Brecht to the English stage. We did the first productions of Brecht here.'

8 L. Maltin (1997) *The Great American Broadcast*, New York: Dutton, p. 92.
9 H. Matheson (1933) *Broadcasting*, London: Thornton Butterworth.
10 Transcript from special edition of *Kaleidoscope* on BBC Radio 4, interview between Ronald Harwood and Martin Esslin, *The Listener*, 6 January 1977, pp. 22–3.
11 Matheson, *Broadcasting*, pp. 112–13.
12 Ibid., p. 113.
13 F. de Saussure (1974 [1915]) *Course in General Linguistics*, London: Fontana.
14 C. S. Peirce (1960) *Collected Papers*, vols I and II, ed. C. Hartshorne and P. Weiss, Cambridge, MA: Harvard University Press.
15 R. Firth (1973) *Symbols Public and Private*, London: Allen and Unwin.
16 Ibid.
17 Crisell, *Understanding Radio*, p. 48.
18 Ibid., p. 143.
19 M. E. Cory (1974) *The Emergence of an Acoustical Art Form: An Analysis of the German Experimental Hörspiel of the 1960s*, Lincoln, NB: University of Nebraska Press, p. 57.
20 M. Esslin (1987) *The Field of Drama: How the Signs of Drama Create Meaning on Stage and Screen*, London: Methuen, p. 30.
21 All of Chion's references to textual speech are to be found in his *Audio-Vision Sound on Screen*, pp. 172–6.
22 Ibid.
23 *Radio Times* (16 September 1995) described *Burn Your Phone* as a 'black comedy' and part of the last young radio playwrights' festival funded by the BBC. Directed by Mairi Russell, the cast included Alan Cumming, Jonathan Keeble, George Allonby, Stephen Critchlow, Zuleme Dene, Becky Hindley, Sandra James-Young and Geoffrey Whitehead.

10 The cinematic and musical inspiration

1 *The Listener*, 24 May 1956, pp. 673–4.
2 A. Briggs (1995) *History of Broadcasting in the United Kingdom*, vol. 1, Oxford: Oxford University Press, p. 183. Quoting from the *BBC Yearbook* (1930) 'The Old BBC', p. 169.
3 H. Matheson (1933) *Broadcasting*, London: Thornton Butterworth, p. 118.
4 The sound mixing panel was introduced to BBC operations in 1928 and represented a divergence from German production practice which continued

to have all the performance and playing components organised in one large studio with the balance being decided by a 'pot' control determining the level for each microphone input. Orson Welles and his Mercury Theatre On The Air produced his plays at CBS from one studio with Orson as the director conducting the components from a podium in the performance area of the studio.

5 D. J. Burrow, R. Middleton and W. Strang (1992) 'Cultural uses of sound', in *Introduction to Music*, Arts Foundation, Milton Keynes: Open University, pp. 6–7.
6 Ibid.
7 Ibid.
8 Ibid.
9 Ibid.
10 Ibid.
11 Ibid., p. 8.
12 R. Arnheim (1936) *Radio*, London: Faber and Faber, p. 55.
13 Ibid., p. 46.
14 Ken Garner, 'Putting the drama into dramatisation: in search of the source of current British radio drama', Radio Drama Conference, Kent University/ Goldsmiths College joint conference 16 January 1999. This is an excellent paper now published in SoundJournal at: http://speke.ukc.ac.uk/sais/ sound-journal/articleindex.html.
15 Burrow *et al.*, *Introduction to Music*, p. 15.

11 Blurring fiction with reality

1 H. Cantrill (with H. Gaudet and H. Herzog) (1966) *The Invasion from Mars: A Study in the Psychology of Panic with the Complete Script of the Famous Orson Welles Broadcast*, Princeton, NJ: Princeton University Press, p. 96.
2 P. F. Lazarsfeld, B. Berelson and H. Gaudet (1944) *The People's Choice: How the Voter Makes Up his Mind in a Presidential Campaign*, New York: Duell, Sloan and Pearce.
3 E. Katz, M. Gurevitch and E. Hass (1973) 'On the uses of the mass media for important things', *American Sociological Review* 38: 164–81.
4 Cantrill, *The Invasion from Mars: A Study in the Psychology of Panic*, p. 190.
5 Ibid., p. 202.
6 Ibid., p. 204.
7 O. Welles and P. Bogdanovich (1993) *This is Orson Welles*, ed. J. Rosenbaum, London: HarperCollins, pp. 18–19.
8 Ibid., p. 20.

9 F. Brady (1990) *Citizen Welles: A Biography of Orson Welles*, London: Hodder and Stoughton.

10 C. E. Shannon and W. Weaver (1949) *The Mathematical Theory of Communication*, Urbana, IL: University of Illinois Press.

11 *Theatre of the Imagination: Radio Stories by Orson Welles and the Mercury Theatre* (1995) CD-ROM, New York: Voyager Company.

12 Ibid.

13 H. Koch (1970) *The Panic Broadcast: The Whole Story of Orson Welles' Legendary Radio Show, Invasion from Mars*, New York: Avon, pp. 111–12.

12 Radio drama panics: a cross-cultural phenomenon

1 Sleeve notes for *Independence Day UK: Twentieth Century Fox Presents a BBC Radio 1 Audio Movie* (1996), London: Polygram Record Operations Speaking Volumes.

2 Ibid.

3 Ibid.

4 Cassette of broadcast programme submitted to International Radio Festival of New York 1996. Catalogued in Goldsmiths College Library, University of London.

13 Moving from burlesque to propaganda and news

1 M. Hilmes (1997) *Radio Voices: American Broadcasting 1922–1952*, Minneapolis, MN: University of Minnesota Press, pp. 212–18.

2 Ibid., pp. 218–29.

3 *Why Bother?*, BBC Radio 3 1993 and repeated in 1995 shortly after Peter Cook's death. Morris interviews Cook as Sir Arthur Streeb-Greebling on his legendary career. The complete series (edited into one 50-minute item) was released on a single cassette or CD by the BBC Radio Collection on 1 March 1999. ISBN 0563557478 (cassette); 0563558601 (CD).

4 H. Thompson (1997) *Peter Cook: A Biography*, London: Hodder and Stoughton, p. 457.

5 Thompson, *Peter Cook*, p. 402.

6 S. Hall (1973) *Encoding and Decoding in the Television Message*, reprinted in S. Hall, D. Hobson, A. Lowe and P. Willis (eds) (1980) *Culture, Media, Language*, London: Hutchinson.

7 J. Fiske (1990) *Introduction to Communication Studies*, 2nd edn, London: Routledge.

8 J. Fiske and J. Hartley (1978) *Reading Television*, London: Methuen.

14 The *War of the Worlds* effect: *Spoonface Steinberg*?

1 Quoted from the sleeve notes of the BBC Radio Collection edition *Spoonface Steinberg*, BBC Worldwide 1997. ZBBC 2058.

2 The extent of the audience response is difficult to validate externally. I had made a request to Kate Rowland, but access to the letters received and telephone calls logged by the BBC appeared to be dependent on a number of factors such as the issue of correspondents' privacy and the question of approving the 'context' of the paper's discourse. I have not been able to determine whether the broadcast of the series *Bomber* in 1995 generated more telephone calls and letters. When I attended a programme review board just after the broadcast references were made to a considerable reaction from the audience which included 'hundreds of calls'.

3 Interview with Kate Rowland at Broadcasting House 5 December 1997.

4 L. Hall (1997) *Introduction to Spoonface Steinberg and Other Plays*, London: BBC Books.

5 Interview with Kate Rowland.

6 Televised on BBC 2 9.50 to 10.30 p.m. 16 June 1998.

7 On 20 June 1998 the *Guardian*'s radio critic Anne Karpf wrote: 'R4's "Spoonface Steinberg" became BBC2's Spoonface Steinberg. Lee Hall's remarkably successful monologue about death and life reprised young Becky Simpson's fine performance over silent footage and stills. But though sensitively and imaginatively done, it was never really more than radio with pictures. Like so much television' (Review Section, p. 5).

8 *Radio Times* 13–19 June 1998, p. 4.

9 Interview with Kate Rowland.

10 H. Cantrill (with H. Gaudet and H. Herzog) (1966) *The Invasion from Mars: A Study in the Psychology of Panic and with the Complete Script of the Famous Orson Welles Broadcast*, Princeton, NJ: Princeton University Press.

11 Fiske, *Introduction to Communication Studies*.

12 R. Barthes (1967 [1957]) *Mythologies*, trans. A. Lavers, London: Cape.

13 V. Walkerdine (1996) 'Popular culture and the eroticisation of little girls', in J. Curran, D. Morley and V. Walkerdine (eds) *Cultural Studies and Communications*, London: Arnold.

14 It is ironic that the expression 'Queen of People's Hearts' as an association with Diana was originally coined in a headline by News International's *Sun* newspaper, which is Britain's biggest selling newspaper.

15 R. Barthes (1968) 'The death of the author', in (1977) *Image, Music, Text*, trans. S. Heath, London: Fontana, pp. 142–8.

16 W. K. Wimsatt and M. C. Beardsley (1954) 'The intentional fallacy', in *The Verbal Icon: Studies in the Meaning of Poetry*, London: Methuen.

15 *Spoonface Steinberg*: constructing the Holocaust as a means of identification

1 L. Hall (1997) *Spoonface Steinberg and Other Plays*, London: BBC Books, pp. 149–50.
2 RAJAR research for Quarter Two 1998. BBC Radio 4 was in fact ranked second to 95.8 Capital FM. In the context of national listening Radio 4 had 10.3% share of total listening in a UK adult 15+ population of 47,652,000.

16 The writing agenda for audio drama

1 H. Kingsley (1988) *Soap Box*, London: Papermac. P. Buckman (1984) *Soap Opera*, London: Secker and Warburg.
2 *America Before TV* (1987) Greatapes, 1523 Nicollet, Minneapolis, MN 55403. The entire output of WJSV for Thursday 21 September 1939.
3 The UK Radio Advertising Bureau has been making a great effort to improve the creative content of UK radio commercials. Much credit is due to Andrew Ingram, who tirelessly travels the UK encouraging research into qualitative creation and production of good radio commercials.
4 *25 Years: A History of LBC 1152 AM*, written by Steve Campen and produced by Chris Lowri, broadcast 8 October 1998. The Imperial War Museum Campaign was created by the advertising agency Ogilvy and Mather. It is also available in *A Celebration of 21 Years of Radio Advertising* (1994) CD, Radio Advertising Bureau, RAB21.
5 Study was conducted in 1995. Each panel member received a copy of the *Radio Times* for a two week period with the request that they each listened to as much as they could on the schedule, made a record of what they succeeded in listening to, when they tuned out while listening and a score out of ten for the production values in relation to each play.
6 The teaching session was provided to a sixth form college in Shoreditch in March 1993 during a Media Studies GCSE course taught by writer Manny Draycott-Lai.
7 P. Guennel and T. Zetterholm (1986) *An Illustrated Companion to World Literature*, New York: Excalibur, p. 9.
8 Ken Dancyger has produced two outstanding practical writing guides: *Broadcast Writing* (1991) and *Alternative Scriptwriting* (2nd edn 1995) with Jeff Rush, both Boston, MA: Focal Press.
9 K. Richards (1991) *Writing Radio Drama*, Sydney: Currency Press, pp. 81–2.
10 C. McArthur (1972) *Underworld USA*, London: British Film Institute and Secker and Warburg.

11 Beckett's *Words and Music* was first broadcast on the BBC Third Programme on 13 November 1962.

17 Creating the character and effective use of characterisation

1 V. Propp (1968 [1928]) *Morphology of the Folktale*, trans. L. Scott, 2nd edn, Austin, TX: University of Texas Press.

18 Writing dialogue

1 K. Dancyger (1991) *Broadcast Writing: Drama, Comedies and Documentaries*, Boston, MA: Focal Press, p. 42.
2 The sound of this extract along with the script can be accessed by Internet at http://www.irdp.co.uk/darksound.htm. The entire dramatisation script is available at www.irdp.co.uk/darkness.htm.

19 The phantom distinction

1 Paul Celan, quoted by B. Holmberg, 'Looking for the invisible', paper presented at the International Forum on 'The Quest for Radio Quality: The Documentary' held during the 48th session of the Prix Italia on 26 June 1996 at the Maschio Angioino Castle in Naples. Attended by the author. All the papers were published by the Radio Televisione Italiana, Rome, in October 1996, p. 169.
2 Neil Bohr, quoted by K. Klaanderen, 'The documentary is (a) drama', quoting John Theocharis from the radio documentary festival 'Boundless Sound', Amsterdam 1995, in a paper presented at the International Forum on 'The Quest for Radio Quality: The Documentary', ibid., p. 251.
3 Klaanderen, 'The documentary is (a) drama', ibid., p. 251.
4 L. Sieveking (1934) *The Stuff of Radio*, London: Cassell, p. 26.
5 Lawrence Gilliam, quoted by R. McLeish (1994) *Radio Production*, 3rd edn, Boston, MA: Focal Press, p. 247.
6 S. MacLoughlin (1998) *Writing for Radio: How to Create Successful Radio Plays, Features and Short Stories*, Oxford: How To Books, p. 101.
7 P. Scannell, 'The radio documentary: from profession to apparatus', a paper presented at the International Forum on 'The Quest for Radio Quality: The Documentary', pp. 33–40.
8 L. Gilliam (ed.) (1950) *BBC Features*, London: BBC and Evans Brothers, p. 12.
9 *From Salford to Jericho*, starring Shiobhan Redmond and Alistaire Gilbraith.

Featuring Simon Armitage performing his own poetry created from interviews with over fifty homeless people. Devised and directed by Kate Rowland. *Radio Times* entry: 'Mags has come to find her brother Billy who lives on the street in Manchester. He won't go home. Billy is not alone in the city with a story to tell.' Broadcast 9–10 p.m. 27 November 1998.

10 Klaanderen, 'The documentary is (a) drama', p. 252.

11 Paddy Scannell and John Drakakis have written the most comprehensive and scholarly analyses of the history of the dramatic or aesthetic feature in Britain. P. Scannell (1991) ' "The Stuff of Radio": developments in radio features and documentaries before the war', in J. Corner (ed.) (1986) *Documentary and the Mass Media*, Sevenoaks, Kent: Edward Arnold, pp. 1–26 and 'Features and Social Documentaries' in P. Scannell and D. Cardiff (eds) *A Social History of British Broadcasting, Vol. I, Serving the Nation, 1922–1939*, Oxford: Basil Blackwell, pp. 134–52. J. Drakakis (ed.) (1981) *British Radio Drama*, Cambridge: Cambridge University Press, pp. 1–36.

12 Sieveking, *The Stuff of Radio*, pp. 115–382.

13 Ibid., pp. 383–94.

14 Scannell, ' "The Stuff of Radio" ', p. 6.

15 Drakakis, *British Radio Drama*, p. 20.

16 Ibid., p. 10.

17 Ibid., p. 9.

18 Scannell, ' "The Stuff of Radio" ', pp. 12–13.

19 G. Orwell ([1935] 1975) *A Clergyman's Daughter*, Harmondsworth: Penguin, pp. 138–64.

20 Drakakis, *British Radio Drama*, p. 9.

21 D. G. Brisdon (1971) *Prospero and Ariel: The Rise and Fall of Radio – A Personal Recollection*, London: Gollancz, p. 111.

22 Scannell, ' "The Stuff of Radio" ', p. 21.

23 A. Briggs (1995) *The History of Broadcasting in the United Kingdom*, London: Oxford University Press.

24 Scannell, 'The radio documentary', pp. 38–9.

25 B. Nichols (1991) *Representing Reality: Issues and Concepts in Documentary*, Bloomington, IN: Indiana University Press.

26 Ibid., p. 62.

27 Posted on Radio Studies Mailbase list January 1999.

28 Gilliam, *BBC Features*, pp. 9–14.

20 Making the documentary feature

1 Both quotations taken from Prix Italia Symposium transcript, 'The Quest for Radio Quality: The Documentary', 26 July 1996, Naples, published by Radio Televisione Italiana, pp. 251–2.
2 Ibid., p. 74.
3 Some of these points were eloquently made by the Belgian director Edwin Brys (Head of Features and Drama Dept BRTN) at the Prix Italia Symposium, ibid., pp. 113–18.
4 Submitted in an Internet debate by radio practitioners and scholars on the 'Radio Studies' list, February–March 1999. Peter Everett was also interviewed by the author via email during the same period.
5 R. M. Busfield (1958) *The Playwrights' Art: Stage, Radio, Television, Motion Pictures*, Westport, CT: Greenwood Press.
6 R. Houd (1991) 'Audio space: spatiality and sound', MA Production Theory essay, Goldsmiths College, University of London.
7 K. Frandsen and H. Bruun (1998) 'Radiooestetik og Analysemetode' (Radioaestheic and analysis method), Danish quarterly magazine *MedieKultur* no. 15.
8 M. Woolf, 'The documentary: a genre to be rediscovered', Prix Italia Symposium transcript, p. 8.
9 A. Briggs (1995) *The Birth of Broadcasting 1896–1927*, London: Oxford University Press, pp. 256–7. R. E. Jeffrey's views on radio drama were set out in three *Radio Times* articles, 'Wireless drama' (6/6/24) 'The need for a radio drama' (17/7/25) and 'Seeing with the mind's eye' (5/11/26).
10 H. Kopetzky, 'Information, opinion, provocation', Prix Italia Symposium transcript, p. 73.
11 G. Ortoleva, 'The radio documentary: its language and forms from the past to the future', ibid., pp. 51–6.
12 E. Brys, 'The mechanics of emotions', ibid., p. 114.

21 Directorial responsibility

1 The series was screened in the UK on Channel Four and the quotations are from the episode in the final series when Cicely attempted to present a production of *Bus Stop*.
2 A. Beck (1997) *Radio Acting*, London: A. and C. Black.

22 Managing the production

1 S. Callow (1992) *Shooting the Actor, or the Choreography of Confusion*, London: Vintage, p. 2.

23 Experimental direction and performance

1 K. Richards (1991) *Writing Radio Drama*, Sydney: Currency Press, pp. 115–20.
2 A. Karpf, 'Wave riding', *Guardian* Saturday Review Section, 13 February 1999.
3 Information about Anthony Sloan's radio drama work was obtained through interview and Internet Reports posted on the WBAI website between 1995 and 1997.
4 R. Durham and F. J. MacDonald (eds) (1989) *Destination Freedom: Scripts from Radio's Black Legacy, 1948–50*, New York: Praeger.

Audio drama bibliography

I have endeavoured to discover as many ways as possible for the student and practitioner to access audio drama sources in respect of publication on theory as well as practical audio material.

The International Radio Festival of New York archive at Goldsmiths College is a useful source of programmes not published in the burgeoning spoken word market. Goldsmiths also retains unpublished academic studies of radio drama which could be of considerable interest since theoretical publication of audio art and programming is small compared to film and television.

I have divided the bibliography into the following sections:

Published texts
Giles Cooper Award winners
Morningside Dramas
Contact directories
Newspaper, journal and magazine articles
Published television and radio programmes
Published spoken word, film, video and sound archives and CD-ROMs
Internet publications
Internet and World Wide Web sites
Unpublished MA and PhD theses
Radio Drama Archives at Goldsmiths College, University of London

Published texts

Adams, D. (1985) *The Hitch-Hiker's Guide to the Galaxy: The Original Radio Scripts*, ed. and int. G. Perkins, London: Pan.

Allan, A. (1987) *All The Bright Company: Radio Drama Produced by Andrew Allen*, eds H. Fink and J. Jackson, Kingston, Ont.: Quarry Press.

Alvarez, A. (1973) *Beckett*, London: Fontana.

Arden, J. and D'Arcy, M. (1988) *Whose is the Kingdom: Nine Part Radio Series*, London: Methuen.

Arnheim, R. (1936) *Radio*, trans. M. Luding and H. Read, London: Faber and Faber.

Ash, W. (1985) *The Way to Write Radio Drama*, London: Elm Tree.

Augaitis, D. and Lander, D. (eds) (1994) *Radio Rethink: Art, Sound and Transmission*, Banff, Alta: Walter Phillips Gallery.

Bannerman, R. LeRoy (1986) *Norman Corwin and Radio: The Golden Years*, Alabama: University of Alabama Press.

Barfield, R. (1996) *Listening to Radio, 1920–1950*, Westport, CT: Praeger.

Barkworth, P. (1980) *About Acting*, London: Secker and Warburg.

Barlow, W. (1999) *Voice Over: The Making of Black Radio*, Philadelphia, PA: Temple University Press.

Barthes, R. (1977a) *Image – Music – Text*, trans. S. Heath, London: Fontana.

Barthes, R. (1977b) *Introduction to the Structural Analysis of Narratives*, London: Fontana.

Beck, A. (1997) *Radio Acting*, London: A. and C. Black.

Beckett, S. (1974a) *Oh les beaux jours suivi, de Pas moi*, Paris: Minuits.

Beckett, S. (1974b) *Comédie et actes divers* (including *Cascando* and *Paroles et musique*), Paris: Minuits.

Beckett, S (1974c) *Pas, suivi de Quatre esquisses* (*Fragments de théâtre I et II, Pochade radiophonique, Esquisse radiophonique*), Paris: Minuits.

Beckett, S. (1978) *Pas, suivi de Quatre esquisses*, Paris: Minuits.

Beckett, S. (1989) *Collected Shorter Plays of Samuel Beckett* (includes radio plays: *All That Fall, Embers, Rough for Radio I, Rough for Radio II, Words and Music, Cascando*), London: Faber and Faber.

Bennett, A. (1988) *Talking Heads*, London: BBC Books.

Bentley, E. (1992) *The Theory of the Modern Stage*, Harmondsworth: Penguin.

Berry, C. (1987) *The Actor and his Text*, London: Virgin.

Berry, C. (1990) *Your Voice and How to Use it Successfully*, London: Virgin.

Birney, E. (1985) *Words on Waves: Selected Radio Plays of Earle Birney*, Kingston, Ont: Quarry Press.

Bogdanovich, P. (1993) *Orson Welles and Peter Bogdanovich*, London: Harper-Collins.

Bogosian, E. (1994) *The Essential Bogosian, Talk Radio, Drinking in America, Funhouse and Men Inside*, New York: Theatre Communications Group.

Brady, F. (1990) *Citizen Welles: A Biography of Orson Welles*, London: Hodder and Stoughton.

Branagh, K. (1989) *Beginning*, London: Chatto and Windus.

Branston, G. and Stafford, R. (1996) *The Media Student's Book*, London: Routledge.

Braun, E. (1993) *The Director and the Stage: From Naturalism to Grotowski*, London: Methuen Drama.

Brook, Pamela (1995) *Radio Social Drama: Communicating through Story Characters*, New York: University Press of America.

Brook, Peter (1990) *The Empty Space*, Harmondsworth: Penguin.

Brown, J. R. (ed.) (1997) *The Oxford Illustrated History of Theatre*, Oxford: Oxford University Press.

Busfield, R. M. (1971) *The Playwright's Art: Stage, Radio, Television, Motion Pictures*, Westport, CT: Greenwood.

Caine, M. (1997) *Acting in Film*, London: Applause Books.

Callow, S. (1985) *Being an Actor*, Harmondsworth: Penguin.

Callow, S. (1995) *Orson Welles: The Road to Xanadu*, London: Viking.

Cantrill, H. (with Gaudet, H. and Herzog, H.) (1966) *The Invasion From Mars: A Study in the Psychology of Panic with the Complete Script of the Famous Orson Welles Broadcast*, Princeton, NJ: Princeton University Press.

Carpenter, H. and research by Doctor, J. (1997) *The Envy of the World: 50 Years of the BBC Third Programme and Radio 3*, London: Phoenix.

Carter, A. (1997) *The Curious Room: Angela Carter, Collected Dramatic Works*, London: Vintage.

Chion, M. (1994) *Audio-Vision: Sound on Screen*, ed. and trans. C. Gorbman, New York: Columbia University Press.

Churchill, C. (1990) *Churchill Shorts: Short Plays by Caryl Churchill*, London: Nick Hern.

Cole, Susan L. (1992) *Directors in Rehearsal: A Hidden World*, London: Routledge.

Cox, B. (1992) *Salem to Moscow: An Actor's Odyssey*, London: Methuen.

Crisell, A. (1994) *Understanding Radio*, 2nd edn, London: Routledge.

Cronin, A. (1996) *Samuel Beckett: The Last Modernist*, London: Flamingo.

Crook, T. (1998) *International Radio Journalism: History, Theory and Practice*, London: Routledge.

Crook, T. and Shannon, R. (1991) *Radio Drama, Writing, Acting and Production*, Manningtree, Essex: IRDP/Woolwich Building Society (booklet with cassette pack).

Daley, B. (1994) *The National Public Star Wars Radio Dramatization*, New York: Ballantine.

Dancyger, K. (1991) *Broadcast Writing: Dramas, Comedies, and Documentaries*, (Electronic Media Guides), Boston, MA: Focal Press.

Dancyger, K. and Rush, J. (1995) *Alternative Scriptwriting: Writing Beyond the Rules*, 2nd edn, Boston, MA: Focal Press.

Day, P. (1994) *The Radio Years: A History of Broadcasting in New Zealand*, vol. 1, Auckland: Auckland University Press with Broadcasting History Trust.

Degler, C. N. (1971) *Neither Black nor White: Slavery and Race Relations in Brazil and the United States*, New York: Macmillan.

Donovan, P. (1991) *The Radio Companion: The A–Z Guide to Radio from its Inception to the Present Day*, London: HarperCollins.

Drakakis, J. (ed.) (1981) *British Radio Drama*, Cambridge: Cambridge University Press. (This book includes important chapters on the radio plays of Louis MacNeice, Dylan Thomas, Susan Hill, Dorothy L. Sayers, Giles Cooper, Henry Reed and Samuel Beckett. It contains an appendix listing 'radio plays published', which is useful for an indication of scripts published prior to 1980, but does not include the publishers.)

Durham, R. and MacDonald, F. J. (ed.) (1989) *Destination Freedom: Scripts from Radio's Black Legacy, 1948–50*, Westport, CT: Praeger.

Eckersley, P. (1942) *The Power behind the Microphone*, London: Scientific Book Club.

Ely, P. E. (1991) *The Adventures of Amos 'n' Andy: A Social History of an American Phenomenon*, New York: The Free Press.

Esslin, M. (1987) *The Field of Drama: How the Signs of Drama Create Meaning on Stage and Screen*, London: Methuen.

Felton, F. (1949) *The Radio Play*, London: Sylvan Press.

Fiske, J. (1990) *Introduction to Communication Studies*, London: Routledge.

Frost, E. and Heersfeld-Sander, M. (1991) *German Radio Plays*, New York: Continuum.

Gibson, J. L. (1986) *Ian McKellen: A Biography*, London: Weidenfeld and Nicolson.

Gilroy, P. (1991) *There Ain't No Black in the Union Jack*, London: Routledge.

Gilroy, P. (1993) *The Black Atlantic: Modernity and Double Consciousness*, London: Verso.

Gombrich, E. H. (1977) *Art and Illusion: A Study in the Psychology of Pictorial Representation*, 5th edn, London: Phaidon.

Guralnick, E. S. (1996) *Sight Unseen: Beckett, Pinter, Stoppard and Other Contemporary Dramatists on Radio*, Athens, Ohio: Ohio University Press.

Guthrie, T. (1931) *'Squirrel's Cage' and Other Microphone Plays*, London: Cobden and Sanderson.

Hall, J. (1984) *Hall's Dictionary of Subjects and Symbols in Art*, Introduction by Kenneth Clark, London: John Murray.

Hall, L. (1997) *Spoonface Steinberg and Other Plays*, London: BBC Books.

Higham, C. (1985) *Orson Welles: The Rise and Fall of an American Genius*, New York: St Martin's Press.

Hilliard, R. L. and Keith, M. C. (1997) *The Broadcast Century: A Biography of American Broadcasting*, 2nd edn, Boston, MA: Focal Press.

Hilmes, M. (1997) *Voices: American Broadcasting, 1922–1952*, Minneapolis, MN: University of Minnesota Press.

Hulke, M. (1980) *Writing for Television*, London: A. and C. Black.

Inglis, F. (1990) *Media Theory: An Introduction*, Oxford: Blackwell.

Irving, H. (1989) *The Drama Addresses*, London: Darf.

Kahn, D. and Whitehead, G. (eds) (1994) *Wireless Imagination: Sound, Radio, and the Avant-Garde*, Cambridge, MA: MIT Press.

Keillor, G. (1991) *A Radio Romance*, London: Faber and Faber. Other titles by the same author and publisher include *Happy To Be Here* (1982), *Lake Wobegon Days* (1985), *Leaving Home* (1987) and *We Are Still Married* (1989).

Kuhn, R. (1995) *The Media in France*, London: Routledge.

Lane, R. (1994) *The Golden Age of Australian Radio Drama 1923–1960: A History through Biography*, Melbourne: Melbourne University Press supported by the National Film and Sound Archive, Canberra.

Leaming, B. (1995) *Orson Welles: A Biography*, New York: Limelight.

Lévi-Strauss, C. (1972) 'The structural study of myth', in R. De George and F. De George (eds) *The Structuralists from Marx to Lévi-Strauss*, New York: Doubleday.

Lewis, P. M. (1991) 'Referable words in radio drama', in P. Scannell (ed.) *Broadcast Talk*, London: Sage.

McBridge, J. (1996) *Orson Welles*, New York: Da Capo Press.

McCaffery, M. (1988) *Directing a Play*, Oxford: Phaidon.

MacLoughlin, S. (1998) *Successful Writing for Radio: How to Create Successful Radio Plays, Features, and Short Stories*, Oxford: How To Books.

McLuhan, M. (1995 [1964]) *Understanding Media: The Extension of Man*, London: MIT Press.

Martin, J. (1991) *Voice in Modern Theatre*, London: Routledge.

Matheson, H. (1933) *Broadcasting*, London: Thornton Butterworth.

Miles-Brown, J. (1985) *Acting: A Drama Studio Source Book*, London: Peter Owen.

Mitchell, J. and Maidment, R. (1994) *Culture: The United States in the Twentieth Century*, London: Hodder and Stoughton with the Open University.

Morrison, H. (1995) *Acting Skills*, London: A. and C. Black.

Naremore, J. (1989) *The Magic World of Orson Welles*, Dallas, TX: Southern Methodist University Press.

O'Toole, J. (1992) *The Process of Drama: Negotiating Art and Meaning*, London: Routledge.

Pope, T. (1998) *Good Scripts: Learning the Craft of Screenwriting through 25 of the Best and Worst Films in History*, New York: Three Rivers Press.

Pownall, D. (1998) *Radio Plays: An Epiphanous Use of the Microphone, Beef, Ploughboy Monday, Flos, Kitty Wilkinson, Under the Table*, London: Oberon.

Prix Italia (1996) International Forum on 'The Quest for Radio Quality: The Documentary', held during the 48th session of the Prix Italia on 26 June 1996 at the Maschio Angioino Castle in Naples. All the papers were published by Radio Televisione Italiana, Rome, in October 1996.

Prix Italia (1998) *Prix Italia, Ravenna 1997*, Rome: Radio Televisione Italiana.

Prix Italia (1998) *The Quest for Quality: The Public At Risk*, Rome: Radio Televisione Italiana.

Propp, V. (1975) *The Morphology of the Folk Take*, Austin, TX: University of Texas Press.

Quennel, P. and Zetterholm, T. (1986) *An Illustrated Companion to World Literature*, New York: Excalibur.

Richards, K. (1991) *Writing Radio Drama*, Sydney: Currency Press.

Ruddick, E. (1995) *My Mother's Daughter: A Theatrical Autobiography*, Braunton, Devon: Merlin.

Sayers, D. L. (1943) *The Man Born to be King*, New York: Harper.

Scannell, P. (1996) *Radio, Television, and Modern Life*, Oxford: Blackwell.

Seymour-Smith, M. (1973, 1975) *Guide to Modern World Literature* (vols 1–4) London: Hodder and Stoughton.

Sherman, J. and 29 other playwrights (1996) *Instant Applause II: 30 Very Short Complete Plays*, Winnipeg, Man.: Blizzard.

Shields, C. and 25 other playwrights (1994) *Instant Applause: 26 Very Short Complete Plays*, Winnipeg, Man.: Blizzard.

Shingler, M. and Weiringa, C. (1998) *On Air*, London, New York, Sydney: Arnold.

Sieveking, L. (1934) *The Stuff of Radio*, London: Cassell.

Smulyan, S. (1994) *Selling Radio: The Commercialization of American Broadcasting 1920–1934*, Washington, DC: Smithsonian Institution Press.

Stanislavski, K. (1988) *Creating a Role*, trans. E. Reynolds Hapgood, London: Methuen.

Stoppard, T. (1994) *Stoppard: The Plays for Radio 1964–1991*, London: Faber and Faber.

Straczynski, M. J. (1996) *The Complete Book of Scriptwriting*, 2nd edn, Cincinnati, Ohio: Writer's Digest.

Strauss, N. and Mandl, D. (eds) (1993) *Radiotext(e)*, New York: Columbia University Press.

Thompson, H. (1997) *Peter Cook: A Biography*, London: Hodder and Stoughton.

Thomson, D. (1996) *Rosebud: The Story of Orson Welles*, New York: Vintage.

Todorov, T. (1977) *The Poetics of Prose*, Oxford: Blackwell.

Tracey, M. (1998) *The Decline and Fall of Public Service Broadcasting*, Oxford: Oxford University Press.

Turner, C. J. (1993) *Voice and Speech in the Theatre*, 4th edn, London: A. and C. Black.

Watson, J. and Hill, A. (1997) *A Dictionary of Communication and Media Studies*, 4th edn, London: Arnold.

Watts, H. (1992) *On Camera: How to Produce Film and Video*, London: BBC Books.

Webb, G. (1950) *The Inside Story of Dick Barton*, ed. N. Tuson, London: Convoy.

Whitburn, V. (1996, 1997) *The Official Inside Story: The Archers, The Changing Face of Radio's Longest Running Drama*, London: Virgin.

Whitelaw, B. (1996) *Billie Whitelaw, Who He? An Autobiography*, London: Hodder and Stoughton.

Whitmore, J. (1994) *Directing Postmodern Theatre: Shaping Signification in Performance*, Ann Arbor, MI: University of Michigan Press.

Yoder, A. (1996) *Pirate Radio: The Incredible Saga of America's Underground, Illegal Broadcasters*, Solana Beach, CA: Hightext (book with CD).

Giles Cooper Award winners

A series, Methuen/BBC publication from 1978, including the radio scripts of the winning writers for each year. Methuen pulled out when the sales were too poor and there has been a hiatus in publication apart from years when the BBC was willing to fund the full cost. This was the BBC selection of scripts it considered to be 'Best Radio Plays' that particular year. Rather than list each author alphabetically in the bibliography I have set out this special section which gives year of publication and names and authors of plays. The BBC's venture in 'vanity publishing' for writers it has selected as 'significant' is not restricted to the Giles Cooper Award winners. The BBC World Service and domestic network Radio 4 have run and still run 'new writing' schemes and competitions which result in subsidised publications. These have also been included. In an appendix to J. Drakakis (ed.) (1981) *British Radio Drama*, Cambridge: Cambridge University Press (pp. 256–62), there is a very helpful attempt to list playscripts published between 1924 and 1979. Drakakis modestly qualifies the list by saying that it cannot claim to be complete. However, I would say that for this period it is the most comprehensive.

Best Radio Plays of 1978

Richard Harris: *Is it Something I Said?*
Don Haworth: *Episode on a Thursday Evening*
Jill Hyem: *Remember Me*
Tom Mallin: *Halt! Who Goes There?*
Jennifer Phillips: *Daughters of Men*
Fay Weldon: *Polaris*

Best Radio Plays of 1979

Shirley Gee: *Typhoid Mary*
Carey Harrison: *I Never Killed my German*
Barrie Keeffe: *Heaven Scent*
John Kirkmorris: *Coxcomb*
John Peacock: *Attard in Retirement*
Olwen Wymark: *The Child*

Best Radio Plays of 1980

Steward Parkeer: *The Kamikaze Groundstaff Reunion Dinner*
Martyn Read: *Waving to a Train*
Peter Redgrove: *Martyr of the Hives*
William Trevor: *Beyond the Pale*

Best Radio Plays of 1981

Peter Barnes: *The Jumping Mimuses of Byzantium*
Don Haworth: *Talk of Love and War*
Harold Pinter: *Family Voices*
David Pownall: *Beef*
J. P. Rooney: *The Dead Image*
Paul Thain: *The Biggest Sandcastle in the World*

Best Radio Plays of 1982

Rhys Adrian: *Watching the Plays Together*
John Arden: *The Old Man Sleeps Alone*
Harry Barton: *Hoopoe Day*
Donald Chapman: *Invisible Writing*
Tom Stoppard: *The Dog it was that Died*
William Trevor: *Autumn Sunshine*

Best Radio Plays of 1983

Wally K. Daly: *Time Slip*
Shirley Gee: *Never in my Lifetime*
Gerry Jones: *The Angels They Grow Lonely*
Steve May: *No Exceptions*
Martyn Read: *Scouting for Boys*

Best Radio Plays of 1984

Stephen Dunstone: *Who is Sylvia?*
Robert Ferguson: *Transfigured Night*
Don Haworth: *Daybreak*
Caryl Phillips: *The Wasted Years*
Christopher Russell: *Swimmer*
Rose Tremain: *Temporary Shelter*

Best Radio Plays of 1985

Rhys Adrian: *Outpatient*
Barry Collins: *King Canute*
Martin Crimp: *Three Attempted Acts*
David Pownall: *Ploughboy Monday*
James Saunders: *Menocchio*
Michael Wall: *Hiroshima: The Movie*

Best Radio Plays of 1986

Robert Ferguson: *Dreams, Secrets, Beautiful Lies*
Christina Reid: *The Last of a Dyin' Race*
Andrew Rissik: *A Man Alone: Anthony*
Ken Whitmore: *The Gingerbread House*
Valerie Windsor: *Myths and Legacies*

Best Radio Plays of 1987

Wally K. Daly: *Mary's*
Frank Dunne: *Dreams of Dublin Bay*
Anna Fox: *Nobby's Day*
Nigel D. Moffat: *Lifetime*
Richard Nelson: *Languages Spoken Here*
Peter Tinniswood: *The Village Fete*

Best Radio Plays of 1988

Ken Blakeson: *Excess Baggage*
Terence Frisby: *Just Remembeer Two Things: It's Not Fair and Don't Be Late*
Anthony Minghella: *Cigarettes and Chocolate*
Rona Munro: *The Dirt under the Carpet*
Dave Sheasby: *Apple Blossom Afternoons*

Best Radio Plays of 1989

Elizabeth Baines: *The Baby Buggy*
Jennifer Johnston: *O Ananias, Azarias and Misael*
David Zane Mairowitz: *The Stalin Sonata*
Richard Nelson: *Eating Words*
Craig Warner: *By Where the Old Shed Used to Be*

Best Radio Plays of 1990

Tony Bagley: *The Machine*
David Cregan: *A Butler Did It*
John Fletcher: *Death and the Tango*
Tina Pepler: *Song of the Forest*
Steve Walker: *The Pope's Brother*

Best Radio Plays of 1991

Robin Glendinning: *The Words are Strange*
John Purser: *Carver*
Tom Stoppard: *In the Native State*
Steve Walker: *Mickey Mookey*
Craig Warner: *Figure with Meat*

BBC Radio Drama Young Playwrights Festival 1988

Benjamin Zephaniah: *Hurricane Dub*
Hattie Naylor: *The Box*
Jeanette Winterson: *Static*
Richard Hayton: *One Friday Not a Million Miles Past*
Abigail Docherty: *Listen to my Inside Mind*
Ann Ogidi: *Ragamuffin*

BBC World Service Radio Plays for the World (published 1996)

Diane Ney: *Truckin' Maggie* (1989)
Andrew Verster: *You May Leave, the Show is Over* (1992)
Katy Parisi: *Puzzles* (1995)
Herbert Kaufman: *Last Supper* (1995)
Margaret Bhatty: *My Enemy My Friend* (1995)

Morningside Dramas

Morningside was a mainstream morning sequence programme on CBC in Canada and in 1991 two compilations of radio plays were published bearing the title *The Morningside Dramas*.

Take Five, edited by Dave Carley

Mary Burns: *Yukon Quintette*
Timothy Findley: *Love and Deception: Three by Chekhov*
Richardo Keens-Douglas: *Once Upon An Island*
Thomas Lackey: *The Skid*
Arthur Milner: *The City*

Airborne: Radio Plays by Women, edited by Ann Jansen

Judith Thompson: *White Sand*
Renee: *Te Pouaka Karaehe* [*The Glass Box*]
Anne Chislett: *Venus Sucked In: A Post-feminist Comedy*
Dacia Maraini: *Mussomeli-Dusseldorf*
Sharon Pollock: *The Making of Warriors*
Diana Raznovich: *That's Extraordinary!*

Contact directories

Contacts: Stage, Television, Film and Radio (annually) ed. C. Barry, A. Dean, S. Miall, K. Poynton, L. Sargent, The Spotlight, 7 Leicester Place, London WC2H 7BP.

Writers' and Artists' Yearbook (annually) (directory for writers, artists, playwrights, writers for film, radio and television, designers, illustrators and photographers), London: A. and C. Black.

Who's Who in Commonwealth Broadcasting (annually)(list of public service broadcasters in the Commonwealth and the Handbook of the Commonwealth Broadcasting Association), Room 312, BBC Yalding House, 152–6 Great Portland Street, London W1N 6AJ.

World Radio and Television Handbook (1997: vol. 51) editor-in-chief Andrew G. Sennitt, Billboard Books, PO Box 9027, 1006 AA Amsterdam, The Netherlands.

Newspaper, journal and magazine articles

All are published in London unless otherwise indicated.

Bates, K. G. (1991) 'Boyz with the Black Stuff', feature on young black directors in Hollywood, *Guardian* 27 July.

Billington, M. (1991) 'Of woman forlorn', review of *Anowa* by Ama Ata Aidoo, *Guardian* 5 April.

Coveney, M. (1993) 'Talent proves blind', *Observer* 23 February.

Dugdale, J. (1994) 'Taped up for Auntie', *Guardian* 25 July.

Duncan, R. (1997) 'Sound sites', *Radio Magazine* (Kettering) 295 (6 December): 24.

Esslin, M. (1971) 'The mind as a stage', *Theatre Quarterly* 1(3).

Fry, S. (1997) 'Wilde thing', *Sunday Times* 17 August.

Games, A. and Jones, M. (1994) 'Mayhem and the Muzzling of Morris', *Evening Standard* 8 July.

Hughes, J. C. (1990) 'Dismal man: two radio plays' (The Tanyard Murder and *The Night Creeper*), Cincinnati Poetry Review Press.

Imison, R. (1965) 'Drama at the BBC', *Plays and Players* December.

Johnston, S. (1991) 'Plain dealing', interview with Hanif Kureishi, *The Independent* 7 March.

Karpf, A. (1997) 'Missing the net', *Guardian* 13 December.

McFerren, A. (1991) 'Justice of the peace', interview with playwright Paulette Randall, *Guardian* 29 April.

Naughton, J. (1997) 'Over to Mick, the Internet', *Observer* 14 December.

O'Kelly, L. (1991) 'Explorer of the grey areas of emotion', interview with playwright Winsome Pinnock, *Observer* 18 August.

Q, William George (1996) 'The great Los Angeles opportunity', *The New Playwrights' Trust Newsletter*: full article published in text by permission of the author.

Wilson, M. (1991) 'All the rage', feature on director Pratibha Parmar, *Guardian* 3 October.

Published television and radio programmes

Lumière's Children (1997) Episode Three, BBC Radio 4, May. Sound Design, produced by Mark Burman. Originally produced for BBC Radio 3.

Minghella, A. (1998) *Cigarettes and Chocolate*, BBC Radio 4, 1 January, directed by Anthony Minghella and Robert Cooper, produced by Tony Cliff, London.

Strasbourg, L. (1997) In the *Reputations* series, Channel Four television, September.

Orson Welles (1974) Interview with Michael Parkinson, BBC Television.

Orson Welles (1995) *Arena* documentary, BBC Television, January.

Orson Welles (1995) *Citizen Kane*, BBC Television, 2 January.

The Lost World of Orson Welles (1997) BBC Television, 2 February.

Published spoken word, film, video and sound archives and CD-ROMs

Adams, D. (1988) *The Hitch-Hiker's Guide to the Galaxy (The Original BBC Radio Production)* six one-hour compact discs, London: BBC Worldwide.

America Before Television: September 21st 1939 – A Day From The Golden Age of Radio (1987) twelve one-hour cassettes, Greatapes, 1523 Nicollet, Minneapolis, MN 55403, USA.

Archers, The Vintage Episodes (including the 1955 episode featuring the death of Grace Archer in barn fire) (1988, 1989) BBC Radio Collection, London: BBC Worldwide.

Beachcomber . . . By The Way (1989) with Richard Ingrams, John Wells, Patricia Routledge and John Sessions, BBC Radio Collection, London: BBC Worldwide.

Bennett, A. (1990) *Talking Heads*, BBC Radio Collection, London: BBC Worldwide.

Benny, J. (1990) *Complete, Original Unedited Broadcasts 25/4/48 and 12/2/50*, Great American Audio Corporation, 33 Portman Road, New Rochelle, NY 10801, USA.

Brook, Peter (1994 [1975]) *The Empty Space*, a film by Gerald Feil, a unique film showing the methods and theatrical approach of Peter Brook, New York: Mystic Fire Video.

Cocteau, J. (1992) *Les Enfants terribles*, Radio France 1947 Book and CD, France, Phonurgia Nova Editions, Les Grandes Heures de la Radio.

Garden, G. and Oddie, B. (1989) *I'm Sorry I'll Read That Again*, four episodes from 1968, 1970 and 1973, BBC Radio Collection, London: BBC Enterprises.

Golden Age of Comedy (1990) *The 20 Greatest Stars of Laughter*, Great American Audio Corporation, 33 Portman Road, New Rochelle, NY 10801, USA.

Golden Radio Dramas (1990) *The 27 Greatest Shows on Radio*, Great American Audio Corporation, 33 Portman Road, New Rochelle, NY 10801, USA.

ITMA (1988) *It's That Man Again*, featuring Tommy Handley, Jack Train, Dorothy Summers, Fred Yule, Hattie Jacques and Derek Guyler. Four programmes from the 1940s, BBC Radio Collection, London: BBC Worldwide.

Jarman, D. (1993) Blue Channel Four television and BBC Radio 3, Sound Design: Marvin Black, a Basilisk Communications/Uplink Production, video distributed by Artificial Eye.

Marx, G. (1994) *Love Groucho: Letters from the Legendary Comedian to his Daughter Miriam*, narrated by Frank Ferrante, Telling Tapes, London: Sound and Media.

Mason, E. J. (1989) *Dick Barton: Special Agent*, first story produced again in 1972 for BBC's silver jubilee, BBC Radio Collection, London: BBC Worldwide.

Meredith, G. (1988) *Blue Hills Revisited*, episodes from Australia's longest running radio soap-feature by Ian Doyle, Sydney: Australian Broadcasting Corporation.

Meredith, G. (1992) *A Tribute to Blue Hills*, including the Blue Hills Rhapsody, four episodes from the radio soap and an interview with Queenie Ashton, who played 'Granny', Sydney: Australian Broadcasting Corporation.

Missing Person: A Radio Play (1983) Karen Hunter Anderson, Kathleen Bruegging, John Lance, London: Longman.

Shakespeare, W. (1988) *Macbeth*, directed by Martin Jenkins, originally broadcast on BBC Radio 4, BBC Radio Collection, London: BBC Worldwide.

Shakespeare, W. (1995) *Macbeth*, starring Steven Berkoff, adapted and produced by David Benedictus, Ladbroke Radio Productions for BBC Radio 4, published by Penguin Audiobooks (1997).

Shakespeare, W. (1997) *A Midsummer Night's Dream*, directed by Neville Jason, Naxos Audiobooks.

Star Wars Trilogy (1997) digitally remastered for sound and picture, *Empire Strikes Back*, *Return of the Jedi*, Lucasfilm, Twentieth Century Fox Home Entertainment.

Teliesyn/Memory Palace Production (1997) Hanes BBC Cymru/Wales, A History, CD-ROM, Cardiff: BBC Wales.

Theatre of the Imagination: Radio Stories by Orson Welles and the Mercury Theatre (1995) CD-ROM, Voyager Company, 1 Bridge Street, Irvington, NY 10533 – 9919 at www.voyagerco.com.

Welles, O. (1937) *Les Misérables: The Non-Musical Sensation*, Mutual Broadcasting System USA, distributed by Radiola, Box C, Sandy Hook, CT 06482, USA.

Welles, O. (1938) *War of the Worlds* (copyright Howard Koch 1988) published in cassette by Metacom Inc., 5353 Nathan Lane, Plymouth MN 55442, USA.

Welles, O. (1938) *The Count of Monte Cristo* (29 August), Mercury Theatre on the Air, CBS Radio, distributed by Radiola Records, Box C, Sandy Hook, CT 06482, USA.

Welles, O. (1938) *Rebecca* (9 December), Mercury Theatre on the Air (script by Howard Koch) CBS Radio, script and CD, Phonurgia Nova, 23 Rue de la Madeleine, 13200 Arles, France.

Welles, O. (1938) *Dracula* (11 July), Mercury Theatre on the Air, CBS Radio, script and CD, Phonurgia Nova, 23 Rue de la Madeleine, 13200 Arles, France.

Welles, O. (1938) *Treasure Island* (18 July) Mercury Theatre on the Air, CBS Radio, script and CD, Phonurgia Nova, 23 Rue de la Madeleine, 13200 Arles, France.

Welles, O. (1944) *The Dark Tower* (5 April), CBS Suspense Theatre, distributed by Radio Yesteryear, Box C, Sandy Hook, CT 06482, USA.

Welles, O. (1944) *Donovan's Brain* (May), CBS Suspense Theatre, distributed by Radiola, Box C, Sandy Hook, CT 06482, USA.

Wells, H.G. (1996) *First Men in the Moon*, adapted by Joe Dunlop, directed by Martin Jameson, first broadcast on BBC Radio 4, published by Mr Punch (Audio).

Wyman, L. (1989) *The Navy Lark*, four episodes from 1960, 1961 and 1967, BBC Radio Collection, London: BBC Worldwide.

Internet publications

Beck, A. (1997) 'Listening to radio plays: fictional soundscapes', University of Kent, UK 100600.1343@compuserve.com

Beck, A. (1998–99) 'Radio theory', http://members.tripod.com/~radiodrama/radiotheory/index.html

Conciatore, J. (1996) 'Will research bring comeback for radio drama?' originally published in *Current* (22 April), a biweekly newspaper that covers public broadcasting in the USA, a service of Current Publishing Committee, Washington DC, currentro@aol.com

Ferrington, G. (1993) 'Audio design: creating multi-sensory images for the mind', *Journal of Visual Literacy* and http://interact.uoregon.edu/MediaLit/WFAEResearch/sndesign

Ferrington, G. (1994) 'Keep your ear-lids open', *Journal of Visual Literacy* and Articles and Research Documents section for the World Forum for Acoustic Ecology http://interact.uoregon.edu/MediaLit/WFAEResearch/earlids

James, B. and James, M. L. (1996) 'Modern and post-modern cultural themes and structure in British radio drama', University of Hertfordshire, USA.

Miller, W. (1995) 'Thesis: silence in the contemporary soundscape' (May), http://interact.uoregon.edu/MediaLit/WFAE

Tiessen, P. (1992) 'From literary modernism to the Trantramar Marshes: anticipating McLuhan in British and Canadian media theory and practice', Wilfred Laurier University, published in the *Canadian Journal of Communication*.

Internet and World Wide Web sites

Independent Radio Drama Productions   http://www.irdp.co.uk

Goldsmiths College, University of London MA Radio Site   http://www.ma-radio.gold.ac.uk

CBC Radio in Canada   http://www.radio.cbc.ca

International Radio Festival of New York   http://www.nyfests.com – recognises the best in radio around the world

The Radio Magazine   http://www.theradiomagazine.co.uk

Marshall Cavendish   http://www.mcmedia.com – *The Magical Music Box* and other partworks

WRN   http://www.wrn.org – radio stations around the world

LBC Radio in London   http://www.lbc.co.uk – broadcast radio drama

Classic FM   http://www.classicfm.co.uk – great classical music radio station in the UK with live broadcast available on the website

National Public Radio in the USA   http://www.npr.org – commissioned IRDP to produce original dramatisations of classic tales such as Dracula and Sherlock Holmes

London Arts Board   http://www.arts.org.uk – funds the London Radio Playwrights' Festival

Radio Stations in France   http://www.francelink.com – broadcasts audio on the Internet

MIT List of Radio Stations   http://wmbr.mit.edu/stations – very comprehensive list of radio stations around the world broadcasting audio on the Internet

RTE Radio in Ireland   http://www.rte.ie

Swedish Radio Theatre in Finland   http://www.yle.fi/radioteatern/english/index.htm

ABC Radio in Australia   http://www.abc.net.au/surf/radio.htm

Maxmedia   http://www.achilles.net/~jgreen – great radio plays by the talented Jeff Green: you can read one of Jeff's novels online as well as hear his plays

Atlanta Radio Theatre Company   http://members.aol.com/artcradio – an excellent website full of information, tapes for sale and dramas to listen to in real audio

Yuri Rasovsky   http://www.irasov.com – award-winning American radio dramatist

Ken Armstrong   http://ireland.iol.ie/~kfelix – award-winning Irish writer

Ken Armstrong, Writer in Residence, Claddagh Films   http://www.claddagh.ie/people/ken.html

London Screenwriters' Workshop   http://www.lsw.org.uk – useful for writers in all media

The Radio Academy   http://www.radacad.demon.co.uk – UK organisation for the radio industry

Peter Ferm's Gravel Walk to Theatre on the Net   http://www.oden.se/~pferm/radioen.htm – more links to radio drama sites

Jack Mann's List of Old Time Radio Pages   http://www.pe.net/~rnovak/jack.htm – lots of useful links here

Radio Sweden   http://www.sr.se/rs/index.htm

NRK Norwegian Radio   http://www.nrk.no

Jerry Stearns' Radio Theater on the Web   http://www.mtn.org/~jstearns/Radiodrama.html

60 Second Theater   http://www.letusout.com/index.html

Prix Italia   http://www.grr.rai.it

Screenwriters   and   Playwrights   http://www.teleport.com/~cdeemer/scrwriter.html

Radio   Archive   of   the   University   of   Memphis   http://www.people.memphis.edu/~mbensman/welcome.html

Page about Orson Welles at Autographics   http://www.autographics.com/welles.html

Media History Project Radio Page   http://www.mediahistory.com/radio.html

Télégraphie   sans   fil   http://ourworld.compuserve.com/homepages/PascalSimeon

All India Radio   http://air.kode.net/index1.html

The Radio Directory   http://www.radiodirectory.com

UK Radio Authority   http://www.radioauthority.org.uk

Poets and Writers Online   http://www.pw.org

Poetry Daily   http://www.poems.com

Online   Resources   for   Writers   http://webster.commnet.edu/writing/writing.htm

Radio Space   http://webster.commnet.edu/writing/writing.htm

The Quill Society   for young writers http://www.quill.net

Shoestring Radio Theatre   http://www.shoestring.org

White   Rock   Taletellers   Society   http://web.radiant.net/sheppard/taletellers.html – non-profit society in British Columbia, Canada

Lewis   Smith,   Victor   –   Audio/Radio   Hoaxer   www.lewis-smith.com/newindex.html

Unpublished MA and PhD theses

Held at Radio Section, Department of Media and Communications, Goldsmiths College, University of London, New Cross, SE14 6NW, for scholarly reference and research. Tel: 0171 919 7611. Fax 0171 919 7612.

Burgess, C. (1998) 'Sight to the "blind": the stimulation of the imagination through techniques of audio drama production for radio', MA Radio, Goldsmiths College.

Dann, L. (1993) 'No more masterpieces, new copying technology, plagiarism and the death of genius', MA Radio, Goldsmiths College, submitted for *Issues in Media and Culture*.

Dietrich, S. (1992) 'Tennessee Williams, New Orleans and the radio feature', MA Drama, Goldsmiths College.

Fenn, I. (1994) 'Historical cycles in British radio comedy', MA Radio Goldsmiths College.

Houd, R. (1998) 'The documentary and the documentarist today: how can the radiodocumentary justify its further existence?' MA Radio, Goldsmiths College.

Houd, R. (1998) 'Audio space: spatiality and sound', MA Radio, Goldsmiths College.

Knight, P. (1992) 'The search for a contemporary approach to radio drama', submitted for MA Contemporary Approaches to English Studies, Goldsmiths College.

Kyte, A. (1994) 'Radio drama and the Theatre of the Absurd', MA Radio, Goldsmiths College.

Mantle, E. (1994) 'Radio drama, voices in the mind', MA Drama, Goldsmiths College.

Nicholas, J. (1993) 'Radio Nova: an essay on the creative tension between avant garde traditions at Radio Nova in Paris and commercial imperatives', MA Radio Production (documentary, interview transcript with Andrew Orr also available).

Shaw, E. (1994) 'Radiovision', MA Radio, Goldsmiths College.

Radio Drama Archives at Goldsmiths College, University of London

All entries for Best Drama Special, Best Drama Series, Best Writing, Best Directing, Best Narration and Best Sound, to the International Radio Festival of New York for 1994, 1995, 1996, 1997, 1998 and 1999.

All radio drama entries for 'The Race in the Media Awards', Commission for Racial Equality, 1994, 1995, 1996, 1997 and 1998.

Productions for LBC 1152 AM in London and independent radio referred to in the text.

Broken Porcelain by Tim Crook (1989) for LBC.

Coffee and Tea 90p by Tony Duarte, directed by Richard Shannon (1991) for LBC.

Farewell Little Girl by Anna Hashmi, directed by Tim Crook (1992) for LBC.

The Great Los Angeles Opportunity by William George Q, directed by Tim Crook (1996) for LBC.

Heart of Darkness by Tim Crook, directed by Richard Shannon (1989) for LBC and NPR, USA.

Restless Farewell by William George Q, directed by Tim Crook (1997) for LBC.

Saddam's Arms by Simon Beaufoy, directed by Richard Shannon (1993) for LBC.

Shiver Breathing by James Payne, directed by Tim Crook (1995) for LBC.

Vissi d'arte by Paul Sirett, directed by Richard Shannon (1991) for LBC. Special mention for radio fiction at Prix Italia 1992.

Wolf and the Woodcutter by Martin McDonagh, directed by Richard Shannon (1996) for LBC.

Index

288